COMMON GENIUS

GENIUS

Guts, Grit &
Common Sense

COMMON GENIUS

Guts, Grit &
Common Sense

How Ordinary People
Create Prosperous Societies
and How Intellectuals
Make Them Collapse

by Bill Greene
Illustrations by
Bruce Greene

Laissez Faire Books
a division of
the Center for Libertarian Thought, Inc.
LITTLE ROCK, ARKANSAS

Laissez Faire Books is a division of
the Center for Libertarian Thought, Inc.
7123 Interstate 30, Suite 42
Little Rock, Arkansas 72209
www.LFB.com

ISBN 978-0-930073-37-4

Library of Congress Control Number: 2007934864

Printed in the United States of America

To Cathy

Table of Contents

Preface

THE SEARCH FOR A PATTERN in history has concerned many of the world's best minds and remains a puzzle, because no one before has ever gotten to the bottom of it. Many have said religion had a role, or geography and climate mattered, or the language and education in different locales, etc., mattered. But most scholars have suggested that each such factor played only a part. Almost nobody argues that climate or geography or religion alone was determinant. Many point to the great philosophers such as Locke, Plato, Hegel, or Montesquieu, but a cursory look reveals that these writers only played supportive (or unsupportive) roles. However, this melange of possible causes is so fixed in most people's minds that it may be difficult for such a reader to accept a wholly new approach. And yet, throughout history, many blind alleys standing in the way of knowledge were only overcome by taking a radically different approach. That is what *Common Genius* endeavors to do.

Because the theme of this book is so controversial and can only be convincingly demonstrated by overturning a vast number of misconceptions, the reader must bear with the historical facts laid out herein, until gradually and inexorably, the fundamental lessons of history are fully revealed. Some readers may still, at the end, remain unconvinced, but it is my fervent belief that the journey will open their eyes and give them food for thought—a worthy objective for any author.

A recurring dilemma in outlining this new theory is that in order to establish the essentiality of the common people's role, it is necessary to disabuse readers of the false notion that it was the best and brightest that made all good things happen. This disabusement should not be read as an "attack" on those of great intellect—it is merely suggesting that the fundamental push to progress came from somewhere else. The essential point is that, helpful as some of the geniuses may have been, even their best efforts relied fundamentally and initially on the physical and financial settings established by ordinary people. After all, we are looking for the primal cause of progress; we must not be satisfied with merely identifying contributing factors.

The extraordinary accomplishments of a Galileo or Einstein didn't occur in the bush—they were only empowered by the glories of the Renaissance and the Industrial Revolution, societal peaks that we will show were the product of more ordinary beings. This underlying truth explains why Madame Curie's lab was not housed in a tent, a manyatta, or an adobe structure.

My research for this book leads me to the belief that students in all the humanities would benefit greatly from using the case method, the educational device used in schools of Law and Business, which forces them to remain grounded in reality. Unfortunately, many professors prefer to teach abstract concepts that can only pretend to capture actual historical experience. Because almost everything in the science of government has been tried at least once somewhere, it is imperative to examine the results of those experiments rather than talk about speculative concepts. Such a course led me to compare the actual dates of such experiments in government to the publication dates of the great philosophers' treatises. Surprisingly, the record shows that the great thinkers were always "playing catch-up" with the common people!

Understanding the hypothesis presented here relies heavily on coming to grips with a certain fuzziness of thinking when we talk about intellectuals, geniuses, innovators, pioneers, etc. This is not a homogeneous class of characters. Thomas Sowell has written about the differences between "hard-scientists" and "soft-scientists." These two types of deep thinkers are well exemplified by two legendary Greeks—Pythagoras and Plato. The former was a physical or hard scientist who developed useful mathematic models in the heady early days of Greek civilization; Plato was a soft-scientist who emerged 150 years later, in the final declining days of Athens, and wrote interesting but relatively useless material on vague topics like the nature of good and evil. Pythagorus relied on the scientific method—observation, tests, repeatable experiments or formulas that proved timeless. Plato speculated on vague undefined subjects, using abstractions and conceptualizations that were not based on reality or provable, and which, when employed later by his readers often did great harm.

In following the theory presented in *Common Genius*, it is important to keep this distinction in mind. There is no denigration of hard-scientists as long as they stick to the scientific method of observation and demonstration. Indeed, they have played a vital role in helping alleviate the work and discomforts inflicted by life on the common people. But, while they may have accelerated progress in already advancing societies, they were never the fundamental underlying cause of advances in freedom or prosperity.

Furthermore, even the soft-scientists are not as a group harmful. They also are not a homogeneous group, but can be divided into three levels of competencies, as described in Chapter 3. But even the best of these, "giants" like John Locke or Adam Smith, were merely "reporters" attempting to describe what common people had already done. Comparative dates are used to demonstrate that nothing "original" was ever included in such philosophers' writings. They did try to summarize general principles from what had occurred, but most of them did even that poorly, and too frequently wandered off into idle speculation.

Many such reporters and analyzers played a useful role in mankind's advance, but they never were the cause of the advances. There has never been a useful innovation in government or economic freedom that emanated from an armchair; all such innovations were the product of involved individuals cooperating, arguing, and compromising in a working environment, and very few of these, if any, were ever members of an intelligentsia. The summaries produced in the arm-chairs may have helped promulgate useful ideas, but they never originated the ideas. And unfortunately, many of the philosophers' reports and summaries were so inaccurate or distorted from reality that they led many readers far astray.

In investigating and developing the hypothesis of this book, it became evident that a number of soft-scientists have been more or less accurate in describing societal mechanics and institutions that had helped or hurt advances in freedom and prosperity. Such writers are cited throughout this book as support for specific facts as well as for their interpretations of history. Taken together, there are hundreds of such historians whose observations come very close to the conclusions drawn in *Common Genius*, but they all miss the common denominator—the unifying linkage that goes to the heart of the matter—the doings of the common man and woman.

Above all, the reader should understand that to date all attempts to learn "the lessons of history" have met with no more success than the sixteenth century Hernando de Soto's search for the fountain of youth. The subject has absorbed many great minds and no clear pattern has ever been established. The cyclical "Rise and Fall" paradigm has been often referred to but never with a satisfactory explanation of "why" societies rose or fell. In light of that record, this book is undertaking to do what has never been done—in Captain Kirk's words, "to go where no man has gone," never an easy task. In an ironic twist, it is the legendary Spanish explorer de Soto's namesake, the current eminent Peruvian economist, who has ventured closest to the source of mankind's progress. He is mentioned more specifically in my "Acknowledgments" and in numerous citations referenced in the Notes.

In *Common Genius*, I outline a revision of the rise and fall cyclical explanations and replace those with a "stepping stone" pattern. The rise and fall of the Greek and Roman eras, as well as the decline of Italian city-states and eventually most of the subsequent European societies, should be looked at as the stepping stones to Western civilization. Each fallen nation state was irreparably set back, but the forward march of Western progress continued unabated. Quite differently, when most of the great non-European empires grew and then stagnated, or were rolled over with new leaders, there was no over-all gain and little progress—the stagnation was virtually timeless. By contrast, in the West, even when one flourishing society collapsed, another nearby locale rose to begin the upward course anew. Indeed, the nature of each such "new" enclave is what establishes the Radzewicz Rule: each new enclave was a fresh young community, populated by ambitious citizens, and relatively unhindered by intellectuals or aristocracies.

When viewed this way, the rise of the West continues, surviving the fall of many predecessor stepping stones, always simply sidestepping to another more enabling locale. But this beneficial historical sequence should not be labeled "The Rise of the West." It has been more precisely "The Rise of Freedom"—because it was always the freedom of the populace that made a society rise.

It has never been a purely ethnic matter. The peoples of Phoenicia, Greece, and the Basques were quite different from those who populated Iceland and Scotland. If the Chinese, the Kenyans, the Argentines, or even the Iraqis adopt the mechanics and institutions that built progress in the West, the next stepping stone could well be theirs to stand upon. There are ten "tipping points" in world history that are referred to in *Common Genius* and each one went in the direction of the emerging Western nations. The next divergence could favor a different region—the blueprint is there for all to see—carved out by the enterprising free common men and women that built each ascending step during the past 3,000 years of history.

The conclusions drawn and the theory presented herein represent a suggested solution to the problem of interpreting mankind's history. The theory outlines what worked and, equally important, what did not work. It is comprehensive, encompassing most of the significant societies of the world during the past 3,000 years, but it remains a hypothesis that may or may not bear up forever. But in reading along, keep an open mind and share the adventure of a great search. There may be a sense of discovery—there will be "Aha!" moments, and even if you end in disagreement, you will comprehend the inherent weakness of most currently popular explanations.

—WCG
Lancaster, New Hampshire
www.thecommongenius.com
June 20, 2007

Chapter 1
The Theory of History

*"The search for beginnings, no matter how far
pressed, usually serves only to open more distant
vistas of earlier developments."*
—Alpheus Thomas Mason & Gordon E. Baker

Interpreting the broad sweep of history is a venture many have
written about, and, as Niccolo Machiavelli admitted 500 years ago, I
may be "deemed presumptuous, since I depart from the methods of
the scholars and academics who have tried before."

But a new approach is as necessary today as it was in the day of
Machiavelli, for the current crop of academics are almost universally
blinded by the current winds of political correctness. They have been
seduced by intellectual conceits that we will reveal in this book to be
based more on emotion than on reason, and this seduction has
created a demand for economic interpretations that support only
prevailing notions and preconceived conclusions. This book goes
against the grain, rejects current agendas, and presents a new theory of
history. As Machiavelli observed, "Since my intention is to write
something of use for those who understand it, it seemed more suitable
to go after the effectual truth of the matter than after an imagined
one."[1]

There is an urgency to this search for the root causes and mechanics of historic advances: the answer will show how all nations can join
the modern world of freedom and prosperity. Too many people have
been excluded from today's economic progress for much too long.
Over half of the 161 nations ranked in the Heritage Foundation's *2005
Index of Economic Freedom* are measured as mostly "un-free or repressed."[2] It is no coincidence that they are also the most impoverished nations in the world. And yet all they need is Economic Freedom

to gain prosperity, for only open economies can unleash the creative efforts of a broad spectrum of a population.

During the past half-century, the scholars and academics, descendants of those disparaged by Machiavelli, have failed abysmally to advance the lot of the poverty-stricken people of the Third World. They have relied mostly on handing out charity, much as they might give crumbs to beggars. And, being scholars, they have held conferences, written monographs, and given talks, none of which has helped one whit. One of the most damning records in intellectual history is this sixty-year failure to remedy the ongoing human misery in much of the world. So we must forget for a moment the abstract theories and ideologies that have failed, and seek the effectual truth. If economic history is to serve some practical purpose it must identify the fundamental lesson that has lain hidden beneath the jumble of history and academic jargon. Most of the academics who study and write about history have never been able to accept the truth, although it has always been there before their unbelieving eyes.

A major theme of these pages is that all historical progress has bubbled up from the bottom—from the actions of common men and women. A secondary theme is that most of history's evils have flowed from the top—from the intelligentsia, organized groups, and soft-science experts who arise in mature societies and are the pied pipers of their decline. In the final chapters, we will examine how the decline of free societies has often resulted from the transfer of authority and leadership from those who built the society to a destructive intelligentsia who arrive after the heavy lifting is done. The arrival of the intellectuals also marks the time when knowledge and decision-making appears to enter a steep decline. The notion that intellectuals are wise and should be listened to is a persistent, recurring, and insidious error that has doomed most past civilizations.

I do not mean to demean all people of intellect—most of them are great assets to their communities. However, there is reason to beware those with little practical experience in any field, who parade their "expertise" before the public, and operate primarily as critics rather than participants. As Richard Posner writes, many of the major contributions by such intellectuals "Are negative in the sense of combating the fallacies and follies of other public intellectuals."[3] Just read *The Nation*, then *Commentary*, and you will understand how these intellectuals disagree. With such differences, they engage in constant squabbling over their labored arguments and abstract ideas—how can any sane person guess which if any of them are right? Such are the intellects that do not produce anything concrete or useful, but merely broadcast abstract ideas and critiques that are rarely born out by subsequent events. Their dismal record throughout history illustrates the maxim that ideas don't have to be sound to be influential.

Any history of mankind and its successes must begin at the beginning; and in the beginning, there were no intellectuals. However, there were people struggling to exist and improve their lot in life, and mankind made magnificent strides, advancing from harsh and primitive tribal and nomadic life to complex and prosperous civilizations. The growing influence of intellectuals in the relatively recent past has served only to confuse, divert, and subvert that progress.

A century ago, some writers saw historical progress as primarily a function of climate and geography. That "answer" to the question of why some societies do better then others was later discredited by a number of historians. Unfortunately, and against all reason, geography-based theories of history have resurfaced as part of the multiculturist zeal to treat all societies as equally praiseworthy. Thus, Jared Diamond offers the following one-sentence summary of his 450-plus-page book *Guns, Germs, and Steel*: "History followed different courses for different peoples because of differences among peoples' environments, not because of biological differences among peoples themselves."[4] This is at heart just another variation of the "nature versus nurture" question that had already been thoroughly covered by Thomas Sowell in works like *Race and Culture* and *Conquests and Cultures*. Sowell presents convincing detail to show that for thousands of years, all races of people around the world have possessed roughly comparable levels of intelligence and that societal progress arose from other causes. And yet Diamond, who cites hundreds of other historians, makes no reference to Sowell's work.

Professor Diamond reports that "to me the strongest argument for writing this book [is that] until we have some convincing, detailed, agreed-upon explanation for the broad pattern of history, most people will continue to suspect that the racist biological explanation is correct after all."[5] Thus he is conforming to the current politically correct need to attack racist or biological explanations even though they have been dead in the water for many years. It would have been more praiseworthy to seek the truth—the real explanation of historical progress—for its own sake, rather than merely reengage a heated but past battle.

The crux of the matter is that there are two answers: geography and climate for Paleolithic times, and another for the past three thousand years. The most primitive societies clearly were affected by environment. But once mankind advanced sufficiently in skills to overcome "nature," environmental conditions became less important. For example, the hunter-gatherers of the Paleolithic Era had to move around to accommodate such forces as the advancing and retreating glaciers of the Ice Ages. Fertile land and waterways were of great importance. But geography cannot explain how political and economic advances occurred for at least the past three thousand years; nor why, in fact, some of the most notable advances arose in some of the least hospitable locales.

Three thousand years ago, over ten major civilizations around the world possessed the geography, climate, governmental structures, and communication systems needed to progress to current levels of prosperity—but the major progression occurred in only one area, scattered first around the Mediterranean Sea, then moving gradually into isolated enclaves in North-Western Europe, and finally across the sea to the United States. Geography may have played a part in enabling those ten civilizations to emerge. But it had little to do with the course those civilizations took over the past three millennia.

Both Sowell and Diamond are correct that there was a lower chance for technical progress in regions with great physical disadvantages, especially if isolated from other societies and functioning only as thinly populated outposts. Thus the primitive people of sub-Saharan Africa, the Inuits of the Arctic regions, the Aborigines of Australia, the cannibals in interior New Guinea, and peoples in similarly remote areas of the South Pacific were all handicapped by geography. However, for the ten or more civilizations that reached relatively sophisticated levels around 3,000 years ago, and each of which enjoyed reasonably favorable environments, a new factor determined success and failure. The difference lay in how the large and growing populations of those societies were organized, controlled, and motivated.

When we look at the times and places where freedom and material comforts emerged most strongly we find that the main drivers of societal progress were the individuals making up the population. When free from oppressive forces, and armed with free will and initiative, these multitudes are the key in any search for historical causation.

This is the position taken by P. T. Bauer when he challenges the "prevailing notions" of established economists and academics and, instead, credits the "individual voluntary responses of millions of people."[6] And Julian L. Simon documents how throughout history, sufficient natural resources have been made available by hard-working populations regardless of natural endowment. Simon contrasts "cornucopians," who believe that "natural resources are available in practically limitless abundance," with "doomsters" who declare that the end is near because we are running out of some vital resource—whether arrowheads, buggy whips, whale oil, firewood, or, now, oil. He rejects both approaches, pointing out that "human imagination and human enterprise" have always manipulated the elements to provide all the resources needed. "In short," he concludes, "our cornucopia is the human mind and heart." . . .[7]

Because the prevailing notions of the experts and intellectuals favored the doomsday scenario, Simon had to struggle for years to find a publisher for his book laying out these ideas. Academics are by nature very unlikely to give credit to the actual workers who make it happen, and prefer grandiose projections of future problems. And, of course, modern media invariably trumpet bad news and ignore good news. Simon writes of "the difficulties of espousing this unpopular point of view [and how] they were near the point of shutting me up and shutting me down."[8] Such is the power of monolithic thinking in academic circles. When he published the first edition of *The Ultimate Resource* in 1981, Simon had the advantage that all the oil experts of 1974, who had calculated that the world would run out of oil in ten years, were being proven 100 percent wrong. (The geologists working in American oil companies hadn't been consulted—they were out finding new oil fields.) History is replete with similar examples of the best and brightest being proven wrong. Yet their influence continues and their warnings are still taken seriously.

Professors in today's colleges rarely assign Simon's books—they prefer more politically correct (i.e., Pulitzer-Prize-winning) tomes that belittle Western civilization and the role of individuals. But the "environmental" theories can't explain the fate of a single major civilization of the past 3,000 years. Equally fallacious is the approach taken by those historians who, recognizing the inadequacy of the environmental theories, merely argue that all societies are equally good—that there have been no winners or losers. George Will has pointed out the ridiculous extent to which this "nonjudgmental" fad has gone: "In 1991 Florida, in a fit of modern 'nonjudgmentalism' and 'multiculturalism' and all that, enacted a statute requiring public schools to teach that no culture 'is intrinsically superior or inferior to another.' . . . [T]his told Florida's immigrant communities something they knew to be preposterous—that they might as well have stayed in Cuba or Haiti or wherever."[9]

Such efforts to avoid moral or even rational comparisons have debased instruction at America's schools and colleges, many of which are guilty not only of bad teaching but also of purveying patently nonsensical rewrites of history. The revisionism is not about legitimate areas of scholarly debate; it seems to be designed simply to discredit America, its institutions, and Western culture in general. Too many students accept this anti-Western teaching and lose any desire to participate constructively in current affairs. Of course, the wiser ones will quickly see the illogic of their teachers and the bias of the textbooks. There is no denying the obvious and gargantuan techno-logical, military, and economic supremacy of the West and especially the United States—not to mention the freedom and safety that is the envy of all peoples. When a constant stream of people from all over the world flows to a single destination and continues unabated for 400 years, even the dullest student should be able to connect the dots. People seek to become a part of the American civilization because of the advantages it has to offer; they're better off here than they would be elsewhere.

For those who seek to get around the obvious and incontrovert-ible fact that the West "won," another pathetic but politically correct answer has been to admit the "win," but argue that the West's victory was simply the result of chance—of good luck, the fates, Karma. This is the message conveyed in Kenneth Pomeranz's *The Great Divergence*,[10] which attempts to establish that the British and Chinese were equals in 1850 when the former somehow pulled ahead by the chance discovery of coal! Lucky it was lying around. Yes, and a good thing for Muhammed Ali that his gloves kept connecting, somehow, with his opponents' chins . . .

Professor Pomerantz's simplistic "explanation" has been deci-mated by Professor Ricardo Duchesne in a technical analysis.[11] But for this author, the simple exploits of one English adventurer in that same decade, Charles Gordon, provide clear enough evidence of English absolute supremacy over the Chinese. In September, 1860, the twenty-seven-year-old officer, fresh from military adventures in the Crimea, arrived in China to convince the Sun God emperor of the advantages of free trade. In the two Opium Wars of the mid-nineteenth century, the English had seized the island of Hong Kong, gained immunity for all foreigners on Chinese territory, demanded freedom to propagate the Gospel throughout the Empire, gained navigation rights on the Yangtse, and won the right to settle, trade, and maintain military forces in seventeen Treaty Ports including Shanghai.[12] These "negotiated settlements" give an indication of which society was the strongest at the time.

Part of Gordon's mission was to retrieve a few British envoys who had been seized even though carrying a flag of truce. When it was discovered that some had been tortured and beheaded by the Sun God's deputies, the British troops, marching unmolested before the Grand Palace, decided to pillage and destroy the Emperor's Summer Palace. British and French gun-ships controlled the rivers of China. Meanwhile, the Chinese peasants were revolting against the Sun God, who ruled the land with a totalitarian grip. The Empress had to pay the British to defend her remaining palace from the rebels. The British and French soldiers did so and sent barrels of souvenirs home to their families. Such was the unequal status of China and the West at that time. It is unlikely that the Sun God's peasants, if they had somehow discovered some coal and learned how to use it, could have inaugurated the Industrial Revolution, founded colleges, built ocean-going vessels, colonized the globe, and outpaced the West. They were already 700 years late on universities and 400 years late on ships and colonies. And as Professor Duchesne points out, coal wasn't all that critical anyway: French mechanics and engineers, lacking coal, had simply developed water power sufficient to keep up with English industrialization. Societal cornucopias obviously lay not in natural resources as such but in the freedom, initiative and enterprise of lowly individuals.

Professor Pomerantz's theory based on coal and chance also fails to recognize that in 1850 the relevant comparison was not England versus China, but the United States versus China. The fundamental and irresistible strength of the West has been its multifaceted independent nations, so unlike the Orient. In the West, if one region failed to keep up, another led the way. The situation around 1850, and the alleged importance of coal, is well illustrated by the Carnegie family. In 1848, they left Scotland and brought their children, including twelve-year-old Andrew, to America and "settled in the former Fort Pitt at the confluence of the Allegheny and Monongahela Rivers, which had been renamed Pittsburgh."[13] For reasons that will become clear in later chapters, the Carnegies did not choose to emigrate to China, nor Africa, nor South America, nor to the Islamic states of the Middle East. They were shrewd Scots and wanted to better themselves. Starting as a messenger boy, young Andrew did just that, quickly availing himself of the opportunities enjoyed by all in America. In 1873 Andrew Carnegie met Henry Bessemer during a trip to England and adapted his ideas for making better steel. In less than twenty years, by 1892, the Carnegie Steel Company, in America, was producing steel equal to half the entire production of Great Britain."[14] In 1901, Carnegie sold his steel enterprises to J. P. Morgan for $480 million. Clearly, the vital factor was the common man himself, free to "vote with his feet" and, in the right environment, to exercise his genius. He didn't need a land of soft gentle breezes—he merely needed freedom from oppression, an open door to opportunity, and equal protection under the law. This was the unique empowering environment created by Western civilization alone. It is the only kind of "environment," at least since the last Ice Age that could determine where human potential flourished rather than languished.

While lady luck has played a role in history, it has never created a consistent pattern. Most men have attempted to control their destiny and "make their own luck." Historical theories based on chance are agenda-driven. As Edward Hallett Carr writes, "In a group or a nation which is riding in the trough, not on the crest, of historical events, theories that stress the role of chance or accident in history will be found to prevail."[15] Carr recalls Gibbon's observation that the Greeks, "'after their country had been reduced to a province, imputed the triumphs of Rome not to merit, but to the fortune of the republic.' Tacitus, also a historian of the decay of his country, was another ancient historian to indulge in extensive reflexions on chance."[16] Ironically, in our own day those who seek to deny the merits of Western civilization, but undeniably finding themselves riding on the crest of its success, are driven to attribute that success to mere chance. This is an intellectual's game to be avoided, for we can only help the poorest nations to succeed if we identify the causes of economic success. Intelligentsias more concerned with abstract ideas than with reality—who deny or recast the real causes of history just to promote pet ideologies—do harm by denying progress to millions of suffering people.

Financial Times columnist Tim Havaford suggests that we still lack a good word "to describe what is missing in poor countries across the world. But we are starting to understand what it is. Some people call it 'social capital,' or maybe 'trust.' Others call it 'the rule of law,' or 'institutions.' But these are just labels."[17] He talks about motivations and incentives, and comes close to the answer: What is missing in backward economies is what is present in successful societies—the common genius of ordinary people. It's not that the people in those countries aren't able to do everything the people in Western nations have done—the genius is there. It's there, but it must be unleashed to operate effectively. It can only work its magic as a self-motivated force when secure and free of excessive restraint. Such empowered common genius is the essential "social capital," the "ultimate resource" of prosperous nations.

The explanation of why the West won lies almost exclusively in how and why that empowerment of each individual came to blossom so fruitfully in only a few places. We will study its origins and growth from King Solomon, Homer, the farmers in Iceland, and the merchants of Phoenicia to the more recent miracles of Florence, Amsterdam, London, Paris, and New York, and, still more recently, Eastern Europe and some of the Less Developed Nations where entrepreneurs are at last building free lives and material well-being. We will survey a steady progression that culminates in America's pinnacle of wealth, freedom, and leisure, spread more richly and widely among its citizens than ever seen before in history.

There are many statistics to prove America's success, but more convincing than data is the fact that so few are leaving. Scholars would do well to chart the movement of people—common people—for it is obvious that the overwhelming wisdom of a multitude of enterprising individuals will choose the best social environment. And they come to America, freely and deliberately choosing the best destination available. If multiculturists were right, historical emigration trends would have shown equally large numbers of people fleeing to Samoa, Tanzania, Peru, Bulgaria, Mongolia, even the Artic lands of the Inuits and Laplanders. But the vast majority chose Western nations, and especially the United States of America.

In a brilliant exposition of the road that lies ahead for the American experiment, Thomas B. Carson describes the American Dream as "a term used to describe commonly-held beliefs, assumptions and expectations of political freedom, economic opportunity, and material progress in the U.S."[18] These are the three blessings that all immigrants sought. They frequently arrived in America ragged and poor in a financial sense, but with a wealth of initiative and imagination. Once ashore, they ceased being "huddled" masses and became Americans—individuals—their new land's "ultimate resource." Carson's simple definition of the American dream neatly summarizes the goals of these immigrants, as well as the goals that most of mankind have been seeking for several thousand years.

Political and religious freedom and economic opportunity have been exceedingly rare during these millennia. Since the first stirrings of civilized society in the Tigris-Euphrates Valley and the days of King Solomon, freedom and opportunity were only a dream, out of reach of the common man. Instead, his lot was to labor under tyranny and oppression that were ever present and that in much of the world still linger malevolently. This dream of freedom, the dream that became reality in America and has endured to this day, is borne of the uniquely human characteristics of man—his ability to reason, his natural

curiosity, his instinct to innovate, his independence of spirit. These qualities, sometimes summed up as "free will," distinguish man from the beasts, and they set his destiny. Only one thing has stood in his way: the lust of other men to rule and appropriate for themselves all the good things in life.

Throughout history, such leaders have made life as difficult as possible for the bulk of humanity. The expression of man's genius had to be fought for, and opportunities for its release have been restricted to a few brief moments and places in time. Such moments were the "accidents" of history, but there was nothing accidental about what subsequently happened. The achievements were never pre-ordained but arose from a long-term struggle by ordinary people to advance, one step at a time, over thousands of years. But wherever individual men and women got even a little such opportunity, freedom and prosperity followed. They built it piece by piece, not by trying to apply utopian theories, but by solving one problem at a time and moving ever forward.

It is a mistake to glorify these achievements as issuing from some kind of brilliant philosophy. They are more like the parts in a "mechanical system," and are the simple products of common workers solving problems. Thus, one can compare such empowering systems to the parts of an internal combustion engine. Just as an engine requires a fuel pump, a water coolant, an igniter, and a drive shaft, so a free governmental system requires courts, deeds to property, coinage, patents, corporate entities, juries, and representative assemblies. The availability and quality of such "parts" represent a vital aspect of economic history. They are what have allowed freedom and business activity to flourish. Many intellectuals, like Plato, have no affection for the ordinary people who developed these things; indeed they frequently oppose democratic forms of government. Needless to say, Plato and other "soft-science" intellectuals never invented a fuel pump or a spark plug; nor did they develop any essential parts of a free governmental structure; or, for that matter, anything of use in the real world. It can be argued that many of the huge advances in man's economic and social well-being over the past few thousand years were achieved more in spite of the intellectuals' ideas than because of them.

Now, this is a revolutionary idea and perhaps in a perverse way, will delight most of the average Joes out there who are pestered by those "beautiful people" who want to tell them what to do and how to do it. I know this discovery has emboldened me to set forth this hypothesis; a hypothesis passed on to me by my wife's uncle, a simple Polish immigrant named Harry Radzewicz. I suspect many of the best and brightest will scoff at my message, saying that I simplify too much, that things are much more complex than I can comprehend. But that is okay with me, for as observed earlier, it is better to seek the "effectual truth" than to build vast conceptual edifices or perpetuate grandiose theories that don't work.

An advantage of the Radzewicz Formula is its ability to simplify a complex question so that it is easily understood. It was explained to me as follows: "History's progress," I was told, "can actually be reduced to a simple equation. It's easy, like simple algebra, or Polish notation." He put it on paper: CM + S - O = EF

Mr. Radzewicz, circa 1940, just before enlisting in the US Air Force, standing next to his own JN-4 World War I Bi-Plane.

"CM, the common man, with Security, minus Oppression, equals Economic Freedom, and that leads to Prosperity. It also subsequently leads to Political Freedom."

And there it was—neat and simple. A fundamental principle missed by all the intellectuals. Deliberately missed, perhaps, because there is no "I" in the formula—intellectuals have never had anything to do with progress.

In the early chapters of this book we will consider the degree of security men have enjoyed and the degree of regulatory oppression they have suffered, for these have been key determinants of historical economic progress. There is a rather fine balance required of each factor if individual opportunity is to be maximized—too much of either can be detrimental. The burden of oppression, whether in the form of an autocrat's tyranny or the weight of regulations and legal threats, has been given too little attention by classical economists.

In *Conquests and Cultures*, Thomas Sowell points out that "modern Western industry and commerce developed at a time when the intelligentsia were a small and relatively un-influential group."[19] Fortunately, most Americans are viscerally aware of the failings of the so-called best and brightest. Raymond Aron has extolled America and "the simple, modest ideas which it continues to cultivate," and the fact that "it is still basically hostile to authority, to the pretensions of the few to know all the answers better than the common man."[20]

Aron's praise for these "simple modest ideas" was penned half a century ago. We can only hope that the basic good sense of the average American has remained hostile to the bad ideas of the intellectual experts. This defensive hostility is crucial, because the intelligentsia are putting out more bad ideas than ever. As George Orwell once noted, many of their notions are "so absurd that only an intellectual could believe them." But inasmuch as the intellectuals have come to dominate the major foundations, colleges and media, it is their bad ideas that get drummed into everyone's brains.

Which is why it is so important to get to the truth of economic history. The evidence will show that it is these bad ideas that have brought on the decline of hitherto successful nations.

Chapter 2
Past Summaries of the Past

"A whole new class of intellectuals has arisen to supply a history geared to what people currently wish to believe, rather than to the record of the past."
—Thomas Sowell, *Race and Culture*

ARNOLD TOYNBEE'S TWELVE-VOLUME *Study of History* lists twenty-three advanced civilizations that emerged within the past several thousand years, of which twenty-two were literate and nineteen were Eurasian. Jared Diamond faults Toynbee for omitting pre-Columbian Native American societies and small outlying areas like the South Pacific islands and the Australian outback, saying he thereby fails to "come to grips with what I see as history's broadest pattern."[21] Toynbee might answer that since there was virtually zero progress beyond the stone age in those isolated locales, they are not very useful in evaluating mankind's progress. And, in all fairness to Toynbee, a twelve-volume analysis of twenty-three civilizations over thousands of years does represent a fairly broad overview of human history.

Most historian have, like Toynbee, found it appropriate to compare the record of the dozen or more major civilizations and attempt to draw conclusions from their successes and failures. Using that approach, the historical record has been generally viewed optimistically, showing a gradual thread of progress from the earliest times to the present. And there can be no question that the affluence and comfort of virtually all people have improved exponentially during the past few hundred years. However, with the undeniable horrors that engulfed the European continent in the twentieth century, "belief in the meaning of history has become a heresy. After the First World War, Toynbee made a desperate attempt to replace a linear view of history by a cyclical theory—the characteristic ideology of a society in decline.

Since Toynbee's failure, British historians have for the most part been content to throw up their hands and declare that there is no pattern in history at all."[22] Toynbee ended by espousing Spengler's concept of the recurring rise and fall of nations, which in turn echoes Marcus Aurelius, who "in the twilight of the Roman Empire consoled himself by reflecting, 'how all things that are now happening have happened in the past, and will happen in the future.'"[23]

It is this recurring pattern among the larger nations that calls for study because if we can determine the reasons societies "rose" we can emulate those techniques, and if we find out why they "fell' we can avoid repeating those historical mistakes. It is not clear what is to be gained by looking at small isolated communities that neither rose nor fell. Granted, such outlying societies permanently mired in stone age cultures were the unfortunate victims of geography, isolation, and lacked the enabling habits of mind that developed elsewhere in the world. But many societies did advance. And since they represent the vast majority of mankind, and since only one of them "triumphed," it is among these that we must look for the causes of man's progress— just as a study of the strategies and techniques that succeed at Wimbledon should focus not on first-round dropouts, but on finalists.

Professor Diamond observes that, "Since Toynbee's attempt, world-wide syntheses of historical causation have fallen into disfavor amongst most historians, as being an apparently intractable problem."[24] In fact, since Toynbee's volumes were published from 1934 to 1954, many scholars have sought the same answer. Thomas Sowell, E. L. Jones, Nathan Rosenberg, L. E. Birdzell, Jr., David Landes, and William McNeill in particular have addressed the causation of historical progress in recent years, and have found hundreds of other writers to compare and contrast on the subject. And, there emerges at least one area of agreement: Most writers of the past half-century contend that neither the environment, climate, nor race have had any significant importance in determining modern progress in freedom or prosperity.

Jeffrey Sachs makes this point emphatically: "It is time to banish the bogeyman of geographical determinism, the false accusation that claims about geographical disadvantage are also claims that geography single-handedly and irrevocably determines the economic outcome of nations."[25] In passing, Sachs refers to Jared Diamond's account of "how geography helped shape the early stages of human civilization."[26] He observes that such factors "became much less or not at all important with the advent of modern transportation and communications" and concludes that "none of these conditions is fatal to economic development. . . . Economic development requires a government oriented toward development. . . . The government must create an environment conducive to investments by private businesses."[27] Why did the industrial revolution come first to Britain? Because "British society was relatively open, with more scope for individual initiative and social mobility. . . . Second, Britain had strengthening institutions of political liberty. Britain's parliament and its traditions of free speech and open debate were powerful contributors to the uptake of new ideas. They were also increasingly powerful protectors of private property rights, which in turn underpinned individual initiative."[28]

In *The European Miracle*,[29] E. L. Jones traces the rise of the Western European nations. The West's unique progress has been the study of many great scholars, and Jones finds no magic bullet to explain it. In the course of his review, he cites over 400 sources, which represent only a fraction of the books and articles he consulted. He faults almost every known explanation and offers only a few tentative causes. This is clearly an area where wise men are cautious.

Jones points out that since Europe was the only place in the world with "sustained economic progress leading to the first industrialization—by definition a unique case—there is no such class of phenomena . . . for comparison." However, by looking at other areas of the world, contrasts can be made. Jones is emphatic about one factor. The failure of the great Imperial Middle East and Oriental civilizations was largely caused, he argues, by despotic rulers exercising too much centralized power over the lives of their people. "Whatever their cultural virtues, the Asian empires never overcame for long enough the liabilities of negative decisions at the top, the lack of incentive for those who held power to invent or innovate anything productive, and the disincentive for those without power to risk setting up production plant."[30]

In other words, in those cultures, the common man was never allowed to exercise his genius. What was needed was simply the safety and incentive of secure private property, free of interference and regulation from above, so that the common man would be motivated to create prosperity. Jones comes close to saying so, but it would have been unprecedented to attribute all progress, or lack thereof, to such a simple explanation.

In 1947 Henry Grady Weaver borrowed from and amplified the ideas of Rose Wilder Lane and argued that human progress came solely from the "energy" of individual human beings. In his book, Weaver refers to the mathematical Equation suggested by the American Economic Foundation : MMP=NR+HE x T—"just a shorthand way of saying that 'man's material progress depends on natural resources plus human energy multiplied by tools.'"[31] Weaver goes on to indicate that the middle factor—human energy—is really the whole story. Tools, of course, are simply inventions by individuals seeking to make their toil less onerous. And natural resources only are important when individuals have found ways to exploit them. By their analyses Weaver and Lane have laid the basis for this book by presenting the logic that ordinary people, when their energy was freed and enabled to operate, created all progress. However, their emphasis was on how this unleashing occurred rather suddenly in America a couple hundred years ago, while the Radzewicz Rule relies on the historical evidence of three millenniums.

The question of when the West pulled ahead of the rest has been the subject of many academics. However, establishing a precise date is really very difficult, as well as unnecessary. Indications of Western success were first discernible long ago, and evolved gradually and witnessed so many reverses and dead ends, that it is impossible to pick out a single point in time. In fact, we refer to ten tipping points in this volume, scattered over the past three millennia, each of which helped lay the foundation for Western supremacy. For E. L. Jones, the giant step forward in economic progress occurred from 1400 to 1800 in Western Europe, "the birthplace of the industrial world."[32] He rightly suggests that the advances of that period were deeply rooted in the past. Respect for the individual person dates to the early Greeks, and even earlier Jewish thought. Such respect for and encouragement of individual initiative proved vital to the recurring innovations capitalized on in the West. But why was this valuable way of thinking so conspicuously absent or suppressed in most of the rest of the world?

Jones again approaches the viewpoint of the present work when he suggests that "very long term growth was less the result of a conjunction of growth-promoting forces than of the removal of impediments."[33] But he still doesn't quite recognize the essential contribution of the individual person—that once impediments have been removed, it is still up to the common men and women to "make it happen." According to Jones, "advances were first conspicuous in the trading cities of Italy, in the Netherlands, Britain, Belgium. . . . They were creations of the market."[34] That is like saying Picasso's masterpieces were the creation of the French artistic movement, or that the Mona Lisa emerged from the artistic genius of the Renaissance. In each case individuals were needed—flesh-and-blood workers. If accomplishments were in fact the pre-ordained spawn of an anonymous culture, wouldn't that mean that someone else would have written the Ninth Symphony, had Beethoven died at as young an age as Mozart did? Or that some other woman in Avon would have conceived an equivalently brilliant and poetic child to replace Shakespeare, had the Bard never been born? Clearly "culture" cannot direct its own development. It is only from the vast numbers of people, under conditions in which they may develop their talents and prospects that genius emerges.

Charles Murray also comes close to asserting the importance of unshackled individuals when he identifies the "sources of energy" that enabled the burst of human genius in the fields of art and science. He concludes from a vast statistical analysis of notable human achievement throughout history that what it requires is a culture 1) in which people believe that life has a purpose and that the function of life is to fulfill that purpose, 2) that encourages the belief that individual citizens can act effectively and independently, and 3) that enables them to do so.[35] Thus, human initiative, combined with an "enabling society," permits and supports the innate capabilities of the common man to act. These are precisely the hallmarks of both the Greeks' affinity for heroes and the Judeo-Christian emphasis on free will and personal responsibility that found renewed expression in a few pockets of Western Europe after 1000 A.D.

In the eighteenth century, Adam Smith observed that "little else is required to carry a state to highest degree of opulence from the lowest barbarism, but peace, easy taxes, and tolerable administration of justice; all the rest being brought about by the natural course of things."[36] This "natural course of things" is of course the blood, sweat, and tears of many ten-hour days put in by millions of lowly workers and innovators. Smith was right about the need for security and a reduced level of oppression; but, the rest is up to each individual worker.

In this book, frequent reference is made to Mancur Olson and Hernando de Soto, who avoid Smith's vagueness about causation. They spell out the need to empower the multitude of individuals to create entrepreneurial activity. They come closer to saying, "It's the average Joe." This is not a petty distinction; voters and administrators must not think that prosperity comes from governmental efforts, the market, or some invisible force, lest they lose sight of the importance of supporting the individual worker and risk taker—as well as the need to stay off his back. Adam Smith's legendary "invisible hand," if examined thoughtfully, would be seen as the common man's hand, rough and calloused, perhaps scarred, by years of toil. Many such hands operate in a free market to create spontaneous order and efficient economic activity. Every society must be careful not to tie those hands.

The "removal of impediments" allowed individuals to escape the grasp of controlling rulers and conduct business, innovate, and create market enhancing systems to promote economic growth. It must be noted that political freedom was not an essential part of this process; but it is closely allied. Without some degree of political freedom individuals may not be able to retain their freedom to act unrestrained by those above them. However, even limited freedom, such as the freedom made possible by a ruler's benign neglect, may be freedom enough to permit economic progress. On the other hand, political freedom without economic freedom is hollow and useless. Democratic but over-regulated India, with its huge bureaucracy, has fallen behind undemocratic Hong Kong. In Third World countries it is not unusual to see representative governments and parliaments and popular elections in full swing, even as citizens are prevented by overreaching regulations and inadequate property rights and financing opportunities from exploiting any significant degree of business opportunity. Such democracies, where the individual is denied economic freedom, will stagnate in poverty, and their citizens will enjoy little benefit from their votes.

Charles Murray points out that man has achieved great things even during times of strife and under autocratic governments provided only that he enjoys freedom of action: "Political freedom technically defined fails to explain anything—it is de facto freedom, autonomy to act, that counts."[37] In the 2004 edition of *Economic Freedom of the World*,[38] Hong Kong and Singapore are ranked first and second in economic freedom, though neither is a democracy. More democratic countries like the United States, New Zealand, Switzerland, and Great Britain are tied for third place. It should surprise no one that these six nations, including the two top-ranking non-democracies, also enjoy great prosperity—for they are all ruled by market-enabling governments. Another proof of this principle is that, thanks to the stifling regulatory restraints imposed in the advanced welfare states, there is less de facto freedom today in many democracies than in some autocracies. Thus, Kuwait, Oman, and the United Arab Emirates rank higher in the EFW Report than do Germany, France, and Sweden. We will examine how such self-inflicted injury to their economic vigor signals a continued decline for Continental democracies as they slide into the third and final declining phase of free societies.

In Chapter 5, we will examine those historical periods during which political order and economic opportunity most robustly emerged, and observe how it was the individual man, working at the micro-level, who, contrary to what is implied by so many sweeping interpretive studies of mankind's progress, gradually built the framework for both political and economic freedom. It is that preeminent "lesson of history" that provides hope for the future. As Jeffrey Sachs has written, "When the end of poverty arrives, as it can and should in our own generation, it will be citizens in a million communities in rich and poor countries alike, rather than a handful of political leaders, who will have turned the tide. . . . We have exciting times ahead, and no time to lose."[39]

One of history's biggest obstacles to continued progress, and to the dissemination of economic benefits to all people, has been the time lost and wrong paths taken by adherence to the faulty ideas of soft-science intellectuals. If we are to succeed as a people, we must sort out the right ideas from the wrong ideas. So we must, first, clarify what is meant by intelligence and rational thought. Then we will illustrate the difference between intellectuals and ordinary people, in order to distinguish the constructive forces in mankind's advance from the destructive forces.

Chapter 3
The Nature of Intelligence

"An intellectual . . . takes ideas as seriously as an orthodox religious person takes . . . doctrine or dogma . . . Not for nothing have we been called the 'clerisy' of a secular age, and not for nothing are we unable to live amicably together when disagreements arise over the ideas that are so vitally important to us."
—Norman Podhoretz, *Ex-Friends*

THE VAST MAJORITY of Americans and Europeans—the happy and wise common people—are gradually losing control of the nations they have built.

We have witnessed a shift in control and decision-making from those with first-hand knowledge of how things actually work to elites that think they know how things should work. It is this shift that explains the current drift and confusion in the West, a confusion representing a serious danger for those who want to continue to enjoy, and want their children and grandchildren to enjoy, the benefits of living in the freest and most prosperous nations in history.

When we examine the historical record of free societies we observe that neither an intellectual class nor a hereditary aristocratic class was involved in the founding or building of any free and successful society.[40] They have helped found tyrannical societies like Communist Russia, Nazi Germany, Maoist China, Peru's Shining Path, and Cambodia's Pol Pot regime. They have also ruined many established or emerging communities. Why do those who have wrought so much havoc continue to gain so much power and influence? To understand this problem it is useful to develop some classifications and definitions of "intellect" and "intellectual," because it is only certain categories and applications of human intelligence that have made for progress.

First, we will distinguish between intelligent individuals, intellectuals, common sense, and creative genius.

It seems that even in definition, intellectuals defy any clear and simple understanding. *Webster's Unabridged Dictionary*[41] provides twelve meanings for "intellectual," and several more for "intellectualize" and "intellectualism." Most definitions of "intellectual" cite "a reliance on the intellect" and "reason" rather than on "emotions or feelings." That correctly describes scientific or scholarly investigations where reason, observation, and rationality are maintained. Currently such application of logic and reason free of emotion is primarily confined to the "hard sciences." Research in most other, softer fields has become so ideological and politicized that emotions and utopian aspirations usually far outweigh logic, intellect, and reason.

Fads in academic circles dealing with such hot topics as diversity, multiculturalism, and moral relativism have created an atmosphere burdened by a political correctness that stifles true debate and any attempt to apply reason. Incidentally, the very need for political correctness as a limitation on debate shows just how insupportable are all positions so protected. Nevertheless, rules governing the range of acceptable thought have become overpowering, a situation reflecting the decline of academia. Recognition and awards go to those "scholars" who most rigorously conform to and find a way to confirm prevailing notions. Jared Diamond's *Collapse* may be widely assigned to students because it deals with the "environment," and asserts that the prime reason that civilizations decline and collapse has to do with environmental damage, climate change, rapid population growth, and the squandering of natural resources. Pollution is in; consumer consumption is out.

In the over 550 pages of Diamond's tome, only a few paragraphs touch on the decline of Greece and Rome (the stories of which apparently couldn't be wedged into his thesis). The rest of the book deals primarily with the failure of obscure islands in the North Atlantic and South Pacific, most of which were harmed by cyclical changes in climate that preceded any of the alleged industrial environmental sins of more recent days. There is little reference to the impact of cultural institutions, forms of government, trade and exploration, religions, or the freedom and attitudes of peoples. Diamond has been praised by Robert H. Waterman for showing that "On lonely Easter Island, humans ignored nature, built astonishing monuments to themselves, and guaranteed their own demise. Other civilizations have done, and are doing, much the same thing." It apparently doesn't matter that the weather on Greenland and the erosion in the Easter islands, whether it affected them or not, has little relevance to the major civilizations that also collapsed or to modern societies that are not collapsing. Thus ideology and fashions trump scholarship and sense. And thus many of those customarily assumed to be "intellectuals" display traits opposite those described by the dictionary, in fact subordinating objectivity and reason to feelings and aspirations. They do employ intellect: to display immense scholarship jammed with hundreds of detailed (if irrelevant) statistics. Exhibit A is Kenneth Pomeranz's *The Great Divergence*,[42] in which such dreary details as the number of cups of tea consumed per capita are accumulated ad nauseam in the ultimate mission impossible: to prove that the China of 1850 was on a par with the England of 1850. In the pages that follow, we will identify ten real divergences in history, each of which shifted the tides of progress in favor of the West—all of which occurred well before 1850—and none of which hinged on climate, geography, or natural resources.

We must also seek an answer to why so many intellectuals outside the fields of hard science repeatedly fail to base their reasoning on observation and rigorous evaluation of results. By eschewing the fundamental requirements of a scientific approach, they violate the very definition of their being. Their lack of reasoned thought is most clearly evidenced by the seven-decade-long support for communism offered by so many Western intellectuals. It is also evidenced by the willingness in academic circles to rewrite history to accommodate current fads on diversity, economics, geography, history, and the environment. Indeed, many of today's intellectual leaders appear to have reversed the definition—they act on emotions, hope, peer pressure, and feelings more than on reason. The clearer-thinking students of Western colleges and universities, obliged to cope daily with the glaring deficiencies and lacunae of today's curricula, no doubt often recall Captain Kirk's famous request, "Beam me up, Scotty!"

In *Koba the Dread*,[43] Martin Amis undertakes to unearth the many evils, wars, and mass murders of the past century. He especially delves into the question of why his father, the renowned author Kingsley Amis, supported the Communist Party in the 1940s and 1950s. "What intrigued Amis about his father's story was its very banality," notes Jack Cashill in his account of intellectual hucksterism. "His father did what everyone seemed to be doing. 'The world was offered a choice between two realities,' he writes . . . and the young Kingsley, in common with the overwhelming majority of intellectuals everywhere, chose the wrong reality."[44]

Unlike many communist sympathizers, the elder Kingsley would eventually admit his error, publicly acknowledging that he had let himself be hoodwinked by the communist cause.[45] Martin quotes his father's diagnosis: "We are dealing with a conflict of feeling and intelligence, a form of willful self-deception whereby a part of the mind knows full well that its overall belief is false or wicked, but the emotional need to believe is so strong that knowledge remains, as it were, encysted, isolated, powerless to influence word or deed."[46] So there you have it—the intellectual's own confession of an "emotional need to believe" in something. A wag once said that "faith is believing in something you know isn't true." Unfortunately, intellectuals apply this kind of faith to their faulty secular goals. Thus, they propose ideas patently not so, as opposed to believing in what is true and can be shown. It is a vision thing—they see what should be, what might be if only people were different, and they pursue such dreams with a religious fervor. But they don't believe in religion, they eschew patriotism, abhor family values, and detest capitalism, so what is left for them to cling to? Only some far out socio-economic utopian theories that, with their huge egos and big brains, they would impose on supposed inferiors—the rest of us. Their knowledge becomes "encysted and powerless." That is why they do so much harm.

Wadje Radzewicz once observed, when asked about his religious beliefs, "It's not so much that I'm 'for' God, but that I'm terrified by those who must fanatically deny a God." He believed that those who totally reject established theologies are prone to move on to more harmful beliefs and to adopt and revere worse Gods. In contrast, there are many thinking people who discount much or all of religious dogma but do not feel compelled to ridicule those who have a faith or to eradicate all expression by the religious of their beliefs. Indeed, many such "agnostics" actually have some vague belief in a greater power or natural forces that operate for them as a kind of substitute faith. The failing of the extremists—the activist atheists—is that they will not live and let live, but feel obliged to carry their thinking to the ultimate conclusion and impose it on others. Such extremists have historically been the same intellectuals who deny and combat religion even as they make "the proverbial leap of faith" to embrace a vision of communal life, free love, or communism. Many leapt joyfully into the arms of "Uncle" Joe Stalin, in thrall with his stated intentions, and ignoring the reality of his evil barbarous acts.

This psychological need borne of spiritual emptiness may explain why intellectuals are often so fanatical and emotional about their big ideas. Instead of being rational as their label implies, they replace religious faith with secular faith, imbuing the latter with all the fervor of the former. Now the common man knows that in secular affairs one needs a hard-headed, no-nonsense approach to get by in this world. He wisely lets his unquestioning faith and hopes and dreams reside in his religion, whatever it may be; and thus he gains peace and serenity and comfort without endangering the well-being of himself and everyone else. This innate wisdom of the common man explains why he is the one who produces progress, whereas the intellectual merely gets in the way.

The dictionary also defines "intellectual" as a person "who places a high value on or pursues things of interest to the intellect or the more complex forms and fields of knowledge . . . especially on an abstract and general level."[47] These "things of interest" could include everything from Einstein's musings on the nature of time to Freud's theories on the meaning of dreams and a male's sexual desire for his mother. Such lofty forms of thought can, in the hard sciences, as Einstein demonstrated, be quite useful; but many practitioners of the soft sciences, like Marx or Freud, tend to turn the term "intellectual" into an epithet.

The dictionary defines "intellectualize" as "to ignore the emotional or psychological significance of an action by an excessively intellectual or abstract explanation."[48] To ignore some elements and obscure others is folly. And that point about "excess abstraction" lies at the root of the weakness of many intellectuals. Their concentration on pure theory severed from practical experience will normally relegate their ideas to utopian exercises that do not work. In his pontificator-skewering *Public Intellectuals*, Richard A. Posner describes his targets as "intellectuals who opine to an educated public on questions of or inflected by a political or ideological concern."[49] He notes the lack of "quality controls that one finds in other markets for goods and services [and] a low average quality—low, and maybe falling, though it would be more precise to say that public-intellectual work is becoming less distinctive, less interesting, and less important."[50] This decline in public discourse suggests a hypothesis to consider: Is there an inverse relationship between soft-science schooling on the one hand, and common sense and wisdom on the other? In Chapter 14, this provocative and potentially explosive proposition is explored by means of the "The Radzewicz Curve."

In contrast to these public intellectuals who merely write and talk, expounding their convoluted ideas and analyzing what's happening around them, another group of people is doing all the heavy lifting, those who actually make or do things: construction workers, technicians, engineers, politicians, corporate executives, nurses, soldiers, small businessmen, doctors, policemen, and firemen. Johan Norberg has called these kinds of people heroes—especially the entrepreneurs: "Despite the risks, the hard work, the hostility from society, the envy from neighbors, and state regulations, they keep on creating, they keep on producing and trading. Without them, nothing would be there."[51] Meanwhile the media and schools heap publicity and praise on the intellectuals.

To help restore the balance, this book aspires to contribute to what Roger Kimball describes as "that most patient and underrated of literatures, the literature of intellectual disabusement."[52] A first step is to outline the five categories of intellect. Some kinds of brain-workers are important assets to our society, and we do not want the harmful ones to escape notice by pretending to be among the useful groups:

1. True scientists, in the "hard-science" fields of math, medicine, physics, and the like
2. Managers, and engineers, who develop and perfect products and processes
3. Creative artists who write, compose, film, and paint "master-pieces"
4. Ordinary workers and politicians who bring initiative and energy to their crafts
5. Soft-science intellectuals who deal in ideas, concepts, and critiques of other classes

This fifth category may be subdivided as follows:

A. Historians, economists and commentators who use reason, logic, and facts to describe our culture and its history, direction, and problems.
B. Zealots who plump for a cause, sometimes ignoring the obvious errors and inconsistencies in their reasoning.
C. Nihilists who call for total revolution, for the removal of all civil traditions and moral boundaries, and who despise and vilify the society they live off.

"Hard" scientists in the fields of math, chemistry, physics, medicine and biology have made extraordinary discoveries that make our lives more comfortable. They are in the number one position. The fact that hard scientists have improved the physical lot of man is obvious and the average citizen has the common sense to accept that without dispute. The achievement of just one of these scientists, known to anyone growing up in the 1940s and 1950s, proves the point: Jonas Salk ended the crippling scourge of polio. Without his vaccine, thousands of children would still be crippled every year and sentenced to life in a wheelchair. In marked contrast, Hegel and Heidegger, Nietzsche, and Sartre, "soft" geniuses all, can point to nothing they did that ever actually helped any significant group. In fact, as we will see in subsequent chapters, their ideas have mostly done much harm.

Second place is awarded to the engineers and mechanics who use their ingenuity constructively to seek answers to real problems. While not Einsteins or Salks or Galileos, they build on the accomplishments of their predecessors to achieve breakthroughs in knowledge and processes. They have produced many of the cures of modern medicine, the comforts and conveniences of modern technology, and all the luxuries we have grown accustomed to and which make our lives so much easier than those of past generations.

The hard-science intellectuals and engineers produce something—a patent, a new technology, a medicine, a vaccine, a new product like nylon or Teflon, color TV sets, and so on. They make useful things. They design the bridges and skyscrapers. They build planes, gigantic metallic things that fly—and the mechanics keep them flying. Some of these "miracles" are the result of true genius, and some are merely technical or mechanical adaptations, but all represent a tangible benefit to mankind. And every mechanic working on innovations plays a vital part in economic history. Barney Rubble and

Two common men
may have contributed to invention of the wheel

Fred Flintstone did not invent the wheel, but no doubt someone much like them did—picture in your mind's eye that very common guy or gal, and you'll envision just how near the bottom many of the fonts of progress really lie.

The third category of intellect and talent that has benefited mankind is the artist. These are the people who compose the great music, write the great books, paint the great pictures. Names like Mozart, Shakespeare, Hawthorne, and Picasso come to mind. Harold Bloom's book *Genius*[53] tells the stories of 100 artists he regards as representing some of the finest geniuses "of language." He includes mostly writers of great plays, poems and novels like Milton, Shakespeare, Melville, Keats, Homer, Dickens, and Dostoyevsky. They make something tangible, useful, and beautiful that ordinary people can enjoy. Now individual tastes vary, and the names mentioned are of the highbrow artists, but others who produce for a wider audience are equally if not more deserving of our thanks—creators like Norman Rockwell, Steven King, Agatha Christie, Ogden Nash, Cole Porter, Charlie Chaplin, and Alfred Hitchcock.

These artists resemble the hard scientists and engineers in that they, too, produce a very real product. They offer enjoyment and generally do not carry overt political or religious messages. These artists are distinct from most of the soft-science intellectuals, who do not even attempt to inform or entertain but only to indoctrinate and proselytize. It is obvious that the one hundred writers chosen by Bloom, and many others, have contributed greatly to the happiness of people and the richness of culture.

Another feature common to the first three groups is they have not done much harm. You may say that is not so much to claim—that it is neither a positive nor a negative attribute, just a neutral one. But doing no harm is almost enough to get them on the honor roll all by itself, once you consider the contributions, both good and bad, of the fifth and last category of intellect.

Before we go there, the fourth category—that of the common everyday workers—should be acknowledged. They are not all necessarily book-smart; their SAT scores, if they took the SAT, would be clustered around the nation's average, or below. Most could not be an "intellectual" even if they tried—which they don't—because they are not adept at conceptualizing abstract ideas. But when they approach life and their careers with dedication, use their talents with discipline and persistence, they become very important. In fact, they can be quite successful and respected for their craftsmanship, generosity, and contributions to civil society. These are the people who make the bourgeoisie beautiful, even when they like NASCAR, baseball, professional wrestling, and hunting; and especially when in their simple innocence they infuriate the ACLU by praying to God and waving the American flag. Intellectuals as a rule hate this group, a prejudice which we will explore later, but "God must love them," as Lincoln famously said, "because he made so many of them."

The common people have another virtue, one that makes them doubly important. It is from this huge group—from the bottom—that all the geniuses in the first three groups emerge. Did you ever hear about Mozart's son, or Edison's daughter, or the children of Madame Curie? No, even such giants were not smart enough to perpetuate themselves. It is the common genius of ordinary people that somehow produces the prime movers. Out of the mélange of commoners many uncommon individuals rise to the top. This "product" is created most frequently among those with sound parenting skills. Human beings require not only ten to fifteen years of physical nurturing, but also ten to twenty years of social and moral training. If each generation were not taught such appropriate values as respect for others, cooperation, self-restraint, the rules of fair play and moral decency, charity, the self confidence to innovate, and the self-reliance to take care of himself— societies would rapidly decline.

Thomas Jefferson explained his view of the American common people in correspondence with John Adams: First Jefferson, "argued that there was a 'natural aristocracy among men' based on 'virtue and talents.' Then there was an artificial or 'pseudo-aristocracy founded on wealth and birth, without either virtue or talents.' Was not the whole point of the republican experiment they had helped to launch in America to provide for the selection of the natural aristocrats and block the ascendance of the artificial pretenders, thereby separating 'the wheat from the chaff.'"[54] Thus Jefferson endorsed the concept that there should be a level playing field and every person should have the right to make of himself what he might.

The life story of James Faraday illustrates one of the more extraordinary contributions of common people who were able to lift themselves by their own bootstraps. James was a blacksmith and had moved to London from North-West England in the 1780s. He managed to send his son to school for a short period to learn the rudiments of reading, writing, and arithmetic, but apprenticed him out to a bookbinder to learn a trade when he was fourteen. That son, Michael Faraday (1791-1867), served his seven year apprenticeship and dabbled in chemistry in his spare time. At the age of twenty-one, Michael met Professor Humphry Davy who encouraged his scientific interest and arranged another apprenticeship—this time in chemistry. During the next few decades, the basically self-educated Michael displayed his genius by discovering and developing the principles of electro-magnetism, which led to revolutionary breakthroughs in electricity, generators, and the motors that powered the Industrial Revolution. This common man possessed a great intellect but his abstractions and theorizing were devoted exclusively to practical hands-on scientific investigations that 1) actually worked, and 2) benefitted mankind. History is filled with similar stories, but they appear to only occur in open and free societies.

The fifth class of intelligent beings, the "soft-science" practitioners, have names and reputations familiar to most educated people. However, except for the rational investigators listed in subgroup A, they do not produce a tangible or beneficial product. In lieu of a product, they are credited by some with directing the advance of mankind by their ideas. This is an exaggeration that later chapters will prove mostly false. Sadly, in cases where their ideas did achieve significant influence, it was more apt to prove detrimental than helpful.

These "soft-science" intellectuals, who produce no useable patents, products, inventions, or services, are deservedly in bottom place. As Professor Sowell points out, those who flunk chemistry, physics, and math usually gravitate to the "easier" soft sciences. But the worst of these soft-headed thinkers are more than just lazy.

The best of the soft-science intellectuals belong in Subgroup A and demonstrate that it is possible to be an honest and productive intellectual. What distinguishes such intellectuals is that they try in their varied research to be accurate and to honor truth, without imposing too much of their own personal agenda. The better ones record and pass on mankind's extraordinary achievements in law, religion, politics, and science. Alexis deToqueville and Adam Smith are among such helpful reporters. In some cases, they present positive analysis and suggestions for improving fine points in a society. They for the most part do little harm, and usually are a positive force. They at least document what is happening and has happened in the real world.

In the scholarly tradition, they try to be objective as they search for meaning or summarize history or political or psychological processes in an accurate organized way for the elucidation of their readers. Barristers like Blackstone and Coke established and organized major features of the English legal system. In the popularization of history, the books of James Michener represent a tangible and beneficial product. Lewis Mumford and Edmund Wilson, praised for their independence and integrity by Russell Jacoby in *The Last Intellectuals*, did the same. Jacoby laments the recent decline in such scholars and points to the growing "careerism and corruption of bloated universities."[55] He differentiates Mumford and Wilson from the new breed of academician: "Mumford mainly wrote, as he would state later, around and past the academics to the intelligent readers. . . . He cherished an independence that he feared would wilt once burdened with university obligations and protocol."[56]

Inspired by Mumford's attack on academic "scholars," Wilson looked at the professors gaining status and found "the same profligate pedantry, a vast scholarly libido channeled into textual annotations mangling America's authors. Thirty-five scholars were busy going through variant texts of Mark Twain; eighteen of them were 'reading *Tom Sawyer* backward, in order to ascertain without being diverted from this drudgery by attention to the story or style, how many times "Aunt Polly" is printed as "aunty Polly." '. . . For Wilson this all demonstrated that the academic establishment had become a bloated boondoggle."[57]

Unfortunately, there are few independent scholars left, for getting promoted in academia—gaining entry to politically correct cliques—has become more a matter of conforming to the accepted agenda than of producing sound and enlightening scholarship. Such censorship of ideas within the academic institutions, along with a rash of plagiarism to expedite professional publication, has tarnished the veracity if not the reputation of this group of intellectuals. Most of them have descended into subgroup B, to become little more than zealots for certain socio-political positions. They might actually believe that the West has flourished simply because of good luck or good climate. As Johnny Cash lamented, "Can you blame the voice of youth, for asking, what is 'truth'?"

The third subgroup, zealots and nihilists, have largely taken over the teaching of the soft sciences—alarming when you consider that three of the most popular majors in American universities are anthropology, psychology, and political science, three of the softest of the soft subjects. It is even more alarming when you consider what is being taught in these courses. While everyone knows that the fundamentalist Islamic schools in Saudi Arabia inculcate hatred for America, its people and values, what's unforgivable is that the vast majority of American professors in the humanities are doing the same thing.

The zealots are educated soft-science academics, journalists, writers, and their followers who cannot separate their heads from their hearts and who resort to biased diatribes, revisionist history, and politically correct tracts on "current events." They fill the schools and colleges, the mass media, the State Department, and most of the large private foundations and special-interest groups. Although representing only a small part of the citizenry, they have come to dominate the leading institutions of their countries. Gertrude Himmelfarb argues that, most recently, their ideas emerged from 1960s counterculture to become today's dominant culture.[58]

A small percentage of these intellectuals-with-a-message are conservatives who stand for traditional values, a free economic system, and smaller government. They are a tiny minority in American schools and colleges, often numbering as few as one in twenty. Such teachers tend to be ineffective because on the social and moral issues they are fighting a culture attuned to hedonism and excessive "compassion" for a broad spectrum of supposed victims. They are helpful perhaps for balance, and for being pro-defense, and pro-American. In foreign policy and military matters, they try to promote the national interest. However, they are still intellectuals, and therefore their writings and talks do not reach the masses. They are also somewhat suspect insofar as many of them were radicals in their youth who changed their minds only after gradually losing faith in Leftist programs. As Norman Podhoretz admitted, with his wonderfully sardonic and self-effacing humor, because he is an intellectual it took him many years to recognize the evils of communism—something he expected an ordinary man would comprehend immediately.

Conservative intellectuals like Raymond Aron and Irving Kristol have indeed contributed outstanding scholarship in support of economic and political freedom. But their books are rarely assigned to American students, for they oppose almost everything the typical academic wants to teach—not history or English or anthropology, so much as watered-down current events. They seek not to enlighten, nor to encourage students to think for themselves, but rather to indoctrinate them in whatever ideas are currently politically correct. In *Crisis and Leviathan*, Robert Higgs observes that "Intellectuals, the specialists in the production and distribution of articulate social thought, are subject to fads; from time to time they are carried away by one notion or another for no apparent reason."[59] Unfortunately, these specialists do indeed produce a type of product, in the sense that a corrosive acid is a product: students who imbibe their teachings leave school believing that there is no right or wrong, morality is relative and undeterminable, religion is bad, big business is evil, and the biggest issues facing mankind involve animal rights or sexual orientation.

Thomas J. DiLorenzo notes one reason for the intellectuals' hatred of capitalism and their attraction to every form of collectivist system: "Under a regime of economic freedom and laissez-faire capitalism there is no role for intellectuals to advise the state on how to best plan everyone else's affairs." He points out that "In a capitalistic market place the choices of consumers matter most, even more than the opinions of experts";[60] so such experts suffer what Ludwig von Mises characterizes as "resentment over frustrated ambition."

Consumer sovereignty is the bane of every PhD angry that people he considers frivolous or unworthy often enjoy greater rewards under capitalism than he does. Most of the common men and women of America would readily admit to their crass and vulgar tastes—personal preferences that somehow result in professional athletes—and, worse still, the guy who dreamed up "SpongeBob SquarePants"—earning more money than professors. But under capitalism, "the customer is always right." That is what is so great about it—that it enables the common people to decide what they want, and get it. Free market processes characterized by open and robust competition provide consumers many reliable means of buying a great variety of goods of their own choosing. The capitalism-hating modern intellectuals, who deplore the commonness of Wal-Mart, would probably restrict the public to operas, ballet, and Kafkaesque theater. Their resentment is the same resentment Plato felt for democracy—there was no role for him, the aristocrat and would-be social engineer. Anti-capitalism reaches fever pitch among intellectuals simply because they had no role in building Western economic supremacy, have no role in maintaining it, and only a poor future in it—unless they can dominate it or tear it down.

Finally, we have the nihilists, the most extreme critics of Western civilization and its cultural heritage. Many are anarchists and degenerates who seek to drag all society down with themselves. Most are revolutionaries at heart—they want to start anew—by throwing out all that has been built. Thanks to how pervasively modern schools and colleges have been infected by these intellectual critics of America and the West, the nihilists are a growing population. Most are political scientists, sociologists, beatniks, Hollywood celebrities, writers, philosophers, and cranks. They can point to no useful products, no enlightening works, no life-saving techniques, no enhanced ways to grow food—they offer only vast quagmires of the mind.

In his memoir *Ex-Friends*, Norman Podhoretz offers graphic testimony of the depravity of such people as Ginsburg, Mailer, and Kerouac. In *Intellectuals*, Paul Johnson describes the irresponsible lifestyles of such radical icons as Rousseau, Shelley, Russell, and Sartre; and he observes that in the wake of the Second World War, "there was a significant change in the predominant aim of secular intellectuals, a shift of emphasis from utopianism to hedonism."[61] These people, who advocated wholesale debauchery to justify their personal lives, were sufficiently glorified in the media that they became role models for the young. Many were openly promiscuous in their sexual-romantic liaisons, neglected the offspring of their couplings, and were financially irresponsible. Their corrupt lifestyles frequently shortened their lives dramatically, but not before they succeeded in spewing geysers of hate.

In defense of intellectuals and philosophers, Bertrand Russell explains that we "should try to understand what philosophers are attempting to say before we set them aside."[62] Russell comes to this task as a sympathetic intellectual himself, but admits one must first struggle to figure out what these geniuses mean to say, and then concedes that the result is usually not that enlightening! This is a very back-handed compliment, and, in fact, a condemnation, since few people have the time to devote to such efforts. And Russell's critique applies to most intelligentsia who suffer the handicap of falling in love with inordinately complex ideas.

The next time you see some expert on TV giving his opinion on something, stop and try to figure out if he or she is a subgroup A, B, or C soft-scientist. Do the same at your childrens' open house when their teachers explain what they are doing in the classroom. When I have tried this, I have found very few fair and honest "A" types out there. You will find most so-called experts to be firmly planted in the "B" and "C" categories. If it helps, for a shorthand reference, consider these three groupings as the "good," the "bad," and the "ugly."

Most people have not taken the time to evaluate the media-dominating intelligentsia and thus may accord them more respect than is due. This modern elite promotes views that rarely apply to reality or the wishes of the common people. Such ideas are frequently harmful and dangerous, so they must be filtered carefully if one is to avoid faulty courses of action.

This subject was addressed by Kurt Vonnegut in his futuristic novel *Galapagos*, wherein we learn that the human race was wiped out simply because their brains had gotten too big—as a result of which, their thinking got so convoluted that they could no longer deal effectively with reality. Vonnegut can be humorous, but here his satire is deadly serious. And it isn't just the depraved and destructive European "geniuses" like Sartre, Hegel, and Rousseau who are guilty. All one has to do is read the major newspapers or watch a few TV roundtables, and you know that, right here in America, we are close to the tipping point Vonnegut warned us about: "The big problem, again, wasn't insanity, but that people's brains were much too big and untruthful to be practical."[63] Thus, with greater mental capacity comes greater capacity to twist meanings into falsehoods. Rhodes Scholars have been especially known to suffer from this disease of the intellect, from which the teaching of economic history has not been exempt. The "twisting" of meaning and "tweaking" of semantics is a recurring curse of the intellectuals, and its absence is the saving grace of both common sense and the common man.

Intellectuals are very comfortable bouncing ideas around, and their extraordinary ability to manipulate the reasoning process leads them to love and promote ideologies.

The dictionary defines ideology as "theorizing of a visionary or impractical nature. . . . A body of doctrine, myth, symbol, etc., of a social movement . . . A cultural plan, as that of fascism, along with the devices for putting it into operation."[64] That last point is why intellectuals love ideologies—they can design and impose them from the top. But, as I will argue, social and economic progress has never come from a blueprint from on high, but has always been developed painstakingly by trial and error from the bottom, by common working people. Like many Americans, I tend to agree with the great labor leader George Meany, who liked to say "Ideology is baloney."[65]

George Meany, the plumber from East Harlem, a high school dropout, chewed cigars and condemned "all the stinking America haters who love Moscow." (Joshua Muravchik, *Heaven on Earth*)

Intellectuals of both the Right and the Left will never understand a George Meany, demonstrating the presence among us of an "Intellectual Elite that is completely out of touch with the attitudes of the average person in this country."[66]

The work of Eric Voegelin is aimed in part at liberating us from the grasp of ideologies. He was an intellectual, but he believed that many of the theories and ideologies of the intellectual elite, being simplifications and distortions of reality, serve to obscure the truth. He developed special terms like "pseudological speculation" to describe any ideology that is "closed to aspects of reality because of adherence to rigid ideological preconceptions such as that seen in 'spiritually diseased' thinkers like Karl Marx. Voegelin created these terms to explain the spiritual depravity that engenders ideological systems."[67]

Voegelin directed attention to the real accomplishments and experiences of the political men of action whose deeds gave rise to the subsequent writings of philosophers. Indeed, he gave up a project on the history of ideas because he decided that looking just at ideas would be "an ideological deformation of reality. . . . Ideas, once separated from their experiential roots, are subject to ideological reconstructions. . . . An idea is, in other words, once or twice removed from the primary substance of reality, i.e., the engendering experience."[68]

Voegelin writes like an intellectual, so let me illustrate his very important point. When the first settlers in Iceland, primitive farmers all, got together in 874 A.D. to set up a parliament to handle administrative matters, that was "an engendering experiential event." In other words, when ordinary people, working at the micro-grass roots level, create something useful, that is a small step on history's many stepping stones to freedom and prosperity. And, when Locke and Hume and Kant wrote about the need for representation for the common man, and his right to have a say in his government, over half a millennium later, such writings often were, in Voegelin's words, an "ideological deformation of reality." Not to mention the tardiness of these tomes . . . a 500-year lag. Another hypothesis to explore: Has the intellectual's permanent role in history been simply to play catch-up with the actual doers of history—the common men and women who forged all the actual steps of progress?

Scholars are still arguing about what the books of the intellectuals of the past actually mean. In fact, there is an entire industry of scholars that has been feasting off their self-appointed mission to interpret and apply the writings of such philosophers. Meanwhile, ordinary citizens and politicians and lawyers have been busy carving out and improving actual political and economic systems. Moreover, if one takes the time to read and try to understand the philosophers, it becomes clear that much of it is a muddle—and that much of it is frighteningly supportive of destructive and fallacious ideas. Mortimer Adler has written about the Great Philosophers and criticizes the many errors in the works of just about every one of them, errors whose influence is not benign: "They all tend in the same direction. They affect our understanding of ourselves, our lives, our institutions, and our experience. They mislead our action as well as becloud our thought. They are not cloistered errors of merely academic significance. They have been popularized and spread abroad in a number of ways."[69] Throughout history, misleading and beclouding action and thought has been the stock in trade of all too many intellectuals; and, once this darkness spreads over a land, decline sets in.

Without expressly acknowledging it, Adler's book outlines a key factor in the rise and fall of nations. He is most critical of the philosophers of the past 400 years: "Like men floundering in quicksand who compound their difficulties by struggling to extricate themselves, Kant and his successors have multiplied the difficulties and perplexities of modern philosophy by the very strenuousness—and even ingenuity—of their efforts to extricate themselves from the muddle left in their path by Descartes, Locke, and Hume."[70]

In the entire book, Adler seems to approve of only two—Aristotle and Aquinas. Even with these two he finds fault, asserting that "it has been my understanding of the underlying principles and the formative insights that govern the thought of Aristotle and Aquinas that has provided the basis for amending or amplifying their views where they are fallacious or defective."[71] This confession suggests just how charitable one must be when reading the writings of most intellectuals. In elaborating my own view of historical progress, I am not anticipating that readers will somehow comprehend its wisdom by their deep understanding of the underlying intent inherent in my thinking, nor do I expect that they will cheerfully "amend and amplify" my views so that they make sense. Instead, I have tried to be simple and clear so that interpretation by academics will not be necessary.

A broad interpretation of economic history must consider both the positive and negative forces that have operated. And so, in the chapters that follow, we will examine the lives and deeds of the worst group of intellectuals. When we disparage "intellectuals," and the "intelligentsia," we are not referring to all people of intellect, but just to that large group who fall in love with their abstract and utopian ideas, care not for actual results, and come to their tasks with no actual work experience. In contrast, Dr. Albert Schweitzer is an example of a person of very high intellect who escaped being an intellectual: By being a physician and treating the sick, he actually did something physically that helped others. And by interpreting Bach in organ recitals, he qualified as an artist who benefitted others with his work. Finally, he kept his feet and head firmly planted in reality and avoided fuzzy abstractions—we will see in Chapter 13 how readily he dismisses Descartes' philosophizing and its catchy but fatuous "Cogito ergo sum."

Unlike Schweitzer, "intellectuals" rarely participate in the productive real world, confining themselves instead to positions where they can advise, direct, or criticize. They can generally be recognized as having never held a job in the private sector and thus have no working experience to guide their opinions. We will see how such illogical people and their more zealous and nihilistic comrades "help" successful economies go under. We will compare their deeds to those of the common men and women who forged the many small steps that advanced mankind's well-being. We will evaluate the harm the intelligentsia have done. We will name more names. And we will sound the warning to beware of the "ugly" ones—the blessed, but blighted.

Chapter 4
Philosophers Versus Scientists

 *"The direct economic drain of supporting an intelligentsia with little to contribute to the economy is by no means the sole or most important cost they impose on the rest of the people . . ."*
—Thomas Sowell, *Conquests and Culture*

IN HIS BIOGRAPHY, *Gentleman Revolutionary: Gouverneur Morris, the Rake Who Wrote the Constitution*, Richard Brookhiser recalls Morris's wise observation that "'none know how to govern, but those who have been used to it . . . and such men have rarely either time or inclination to write about it.' Political books, therefore, 'contain mere utopian ideas.'"[72] He predicted that anyone sitting in a comfortable school room, an "ivory tower," well-fed and well-clothed, might easily come to believe that anything is possible—that all that should be, can be. In such a heady and confused state, and with plenty of time on his hands, such a theorist might confidently scribble his groundless ideas about government and economics. Unfortunately, the resulting books are used to teach students—except in business and law, where the case method imparts a sense of reality to the classroom.

As a successful businessman, statesman, diplomat, and politician, Morris was always too busy to write a book. His wise observation—and the wisdom of his example—illustrates the folly of intellectuals, philosophers, and pundits who second-guess the real players. Anyone actively engaged in the business of forging agreements among a community of men knows the many compromises required merely to get them to live together reasonably peacefully. With that practical knowledge, a working man has the advantage over the intellectual, for he understands the difference between what should be and what is actually possible.

Two other practical men who struggled to establish America as a free nation had little use for the utopian breed of philosopher. John Adams thought Plato's *Republic* was a satire when he first read it; he felt no one in his right mind could seriously propose what Plato described as an ideal society. Thomas Jefferson, like most of the educated colonials of his age, had actually read the Greek and Latin writers as part of his schooling. However, he too had no use for Plato in helping create the American miracle. After all, Plato despised the common man and hated the idea of democracy as a form of government.

Nevertheless, the Greek philosophers of mature Greece have been revered for over 2,000 years for mirroring some of mankind's earliest and greatest achievements on the long march to civilized society. It was the Greek city-states, as ultimately embodied by Athens around 500 B.C., that demonstrated the higher possibilities for man. This small community somehow organized itself around a rudimentary democratic political system that unleashed the creative might of many of its citizens. The result was commercial prosperity followed by a rare flowering of culture with magnificent architecture and sculpture and theater. Individuals of remarkable ingenuity were free to explore mathematics, geometry, astronomy and philosophy. Their varied achievements have rarely been equaled to this day. But how did this happen? Did the philosophers contribute to this achievement? We will see how little the soft-science thinkers gave in the following section.

The historical record shows that Plato and Aristotle, who appear to tower over this grand Athenian society, merely reflected the glory of what was, or had been, Greece. They did not create the flower that was Athens any more than Franklin Roosevelt or Ronald Reagan created modern America—instead they came after other more practical workers had created the setting for their leisurely studies. And, unlike Roosevelt and Reagan, they did little to support or protect the nation they were born into.

Like most intellectuals after them, Plato and Aristotle wrote impressive tomes and created some interesting books about the society they were born into. Aristotle went further, being a practical or natural philosopher, and established new scientific precepts dealing with mathematics and astronomy; and he developed principles of logic and techniques of scientific inquiry that proved of lasting importance. He looked to established fact, and was skeptical of Plato's imaginative theories. However, Aristotle accepted the social world as he saw it—monarchies, republics, slavery, and a subordinate role for women, and his socio-political writings suffered some of the same defects as we find in Plato's work. Plato was never involved with the physical sciences; instead, his interests followed those of his mentor, Socrates, and were devoted to vague questions of order, virtue, and some less interesting observations on the type of society he might want to live in.

By the time such men arose, Greek society had benefited from its island security and relative peace for over three hundred years. Greek genius had already created the high culture that gave Plato the opportunity to be educated, to read and write, to attend the theater, and to live surrounded by the magnificent buildings and art that are renowned to this day.

As early as the seventh century B.C., "the opening of Egypt to the Greeks brought them into contact with a civilization age-old and of tremendous organizational and technological achievement, but set and congealed. . . . The Greeks had the best of both worlds; they were themselves free of the autocratic and theocratic institutions of the Middle East, but they could draw on its accumulated observations. Later on individuals with untrammeled minds could continue the search for general principles."[73] It is the combination of physical security and mental freedom that typically allow individuals and societies to flourish. As we find in most great civilizations, it is the soldier who makes the benign scenario possible—by establishing and protecting an essential pre-condition of progress.

After the battles of Salamis and Marathon, the Athenians found new strength and confidence. "Flushed with victory and the sense of freedom fairly won, the people of Athens did for a time rise towards nobility. Under the guidance of a great demagogue, Pericles, the chief statesman rather of the caliber of Gladstone or Lincoln in modern history, they were set to their task of rebuilding their city and expanding their commerce. . . . For a time they were capable of following a generous leader generously, and Fate gave them a generous leader."[74] The battles that ensured security occurred half a century before Plato was born, and had been preceded by several centuries of emerging Greek culture and arts—centuries that constituted an important tipping point in economic history. For the first time, a society was heavily populated with individuals steeped in an optimism that allowed them to seize opportunity and create progress.

But by the time of Plato's birth, it was all about to end. While engaged in a losing battle with Sparta, Pericles was banished, the Republic collapsed, the Thirty Tyrants took over, and the Golden Age of Greece drew to a close.

The Spartan victory was abetted by Athenian weakness: the city had degenerated into a loose democracy in which the skeptics and intellectuals challenged all the political and religious foundations of its history, with Socrates, the most famous of these, wandering the streets and urging the youth to defy authority. Under the heading of *Countercultural Elitist*, Ken Goffman describes Socrates as "essentially a political dropout who criticized all systems. But like most dissidents and gadflies, he would have directed his harshest opprobrium toward his own society, which happened to be a participatory democracy. So the Socratic polity emerges—both from the literature and as a result of a series of incidents that took place during his lifetime—as blatantly anti-democratic."[75] Indeed, many of The Thirty Tyrants who usurped control were the gadfly's own former students; they were led by the young aristocrats Critias and Charmides, relatives of Plato.[76]

Thus soldiers created the opportunity for Athens during the dynamic rise, or first phase, of the Greek civilization. Scientists broadened man's understanding of natural forces. Creative artists produced great theater. Then intellectuals and social philosophers showed up to shut it all down. With internal division and doubts weakening the citizenry's resolve, and the army no longer able to maintain security, the once mighty republic collapsed. It was a collapse caused not by climate or poor septic systems, but by the gradual rot of internal decadence and cultural confusion.

Before the loss to Sparta, Athens had revered the individual, the heroic individual man, the athlete, the soldier, the doer. The Athenians had their gods, many of them, but it was man whom they put on a pedestal. And it was the ordinary politicians, generals, craftsmen, artists and workers, not to mention all the slaves, who created this world, this swashbuckling era when each citizen was important and at least each freeborn male citizen could participate directly in democracy. This successful society had been built gradually over several centuries. Only by painstaking effort and many incremental steps did it culminate in the age of Pericles. And it was only this already-established, affluent, pastoral, almost bucolic society that permitted Plato, born into a rich and noble family, to study at leisure and engage in philosophical speculation.

And engage in philosophical speculation is all Plato ever did. He joined the school of Socrates and relished the clever and "logical" discussions that his teacher employed to "explore" (not solve) ethical questions. This form of logic, Socratic reasoning, has been much heralded as a watershed event. But in truth it only reflected insights that had already evolved during the preceding several hundred years of Grecian history. After all, Pythagoras had deployed rigorous logic in his geometric calculations, and Hesiod had explored the nature of virtue and the human soul some three hundred years earlier. None of these musings helped Jefferson, Adams, and Morris in 1776; they still didn't know what the human soul might be. And as for virtue, they simply believed that taxation without representation was an evil, and that it was worth fighting, even dying, to be free of such political oppression. They eschewed the spinning of philosophical abstractions as an end in itself and instead relied on a few simple principles and beliefs—"common sense"—that they applied to solve real and urgent problems.

Two thousand years before, Aristotle had also explicitly rejected Plato's philosophy, noting that "if we stray beyond the ground covered by experience we wander into empty talk. . . . Whatever is outside all possibility of experience for us can be nothing for us. We have no validatable way of referring to it, or talking about it, and therefore it cannot enter into our discourse in any reliable way."[77] Thus Aristotle remained true to the scientific and rational tradition of Thales, and provides comfort to all subsequent practitioners of the observable and provable "hard" sciences.

Nevertheless, Western scholars and a good press have deified Plato's reputation for over two thousand years as if his ideas were a vital legacy. H. G. Wells, in his *Outline of History*, joins the chorus, saying, "it is a landmark in this history, it is a new thing in the development of mankind, this appearance of the idea of willfully and completely recasting human conditions. So far mankind has been living by tradition under the fear of the gods. Here is a man who says boldly to our race, and as if it were a quite reasonable and natural thing to say, 'Take hold of your lives. Most of these things that distress you, you can avoid; most of these things that dominate you, you can overthrow. You can do as you will with them.'"[78] This is a common accolade, yet Solon and Lycurgus had already "taken hold of their lives," and carved out giant steps for mankind, much earlier, by creating constitutional governments for the Greek cities. And it was Plato, with his contempt for the republic he had inherited, who helped destroy it.

Indeed, Athens had developed a constitution and banished the despotic rule of kings early in the sixth century B.C. Mortimer Adler points out that "Solon gave the Athenians a constitution which, adopted by them voluntarily, established the Athenian republic. So, too, Lycurgus gave the Spartans a constitution. . . . Aware of this history, Aristotle, after stressing the naturalness of the state because of the natural need it satisfied, wrote that 'he who first founded the state was the greatest of benefactors.' He had Solon and Lycurgus in mind as of the state because, in his view, absolute or despotic rule, carried over from the rule of tribal chieftains, was incompatible with a state—a civil society or political community."[79] The two states, one a republic, the other more of a democracy, had been installed and operated by practical men long before Aristotle or Plato wrote about them; indeed before either was born. Clearly those predecessors had been ready, willing, and able to "willfully and completely recast human conditions," so the concept was well established before Plato played with the idea, and got the credit, many years later. The small city-state of Athens was organized and developed around a historically new idea: respect for the individual. This gradually led to individual claims to one's rights as a member of the democratic polity.

Let us consider key dates in the growth of Greek culture (all dates are B.C.):

Beginnings

c. 900	Simplified alphabet and written language emerge; literacy spreads.
c. 750-800	Homer, first literate European poet, pens epic poems *Iliad* and *Odyssey*.
c. 700-750	The poet Hesiod writes *Works and Days*, celebrating lowly farmers and calling for justice.
750-550	Age of Colonization. Spread of the Greek culture, city-states, coins, trade.
c. 600	Sappho of Lesbos, first great lyric poet, flourishes.

Signs of Greatness—The Beginning of the Golden Age

650-550	Lycurgus, legendary law giver, writes Sparta's republican constitution.
c. 590	Thales, the first great Greek scientist, seeks to explain the physical world by relying on observation and reason, not tradition and myth.
590s	Solon, reformer of Athenian laws, moves toward constitutional democracy.

c. 580-500	The mathematician and logician Pythagoras, founder of quasi-religious brotherhood, flourishes.
561-527	Pisistratus, Athenian ruler, encourages theater, public buildings, temples.
550	Anaximander speculates on human evolution from lower species.
c. 525-456	Aeschylus, first great tragic dramatist, emphasizes traditional values.
508	Cleisthenes adopts new democratic constitution under which the Assembly includes all Athenian citizens from landless laborers to aristocrats.
496-406	The tragic dramatist Sophocles, author of *Antigone*, explores emotions, sobriety, restraint.
490-479	Persian Wars are fought; Athenians stop Persians at Marathon.
477	Spartans delay Persian army at Thermopylae.

The Mature Age—Supremacy of Mind and Might

478	Themistocles commands victorious Greek sea battle at the Bay of Salamis.
C 490-440	The Sophists, the first social scientists, study human behavior, ethics, politics, history, and affect an attitude of sweeping doubt, relativism, and individualism.
479	The Spartan army routs the Persians at Plataea, making Greece safe from foreign wars.
485-406	The tragic dramatist and skeptic Euripides offers psychological insight into man, reason, faith.
477	The Delian League, a central authority that reduces the independence of the states, is established.
484-430	Herodotus emerges as the first major Greek historian.
460-429	The Golden Age ends with the rule of Pericles. Architecture, civilization peak.

c. 469-399	The philosophical gadfly Socrates espouses the views that an unexamined life is not worth living and that knowledge equals virtue.
c. 440	Democritus speculates on atomic structure of the universe.
432	The Parthenon is completed.
460-400	Thucydides, first great critical historical scholar, pens *The History of the Peloponnesian War*.
460-377	Hippocrates, the first major Greek physician and "father of medicine," flourishes.

The Decline of Greece

431-404	Peloponnesian War marks the decline of Athens and its eventual defeat by Sparta.
430-429	Plague wipes out a quarter of Athenian population.
c. 450-385	Aristophanes emerges as first great Greek comic playwright.
427-347	Plato, student and interpreter of Socrates, writes dialogues on order and virtue.
384-322	Aristotle, student of Plato and universal scholar-scientist, teaches at the Lyceum; tutors Alexander, son of Philip of Macedon.
359-336	Reign of Philip of Macedon.
338	Battle of Chaeronea. Macedonians gain mastery over Greece.
336-323	Alexander conquers Greece and much of the rest of the known world.

This four-part chronology highlights some of the pre-eminent Greek thinkers and doers to show the gradual progression of their ideas and deeds—the birth, rise, plateau, and decline of Greek culture. The achievements often credited to Plato had already been accomplished by many predecessors, for the most part before he was born. During four centuries of advances, generations of enterprising individuals forged the stepping stones that paved the way for Periclean Athens. There were great playwrights, soldiers, mathematicians, statesmen, law-givers, architects, and builders, but few soft-science intellectuals—until near the end, when Socrates, Plato, and the Sophists arrived on the scene.

The *Histories of Herodotus* chronicle much of this development through to the time of his death around 420 B.C. Herodotus was a champion of freedom and praised Cleisthenes, who transformed Athens into a democracy by allying himself with the common people against the aristocrats. As we see so often in history, freedom for the common people led to a burst of vitality for the society. "Athens had been great before; now, her liberty won, she grew greater still."[80] He recounts the many bloody battles between neighboring cities and leaders all vying for power and control, and the victory of the common people during the sixth century B.C., almost 100 years before Plato was born. Once free under Cleisthenes, "the father of democracy," Athens, "went from strength to strength, and proved, if proof were needed, how noble a thing equality before the law is, not in one respect only, but in all; for while they were oppressed by tyrants, they had no better success in war than any of their neighbors, yet, once the yoke was flung off, they proved the finest fighters in the world. This clearly shows that, so long as they were held down by authority, they deliberately shirked their duty in the field, as slaves shirk working for their masters; but when freedom was won, then every man amongst them was interested in his own cause."[81] This may have been one of the first written expressions of the insight that the oppression of tyrants stymies the creativity and initiative of a people; and that with the yoke thrown off, a people under freedom can use the cornucopia of the human heart and mind to create success and progress.

The Histories were published in 415 B.C., almost two and a half millennia ago, so the all-important role of the individual's attitude, including the source of his motivation, has been well known all these years. Herodotus repeats the point when he recounts the battle of Thermopylae, explaining how a small band of Spartans could for so long resist the Persian hordes of Xerxes: free men, fighting for their homes and families, represent "the finest kingdom in Greece, and the bravest men." *The Histories* have long been a classic, but its insight into the initiative and enterprise of free common men has been muddied by intellectuals who prefer the ideas of Plato: the convoluted theories that propose that a select few "smart" people should rule from above, telling the rest of us what to do. It is this all too common backsliding in human knowledge that is so frustrating in the study of history. When one reviews mankind's progress, progress that occurred spectacularly but all too rarely, it seems unconscionable that such useful knowledge and successful strategies once enunciated were subsequently suppressed or displaced by the failed policies of so many philosophers and intellectuals. Academics of the past two millennia have been inclined to neglect Herodotus and keep Plato alive to justify their preoccupation with the wrongheaded abstractions of what would otherwise be recognized as a transparently useless occupation.

More than two thousand years after the virtues of Greek democracy and the common man were recognized by Herodotus, the Americans shocked the world by establishing liberty in colonial America. In writing about those more recent times, David McCullough asks, "What were those self-evident truths that so many risked all for, fought for, suffered and died for? What was the source of their courage? Who were those people? I don't think we can ever know enough about them." Reading McCullough's book is an excellent way to learn about the "self-evident truths" the American patriots fought for, but so is the study of earlier history. For the American patriots were, like the Greeks, simply common people who wanted freedom— common people who were sick and tired of haughty aristocrats and power-hungry leaders telling them how to live and what to do. They were the same kind of souls who had rallied around Cleisthenes twenty-four hundred years earlier to topple the tyrants. Despite all the endless philosophical tomes debating the meaning of life, the role of governments, and the nature of knowledge and of good and evil, the ideal of freedom for both the Greeks at Thermopylae and the Americans at Valley Forge was indeed "self-evident." And all too often, the prolix intellectualizing of the intervening millennia has served only to obscure what the common people were doing.

Chapter 5
The Stepping Stones of History

 *"In each period that is marked by historical progress, there exists what one might call a 'laboratory society' where civilization's great inventions are tested."*
—Jean-Francois Revel, *Anti-Americanism*

Alan Dershowitz argues that the rights of citizens in relation to government have been developed or invented over the years by individuals seeking to protect themselves from injustice—"to prevent the recurrence of wrongs."[82] His view is consistent with our thesis that all the great advances—in common law, juries, bills of rights—which are the hallmark of Western legal systems originated not with theorists but with common men and women demanding freedom from oppression.

Man is an imaginative and enterprising creature who responds positively to freedom. No intellectual or philosopher is needed to discover this fact. Anybody who watches children knows that all humans want freedom—indeed, the problem is to get them to restrain themselves, to cooperate. Throughout history, those who would rule from above have resorted to extraordinary methods to hold down the rest of us. Once freed, most men and women respond creatively, and they respond to success with redoubled effort. Such initiative is not a racial or ethnic characteristic. All men desire freedom; all men are willing to work; all men work harder if economic freedom allows them to keep the product of their toil.

Some writers question whether freedom can be "taught" in nations with no experience in its precepts. Freedom need not be taught—it is man's natural state—but it does need a chance to flourish. For thousands of years, almost all civilizations were ruled by autocrats who lived in ease as the great masses of humanity whom they ruled lived in poverty. Throughout this evolving period there were only a few isolated instances when ordinary people were at least relatively free to do as they themselves desired. It was during those precious moments that the common men and women showed what was possible—the heights mankind could reach if only given the chance.

Citizens of the twenty-first century are fortunate that the common men of past millennia created the systems of freedom that we now enjoy. The enabling mechanisms are there for all to see, cherish, preserve, and emulate. But it did not just happen. And it did not come easily. To borrow a phrase made famous by Donald Rumsfeld, "It was a long hard slog and not too tidy." Let's look at the major stepping stones.

Phoenicia: The First Merchant State

The isolated pockets where economic freedom arose in latter days—like Holland in the seventeenth century and the Italian cities in the early Middle Ages—were preceded by the example of Phoenicia some two thousand years before. Similarly isolated, the Phoenicians were mostly free from outside intervention. Ironically, when there has been a geographical element in a nation's success it has often been the *absence* of valuable land that helped. Because no potential aggressors lusted after their remote and barren outposts, the hardy residents were left secure and free of outside oppression. And, to compensate, they became skilled sailors and traders, finding a niche providing many of the goods needed by surrounding empires. Writes historian Glenn Markoe, "As 'favoured cities' in the eyes of the Egyptians, the Phoenician coastal towns clearly benefited from their role as entrepreneurs in such commerce."[83] The competing empires of the area found the cities useful as sources of goods. "During much of their history, the Phoenician cities served as client or vassal states under a variety of political overlords. . . . However, foreign over-lordship appears to have been relatively non-invasive from a political standpoint, geared primarily at ensuring the timely payment of taxes and tribute and the contribution of services."[84]

With the huge empires of Persia, Babylonia, and Egypt to the east and south, and the Greeks to the north, for over a millennium the Phoenicians were restricted to the narrow band of coastline along the eastern edge of the Mediterranean. Indeed, to be safe from attack they built their largest cities on islands and peninsulas off the coast. To avoid land-dependent commerce, they established shipbuilding and trading routes that allowed their merchants to trade throughout the known world. By 1100 B.C., their settlements had spread from one end of the Mediterranean Sea to the other.

In the early years of their exploring and colonizing, the Phoenicians were ruled by kings claiming God-given authority, who established dynasties lasting sometimes a hundred years, until replaced by another family of rulers. However, under the King there was no aristocracy. The scarcity of land to support large estates helped the Phoenicians to avoid the kind of feudal land-systems that afflicted so many other societies. Instead there was a large business class, busily engaged in trade, shipbuilding, and eventually in manufacture for export. Capitalism had found its first expression, uninhibited by either aristocrats or intellectuals.

Excavations at Phoenician manufacturing sites have revealed their extensive pottery works, with separate areas for washing and storing clay, a production room with wheels for spinning, kilns for baking, finishing departments with slip basins for decorating, and storage, packing, and shipping areas. They were also renowned for the production of decorated fabrics and for their use of warp-weighted looms.[85] Because they possessed no natural resources other than timber, they developed widespread trading routes where they could purchase, transport, and resell raw materials throughout the Mediterranean region. However as early entrepreneurs they "not only transported these metals as raw commodities but transformed them into expensive finished goods."[86] As we see so often in tracing historical processes back through time, even the Phoenician exploits were nothing new: "Many of their trade routes and ore sources had already been established by the Mycenaeans before them."[87]

Three thousand years later, Adam Smith wrote a 900-page tome about this kind of entrepreneurial activity. Because Smith's book "is big and dense enough to double as a doorstop" and is full of "meandering sentences and discursive tangents," P. J. O'Rourke recently published what reviewer Joel Miller calls "Adam Smith for Dummies."[88] Joel Miller praises O'Rourke's concision in boiling the entire thing down: *The Wealth of Nations*, O'Rourke writes, "argues three basic principles and, by plain thinking and plentiful examples, proves them. Even intellectuals should have no trouble understanding Smith's ideas (of) . . . pursuit of self-interest, division of labor, and freedom of trade."[89] Thus, the essence of Adam Smith's acclaimed book is a review of this "trinity of individual prerogatives." The free and independent Phoenician traders were among the pioneers of such pursuit of self-interest, division of labor in manufacturing processes, and great exponents of free trade. And as Adam Smith elaborately explained three millenniums later, these manifestations of human enterprise created prosperity in a rather barren land.

The Phoenician middle class built its own utopia. Although democracy was extremely limited, a relatively high degree of economic freedom enabled much of the population to engage freely in their business and private lives, safe from both internal and external assault: "A patriciate of rich merchants, who certainly lived like lords, decided the fortunes of the cities, while all rough work was done by servants and all lowly tasks by slaves," Gerhard Herm reports. "Powerful oligarchies in all Phoenician ports, with councils of elders, acted as a supervisory board in trade transactions. The basis of life was business, which automatically limited tyrannical methods. . . . This was still more evident in the Phoenician colonies. Carthage, the largest, probably never had a king, and was ruled as democratically as any other mercantile republic of later times."[90]

The empowerment of a wide range of citizens was a marked feature of this society. For extended periods the ruler's decision-making abilities were limited by the powers of a council of elders, "an ancient Phoenician institution documented in the Amarna correspondence."[91] In addition to these elder statesmen, there was "a larger, more encompassing body known as the 'people's assembly.' Documented in the mainland Phoenician realm at Tyre and Sidon, this institution was apparently composed of the 'enfranchised' population of the city, i.e. its free male citizenry."[92] These two political bodies anticipated and presumably laid a foundation for the similar forms of democracies that would arise centuries later in the Athenian city-states.

While the powers of the council and assembly may have been limited, such governance was a step toward fuller democratic representation and was, in any case, much different from the absolute rule of a single person. More important, the relatively independent cities were led by an economically enlightened group of merchants, heads of shipping trade syndicates, and shipping magnates. These individuals, pursuing their market activities throughout the Mediterranean and beyond, became the first industrialists and capitalists, promoting trade, efficiency, and prosperity wherever their influence flowed. Their powerful fleets made them valuable to the surrounding powers. When Xerxes invaded Greece in the early fifth century B.C., the Phoenician naval forces helped the Persians, and thereby gained extra privilege and power. Thus, by shrewd alliances and partial deference to the giants around them, for many years the merchant classes were able to maintain a relative autonomy.

The Golden Age of the Phoenicians lasted some 300 years, until about 850 B.C., when empires to their east gained increasing control over the cities of the Lebanon and the expanding Greek colonization of the Mediterranean took over much of the area. Even then, the Phoenicians played a major role in trade for 500 more years until in 350 B.C. Alexander the Great seized their one undefeated stronghold island of Tyre by building a causeway from the mainland to invade the city.

The Greeks had been enemies of the Phoenicians for hundreds of years, competing with them for ports and trade throughout the Mediterranean. With the final demise of the Lebanese cities, the Greeks were able to record history from their perspective: "The Greeks, as voluble as the Phoenicians were silent, saw to it that the people of the Lebanon went down in history as a crowd of avaricious, thieving, deceitful traders. To all intents and purposes they have only been rediscovered through modern research."[93] Setting aside the prejudices of Greek chroniclers, we realize that the Phoenicians were one of the first societies to demonstrate that economic success would inevitably arise from the individual enterprise of free citizens when they were unencumbered by a rigid political, bureaucratic, or theological structure.

Greece: The Roots of Democracy

Louis J. Halle locates the beginnings of the Aegean civilization in Crete around 2000 B.C.[94] Achaean ascendancy on the Greek mainland is assigned to the period from 1300 to 1100 B.C. The siege of Troy memorialized by Homer probably occurred in this latter period, and it was followed by frequent wars among the Greek-speaking peoples of the region. Then, around 800 B.C., classical Greek culture began to emerge.

Halle points out that in the time of Plato, 500 years later, with "the polity of Pericles, the Parthenon, the historical work of Thucydides, the drama of Euripides, and the philosophy of Plato . . . there is no way forward that is not down. If, however, one places oneself in the Greece of Homer, when the nation is beginning to realize itself in its own conception, then the prospect of an upward way is clear ahead."[95] From that early beginning, the advance of freedom was aided by the isolation of pockets of small societies in which citizens were able to secure rights from their leaders.

Victor Davis Hanson has suggested that these enclaves were uniquely enriched by an autonomous class of independent farmers—an agrarian community "neither rich nor poor, but wholly different from either in both conduct and spirit." From the seventh century on, Greek culture was built upon this foundation. Its enterprising nature is evidenced by Hesiod's *Works and Days*, which chronicles a farmer's tasks and obligations, urging hard work and moral precepts that built prosperity for a new middle class of yeoman farmers. The emergence of this group created something unique in Mediterranean cultures that was to empower the city-states: an ennobled new middle class, a free citizenry owning their farms and enjoying economic freedom.

Hanson documents the origin of these independent farmers in *The Other Greeks* and subtitles his book, "The Family Farm and the Agrarian Roots of Western Civilization." These farm families, united and motivated by their ownership of their lands, built the original middle class of early Greece. Because they provided the foodstuffs in peacetime and yoked together as hoplite warriors defended their turf in times of battle, they were accorded the rights of full citizenship. Aristotle praises this middle group of common people in his *Politics*, credits them with providing the city-state with social and political stability, and argues that government by this class provides the best form of government. As the city-states grew in power, shipping and trading came to play more vital roles, and many farmers emigrated to the new Greek settlements, spreading their ideas of private property and citizens' rights throughout the Mediterranean region.

However, the sources of most major societal advances are not merely material or geographic; they are also mental. So it was in the ancient world. This further ingredient did not spring from grandiose theories of intellectuals but from the cosmopolitan outlook of seasoned traders and travelers—businessmen exposed to the diverse cultures of Egyptians, Phoenicians, Israelites, and Hittites. Halle observes that a society living in isolation has little cause to question the revealed knowledge of its religious leaders, which a priestly elite presented "to the common mind as knowledge that, having been revealed to it by a supernatural power or powers, was not to be questioned." But Greek traders must have realized that had they been born in Egypt, Israel, or Tyre, their gods would have been different. "The increasingly wide and varied world of the Greeks who lived from 1000 to 500 B.C., then, tended to liberate them from intellectual bondage to any priesthood or body of religious dogma, freeing them for indulgence in intellectual speculation."[96]

Greek traders and merchants were empowered by their adaptation and improvement of democratic practices drawn from the

Phoenician use of local administrative councils as well as a new and improved alphabet. The increased ease in writing expanded literacy, encouraged the recording of laws in written form for all to see, and facilitated the essential records of entrepreneurs. The resulting rise in sophistication and literacy occasioned something rare in the world: a

great writer, Homer, and the first philosopher, Thales of Miletus. Thales was a "natural" philosopher "concerned with the nature of physical being, rather than with ethics or social and political propriety as Gautama Buddha and Mahavira in India, and as Confucious in China, would be a few years later. It is the tradition of physical science, down to Niels Bohr and Werner Heisenberg in our own day, that stems from him."[97] Such was the dynamism of Greek civilization, spurred by practical men, physical scientists, and shrewd politicians and leaders. It may be wondered whether Buddha, Mahavira, and

Confucious—
praised order and obedience
over dissent and new ideas

Confucious held back their societies by emphasizing "ethics" and "order" rather than more practical sciences, much as Platonic thought would one day impair the progress of the West.

This interest in natural science marked the achievements of the best Greek minds for hundreds of years, until, amidst the full bloom of Periclean Athens, Socrates adopted a new course and emphasized a philosophy that explored the nature of virtue and knowledge, and attempted a perhaps vain search for "truth" and the human "soul." He ushered in the soft sciences that have progressed so little since Socrates and Plato first advanced every what-if imaginable. Since these philosophical what-ifs have no clear answer, their exposition is mainly an exercise in clever, sometimes beautiful, but always ambiguous language. As even Bertrand Russell laments, "we should try to understand what philosophers are attempting to say before we set them aside. It must be confessed, all the same, that the effort sometimes seems out of proportion to the insight achieved."[98]

The reason academics assert that the past 2,300-year history of "philosophy" is merely a footnote to Plato is that no more can in fact be said. Once you discuss the desirability of virtue and justice, and how evil is bad, and question whether we can really trust our senses when we touch and see something, whether knowledge really helps us understand the world, and whether man is selfish and needs some rules to live by, etc., where do you go with it? Especially if, while all this is being debated, ordinary politicians and laymen have actually set up schools to educate the young, given many of the citizens a vote, established courts and juries and laws to regulate behavior, and devised constitutions and Bills of Right to establish freedom and social civility. Anyone watching closely cannot help but perceive that the theoretical speculation has been pre-empted by the deeds of practical men. Russell explains that in itself, "philosophy sets out neither to solve our troubles nor to save our souls. . . . It is, as the Greeks put it, a kind of sightseeing adventure undertaken for its own sake."[99]

Note that, originally, the term "philosophers" referred almost exclusively to investigators of natural science, the hard sciences that produced useful results. Since Socrates, such "physical sciences" have been pursued by investigative minds quite different from those in the soft sciences. The latter have taken over the term "philosophers" and imbued it with the useless and esoteric flavor of excessive abstraction devoid of practical thought.

Some have argued that the philosophers, including Plato, are essential to teach the young, to pass on knowledge, and to maintain the symbols and belief systems of a society. It is true that someone must do this, but Plato and most of the soft-science philosophers who followed him are the last people anyone would want to perform this task. First of all, teaching basic mathematics and grammar is the work of a skilled and patient teacher; and, fortunately, there are many of them. They are the unsung heroes who, hundreds of years before Plato was born, probably taught Pythagorus his numbers; Anaximander his science; and Aeschylus, Sophocles, Herodotus, Thucydides, and Euripedes how to read and write. As for passing on cultural and national values, Plato and Socrates actively encouraged young people to ignore their culture, resist authority, deny the gods, and abandon democracy as a method of government. With "friends" like these, who needs enemies?

In contrast to Socratic investigation of ethics, the natural philosophers, the true scientists, had in the previous centuries developed a way of looking at things hitherto unknown to history. They didn't figure out simple geometry only to help irrigate or layout agricultural lands, as the Egyptians had done; or study astronomy only to make better calendars, as the Mesopotamians had done 2,000 years before Thales. Instead of seeking mechanical answers, the Greek scientists investigated the world around them to discern the unvarying laws of nature. As Halle puts it, "There is a world of difference between the observation of natural phenomena merely for the sake of practical application of the knowledge thereby gained . . . and speculation that aims at undersr!nding for its own sake, representing the need to fill the vacuum of ignorance."[100] Thus, this early Greek thought was more concerned with exploring the "why" of physical events than in exploiting the "how" to solve practical problems. Pythagoras exemplified the new approach by investigating the relationships of shapes and using mathematics to search for underlying rules. Instead of treating knowledge inherited down from the past as sacrosanct, he speculated independently on the possible meaning of his observations. By testing and revising such speculation he was able to arrive at more accurate conclusions, and this way of thinking formed the kernel of future methods of scientific reasoning. The soft scientists also further developed their "alternative" methods of investigation. All too often, what it comes down to is that hard scientists adjust their theories to reflect observed reality, while soft scientists adjust their perception of reality to fit their theories!

In the pre-Socratic period, the Greeks made many advances and fruitful beginnings in mathematics and medicine, chemistry and physics. Then came the age of Pericles. Greek philosophy became divided, with natural scientists continuing their discoveries as the social philosophers, led by Socrates and Plato, misguidedly sought to apply the scientific method to political and ethical subjects. Ever since, the practitioners of the soft sciences have continued to speculate on ethical precepts and questions of truth, justice, and knowledge. Meanwhile, whenever the occasion arose, common men established systems of government and business that leapfrogged such questions with practical reforms that fostered the well-being of millions. A close comparison of dates shows that the historical achievements invariably preceded the philosophical exposition that attempted to explain why the common man should do what he had already done. Moreover, examination of the philosophical writings indicates the frequent distortion of the actual record, leading to such "insights" as the Platonic dictum that the educated elites should use their superior virtue and intelligence to rule over the common people.

Free thinking can be a boon to scientific and artistic innovation, but carried too far, injected into religious or political observances, it can breed ruin. The traditional and pagan religious beliefs of the Greeks ennobled the people without preventing Pythagoras and other scientists from investigating the physical world. "The beauty of Apollo or Aphrodite, the wisdom of Zeus or Athena, constituted models for imitation, not only in stone but in statecraft and in personal conduct."[101] Religion did not hinder the Greeks because, like the Dutch and Americans who would follow, they learned to live nourished by faith while applying strict reasoning and logical processes to scientific and business endeavors. Most ordinary people seem to have no problem living with both faith and reason. This combination marked the great advances of pre-Socratic Greece and laid the foundation for future societies wise enough to emulate the formula.

Unfortunately, after a few centuries of progress, this useful dichotomy was sundered when Socrates condemned "the false belief in the traditional gods and goddesses that [was] imparted to schoolchildren by requiring them to read Homer."[102] What's more, he wandered the streets of Athens questioning authority during the Peloponnesian Wars, and helped spread the loss of faith that marked the end of Greek supremacy. Here was free thought taken too far. The religion as practiced by the Greeks for the past 500 years had certainly not held back progress, and it had lent structure and strength to the culture; so why tear it down? Why must intellectuals come in and ruin every good thing? Was not Socrates guilty of inciting unrest among the youth as charged? What was his religion-bashing going to gain? Free speech is an important right, one that unfortunately is frequently abused or over-indulged in to the detriment of the society allowing such freedom. But in its purest form it allows even the most absurd statements— words that can help enemies and weaken friends. In any case, Socrates can be accused of breaking an old time-tested axiom: if it ain't broke, don't fix it. And his timing was horrible, urging students to resist authority in the midst of a war that his city was on the verge of losing.

A common failing of intellectuals is just such lack of proportion— the inability to recognize the relative significance of things. Instead of tearing down the rather harmless and playful panoply of gods that the Greeks had honored for hundreds of years, intellectual thinkers like Socrates and Plato could have used their brilliance to improve the laws and courts of Athens, elevate the role of women in society, oppose slavery, extend the voting franchise, or improve the financial institutions. How logical or sincere could their search for justice, truth, and virtue have been when they never questioned the suppression of women or the widespread existence of slavery, and opposed equality for all common men? Instead they attempted to apply the rigorous logic of science and the physical world to vague, theoretical, and spiritual questions, and yet denounce the "superstition" of religions. A persistent weakness of intellectuals is this unfortunate urge to demand absolute proof on any question of religious faith, yet then be willing to make the proverbial "leap in the dark" to embrace various nonsensical ideas about governance. They've got it backwards! In science, technology, business and politics, one must be hard-headed and realistic; it is in religion that you can well afford to be more trusting, more optimistic, more hopeful about any available comfort "that helps us get through this thing, whatever it is."[103]

Iceland: Overcoming Geography and Climate

The expansion of freedom in England, fought for and achieved throughout the second millennium, was not, as the Great Gallagher would say, "a totally new concept." The Viking settlement in Iceland was composed of Scandinavians, mostly Norwegians, who claimed the virgin land and who in spite of the harsh climate established a nation of thriving farmers. And these people in 974 A.D. established a Parliament, sometimes referred to as the First Parliament in the world, more than 250 years before the Magna Carta was imposed on the rulers of Britain.

"From the ninth century to the twelfth the concerns of free farmers dominated the spectrum of governmental activity," notes historian Jesse Byock. "Legal and administrative decisions were fashioned within the context of a widespread belief in the inviolability of the rights of freemen. . . . Avoiding warfare, the Icelanders esteemed political flexibility and legal acumen, a cultural focus that is seen in their literature."[104] The common-sense idea of "inviolability of the rights of freemen" is a recurring theme in history; a self-evident truth, if you will, that even these Viking farmers understood. The respect for an individual's rights in Iceland had a beneficial impact on slavery. As Byock states, "The Icelandic respect for freemen's rights was also extended to freedmen (freed slaves) and their heirs. The slaves, many of them were probably of Celtic stock, were brought by the early settlers and were rapidly integrated into the society. . . . Most slaves were freed in the tenth century, although a few instances of slavery may have continued into the early twelfth century."[105]

The first settlers in Iceland, arriving around 870 A.D. from Scandinavian (or Viking) lands, were faced with a barren landscape and a nasty climate. But they had two vital advantages. First, they had left the nobility behind. Second, there were no other nations that coveted their remote and inhospitable land. Like the settlement of New England 750 years later, the first settlers were followed by a rush of kinfolk seeking free land. Within sixty years, a mere three generations after the first settlement, all the usable land had been claimed and settled. Coming from the various Nordic lands, the settlers brought their own laws and traditions with them; it became evident that some organization was needed. As Byock explains, "The problems probably could have been tolerated had not the idea of some form of unified country-wide structure appealed to the self-interest of the colonists. The initiative for establishing the Althing, the national assembly, seems to have come from a large and powerful kin group. . . . Norwegian legal traditions applied only to a limited extent to the society that was being created in Iceland. In many areas establishing new constitutional arrangements and new legal procedures was unavoidable. The innovations were then little by little hallowed by custom."[106]

In the political system that thus emerged, residents elected representatives who would meet, debate, and vote on policies to govern the land. This happy arrangement was abetted by three conditions that were also evident in the American and Dutch miracles: One, the settlers were of one economic class—there was no landed gentry or aristocracy, and, at least at first, everyone worked. Two, there were no intellectuals. Not in primitive Iceland! And, three, religion was kept separate from political affairs, or at least did not exert a controlling influence over political affairs.

The dearth of aristocrats, intellectuals, political scientists, priests, and philosophers did not harm the ordinary people. The simple farmer-settlers managed quite well, working out their problems in meetings, arguments, and negotiations. The complex writings of Locke, Hume, Kant, Montesquieu, and Rousseau would come centuries later, when they would set forth in elaborate prose the proposition that a representative elected government, supported by laws and courts, could best provide freedom. Some of these later writers did a reasonable job of discussing the natural rights of man, the pros and cons of constitutional government, the use of a parliament, the need for laws and courts, and the like. But they write as if it were their idea, giving little or no credit to the peoples that had already by decades of effort actually created such societies.

Certainly the Vikings deserve more credit for their innovative governance than they usually get. Alas, their literary record is restricted to the famous Icelandic sagas, which have become widely available only in the past century. Celebrated names and peoples sometimes owe their renown more to the fortuitous preservation of their writings than to the value of those writings. But the Viking conception of representative government must have influenced the demands of Englishmen many years later for a say in their own government. The national assembly established in Iceland was not the only parliament in Viking settlements. In Torshavn in the Faroe Islands, Europe's smallest capital, one can still walk out on the Tinganes peninsular and observe the original seat of Parliament, dating back over a thousand years. And tourists still visit Toompea Castle where Estonia's Parliament met when its free and prosperous city-state represented the northernmost member of the Hanseatic League. The founding of these parliaments on the remote outposts around England before 1000 A.D. must have been known to inhabitants of the mainland. Thus, even the Magna Carta was not a totally new concept.

For as long as man can determine, the average temperature in Iceland has fluctuated repeatedly over multi-century cycles. But it was always a remote, forbidding, and cold land. As in Plymouth, Massachusetts, 750 years later, there were no comforts to be had except what the settlers built with their own hands. Now, one of the characteristics of intellectuals is that they cannot or will not do much with their hands. You rarely see them doing real labor, growing crops, playing baseball or football, or getting their hands dirty. They were not and could not have been among those people who settled Iceland, the Faroe Islands, or Plymouth, Massachusetts, and created prospering societies, farms, a fishing industry, and established representative governments.

The philosophers and intellectuals came later, in places like Paris, London, and Hamburg. They still could not work, but they sure could write. They proceeded to take everything that had ever happened in human history and present it every which way imaginable. They have elaborated so much on events both real and imagined, that many of their treatises on government obfuscate rather than clarify what is in fact a rather simple proposition, that "a government powerful enough to create and protect private property rights and to enforce contracts, yet constrained enough so as to not, by its own actions, deprive individuals of these same rights, will be a 'market augmenting government.'"[107] A constitution providing for these conditions, combined with a form of representative democracy, has proved to be the best guarantor of such freedoms.

The Basques: The Importance of Undesirable Land

The Basque people were responsible for one of the least-known and least-appreciated stepping stones fostering the development of freedom.

This ancient race has survived to the present day in a small section of mountainous land facing the Bay of Biscay and situated in a small area on both sides of the French-Spanish border. In the millennium after Rome fell, the Basques retained their freedom and made a living by exploiting the one favorable asset of their location—the sea. They fished, traded, and built ships. Because of their isolation and the basic undesirability of their land, they were rarely attacked by foreign forces; and the ruggedness of that land instilled a tough self-reliance in the people. "According to popular myth, their rugged, mountainous terrain made the Basques unconquerable, but it is also possible that few coveted this land," notes Mark Kurlansky.[108] Since the days of the Romans, nearby empires learned that it was better to coexist with the

Basques than to try to occupy their lands. Indeed, for the past 2,000 years the Basques have maintained their own laws, customs, language, and government, making them one of the freest people in Europe. In effect, they operated as a nation, although made up of just two small parts of France and Spain.

The Bay of Biscay was the winter home of whales, porpoises, and dolphins, making possible a thriving fishing industry. As early as 670 A.D., "there was a documented sale in northern France by Basques from Labourd of forty pots of whale oil. . . . The first commercial whale hunters were the seventh- and eighth-century Basques, who found an eager market for this meat in Europe."[109] Whale meat, coming from animals that, like fish, lived in water, was permitted food on holy days (then, about half the days in the year!) and so became a staple of the European diet. As the whales in Biscay Bay became depleted from over-fishing, the Basques ventured further—into the north Atlantic and to Iceland.

By the ninth century, the Basques had met and skirmished with the Vikings and learned to copy the superior hull construction of Viking boats, in which overlapping planks were fastened with iron rivets. The Basques improved the design of ocean-going vessels and eventually brought Viking innovations in ship design to Florence and the other great trading ports of northern Italy city-states. By 1000 A.D., the Basques were venturing to Norway, Greenland, and Iceland to fish for whales and cod. They are believed to have reached parts of the North American continent before any other Europeans. In this way, they became Europe's leading shipbuilders, pilots, and navigators. Capitalists before capitalism, Basques financed most of their shipbuilding through private ventures. . . . Basque ships, large and beamy and known for their exceptionally large hold capacity, were sought after by Europe's maritime peoples. . . . Shipyards emerged in the fifteenth and sixteenth centuries over the entire Basque coast."[110]

Facing little oppression that could impede them, the common merchants and traders pioneered numerous legal and financial mechanisms that allowed for easier and more productive business operations. Their "maritime skills and engineering innovations were supported by legal prowess. In 1351, the Vizcayan fishing port of Bermeo signed a treaty with Edward III of England that was the first international accord to establish the principle of freedom of the high seas."[111] A simple, almost primitive people, with limited natural resources, thus accomplished great things. They were a small community, with trading routes not nearly as happily located as those of peoples living in the Mediterranean or along the shores of the Red Sea, the Persian Gulf, the Indian Ocean, or even many of the South Pacific Islands. Yet they matched the best success stories. They benefited from security; from a scarcity of oppression, aristocracy, and intellectuals; and from a can-do attitude. They were also familiar with and benefitted from exposure to the Greek-Roman cultures and the Christian Church. Finally, their initiative was never dampened by passivity-preaching religions and philosophies. One suspects no Basque ever gave up on a difficult goal because "the Almighty will take care of me," nor accepted adversity without a struggle just because "God wills it," nor, for that matter, lapsed into lethargy the better to "contemplate inner peace and harmony." Of course, such mental burdens are just another form of oppression imposed on people by faulty religions and cultures.

Columbus's four voyages to the New World (1492-1502) included Basque ships and were in part manned by Basque sailors, pilots, and navigators. After the New World was charted, Basques were quick to capitalize on the new opportunities for trade there. In the eighteenth century, Basque merchants elbowed their way into the cocoa trade with Venezuelans, in direct competition with the Dutch. As its share of the world market increased, Real Compania Guipuzcoana de Caracas, a Basque trading corporation, "became the company with which producers sought contracts. Because Basque ports were not in the Spanish customs zone, they could operate like a free zone for trade in the rest of Europe."[112] Shipbuilding boomed, and the Caracas trade expanded to include leather, coffee, beans, turkeys, and tobacco. To fill the ships on their return trips to South America they carried Basque iron products, wine, weapons, chemical products, sardines, and lumber. "In 1751 the company seat was moved to Madrid. But it did not operate as a Spanish monopoly. Its owners were the first pan-Europeans, caring little about the arbitrary borders that split up the continent. At the dawn of capitalism, the company became a multinational. . . . In this new age of capitalism, the Basques were demonstrating what their British contemporary, Adam Smith, would write about decades later."[113] While they were at it, by breaking the Dutch cocoa monopoly, the Basques caused the price of chocolate to plunge; but far from causing bankruptcies, the lower price led to such an increased demand that the greatly expanded market "made the trade far more profitable than it had been under Dutch price fixing."[114] Adam Smith later wrote about this, and university scholars soon preached about the elasticity of demand and the marginal propensity to consume—simple market mechanics that those uneducated but sagacious Basque traders already knew all about.

Like the Norwegians, the Basques were acquainted with how Icelanders governed themselves, for they fished throughout the North Atlantic. Knowledge of Icelandic institutions may help explain why they established similar local assemblies. On the other hand, such assemblies had been in use in scattered communities for thousands of years; the main inspiration for establishing them was simply the freedom to do so. Representatives from the Basque assemblies were sent to Guernica, where a fourteen-man ruling body was chosen by lot to govern the "nation" until the next meeting. The Basques were fortunate to be burdened by almost no tradition of aristocracy, and in only one province—Navarra. The rugged and primitive lifestyle and fierce independence of the populace was never softened up enough to accommodate an elite that could produce nothing tangible. But from time immemorial, the common men did maintain a set of working laws. The first written code of laws of the Basques was established in 1155; it formalized customs and traditions that had been handed down orally for centuries.

Vilhelm Moberg has written of three other isolated and inhospitable terrains the institutions of which nourished the freedom of peasants—Sweden, Norway, and Switzerland. The Swiss League was formed in 1291 and "behind the magnificent ramparts of their mountains its people defended themselves successfully and preserved their freedom. . . . In Norway's mountains and deep valleys, the Norwegian peasants, too, had dwellings inaccessible to outside interference. Mounted men-at-arms found no roads to advance by. Nor had the country any indigenous nobility; and the Danish nobles were few in number, and thereto extremely remote from their own capital in Copenhagen. To keep the Norwegians under effective surveillance was beyond the power of the Danish overlords."[115] Tolstoy theorized that progress often occurred in some of the most undesirable locales because the people had to work harder to overcome adverse conditions. More plausibly, it's because the people were free to work unhindered by either invaders from without or oppressive aristocrats and intellectuals from within. Assemblies like the Viking parliaments were no great "Aha!" discovery—they simply made sense, and similar institutions have been readily adopted whenever people are not prevented from doing so. And, as Herodotus observed, free people are better workers than slaves.

Thus, the Basques maintained a high degree of safety and suffered little oppression throughout most of their history; and, as a consequence, free economic activity blossomed.

Florence and the Italian City States: Drawing on the Past

After the barbarians had sacked Rome, but before the Renaissance, several small enclaves in Italy established successful city-regions that repeated the shipping and trading successes of the Basques and Phoenicians and anticipated the Dutch miracle of the sixteenth century. The great Medieval trading city of Venice got its start in 810 when its "lagoon settlers had asserted their right to exist as an independent entity. . . . The islands of the Rialtine archipelago . . . from their position in the center of the lagoon, almost impossible of access to those who were unfamiliar with the shoals and shallows that surrounded them, were superbly placed to defy an attacker. . . . Their inhabitants, being at once champions of and refugees from practically all shades of political opinion, were collectively impartial."[116] These refugees found safety and freedom by occupying land no one else wanted. They elected Agnello Participazio as their first leader, "whose modest house on the Campiello della Cason (near S. Canciano) became the first Doges' Palace in the Venice that we know today."[117] Thus geography played a role, but only because it was undesirable geography, and then only because that back-water environment appealed to ordinary people who wanted to escape the oppression of superiors.

Most of the Italian cities were governed as democratic republics at some point during the centuries leading up to the Renaissance. Such periods of freedom were interspersed with periods of autocracy, most notably, in Florence, under the rule of the Medici Princes. However, under either form of governance, an enlightened ruling class allowed considerable economic freedom for the citizens. Indeed, Machaivelli's advice to the princes was that if they wanted to maintain order and prosperity, to never take away any citizen's private property. There was a growing understanding of the benefits of free enterprise. This period after the Dark Ages constituted a baby step forward for mankind, one neither widespread nor very long-lived, but demonstrating to any who would notice that there was an alternative to oppressive, centrist governments—greater freedom for the individual that could in turn bring greater economic prosperity to all.

Helped by their strategic location between Europe and the East, these cities enjoyed flourishing shipping and trade. They "obtained a measure of political autonomy by the purchase of charters from their suzerains. The charters . . . conferred varying degrees of self-government, sometimes to the point of virtual freedom from feudal allegiance."[118] Such opportunities could be negotiated in only those regions in which monarchies were unable to establish strong central control. From the twelfth century to the fifteenth century, Italy, being divided into several regions and numerous "independent" cities, was sporadically able to enjoy this small-scale, local autonomy—much as the isolated city-states of ancient Greece had done. Not so in England, France, and Spain, where the towns were obliged to ally themselves with the rising monarchies and landed gentry that held power over them, a situation that was not to be remedied but by force of arms in the seventeenth century in England and the eighteenth century in France.[119]

But wherever the grip of centralized power slackened, local townsmen established a degree of autonomy and escaped the restrictions of feudalism. "The extent of self-government which eventually emerged and persisted for long periods of time in these European cities and city-states was without an exact parallel in other cultures. The closest precedents were European, the Greek city-states which flourished from the sixth to the fourth century B.C. Nothing very similar can be found in the great civilizations of Asia or the Muslim world."[120] A similar power vacuum fostered comparable autonomy, and thus prosperity, in the Hansa towns of the North Sea and the Baltic, and on the Dutch coast.

In the fourteenth century, the bankers, traders, and wool merchants established the businesses that made Florence the richest city in Europe. The resulting wealth and leisure fueled a concurrent interest among church leaders and wealthy merchant families in finding and translating classical scholarship—to restore the great days of Greek and Roman culture. Out of this mix there emerged a new confidence in what man could achieve. The dictum of Pythagorus, "Man is the measure of all things," recalled from an age almost 2,000 years earlier, became the new motto of Florence. The great architects Brunellesco and Alberti designed buildings to honor the "God-like" men of the city. Kenneth Clark emphasizes how well this optimistic spirit worked: "There is no better instance of how a burst of civilization depends on confidence than the Florentine state of mind in the early fifteenth century. For thirty years the fortunes of the republic . . . were directed by a group of the most intelligent individuals who have ever been elected to power by a democratic government."[121] Because there was freedom, upward mobility, and self-confidence in these towns, a group of movers and shakers emerged to inspire their times—and deliver a rebirth of civilization, i.e., the Renaissance.

The artistic geniuses of the period generally emerged from the humble families of artisans, and they were encouraged and financed by the bourgeois wealth of merchants and traders. The belief in the dignity of man was ever-present: in the frescoes of Masaccio, the sculpture of Donatello, and, at the peak of the Renaissance, the sculpture and painting of DaVinci and Michelangelo. Each individual was "conscious of his human powers, as a complete moral and intellectual being."[122] After 60 years of rule by the Medicis family, in 1494 the Florentines re-established a republic. To celebrate their freedom, they commissioned heroic and patriotic art. They engaged a young artist to create a gigantic figure of David, the tyrant killer. "The Michelangelo is vast, defiant, and nude. . . . When we come to the head we are aware of a spiritual force that the ancient world never knew. . . . It is not a part of most people's idea of civilization. It involves a contempt for convenience and a sacrifice of all those pleasures that contribute to what we call civilized life. . . . And yet we recognize that to despise material obstacles, and even to defy the blind forces of fate, is man's supreme achievement; and since, in the end, civilization depends on man extending his powers of mind and spirit to the utmost, we must reckon the emergence of Michelangelo as one of the great events in the history of western man."[123] This ability of free, independent men "to despise material obstacles," to even ignore "the forces of fate," refutes any theory of modern history based on geography, climate, or chance. The greatest flowering of genius occurred in those periods when the reins of government were loosest and a populace could find ways to overcome both fate and material shortages.

Like the Roman civilization of a thousand years and more before, the Italian cities survived for centuries despite recurring swings between republican, democratic, and autocratic governments. The leaders and artistic geniuses of the fifteenth century looked to the past for knowledge of how to regain virtuous and creative times—as had the Romans after the fall of the republic. Paul Johnson writes, "Augustus Caesar, while creating an empire on the eve of the Christian period, looked back to the noble spirit of the Republic, and even beyond it to the very origins of the city, to establish moral and cultural continuities and so legitimize his regime. . . . The empire was never so self-confident as the Republic, subject as it was to the whims of a fallible autocrat, rather than the collective wisdom of the Senate, and it was always looking over its shoulder at a past that was more worthy of admiration and seeking to resurrect its qualities. The idea of a republican renaissance was never far from the minds of Rome's imperial elite."[124] But it took freedom to bring about that renaissance.

In Renaissance Italy, we again witness the virtuous strength earned by men who are free, for the crowning geniuses of her cities had emerged after decades of nurturing Republican rule. It is true that even in the Republican periods, "democracy" was extended to only a relative few, especially in the more aristocratic cities of Urbino and Mantua. But economic freedom and the spirit of humanism encouraged all individuals to excel, and the enlightened rulers did recognize talent from all classes, so there was upward mobility and opportunity for success. Children of ordinary artisan families who learned their trades well could rise to the top. In fact, the attitudes and environment in Florence's working-class neighborhoods were more conducive to individual success than the attitudes and environment of most modern democratic cities. In practice, economic opportunity is more important to most men than democracy—in the short-run, you don't need a vote, so long as you are left alone to peacefully pursue your interests. You do need the vote to keep leaders from interfering in your life. But the vote, when you get it, must be exercised wisely, to deny demagogues and elect people of integrity and common sense—not to extract taxpayer-funded goodies. Indeed, a truly rational electorate would always vote for the candidate offering them the least!

Although democracy in many Italian cities was limited, and their governments often run by autocrats, for the most part these "Princes" came from the wealthy merchant class. What their background in business told them was that free trade and an open, competitive society is the best way to generate wealth for all. These rulers were not intellectuals without real-world experience, but seasoned businessmen who knew firsthand the realities of work and enterprise. Moreover, they were acutely aware of the competition coming from numerous surrounding city-states, each overflowing with ambitious and enterprising traders and entrepreneurs. So although they had the power to impose taxes and confer monopolies and exclusive trading privileges, they also knew that it would be self-destructive to abuse that power.

David S. Landes observes that "European rulers and enterprising Lords who sought to grow revenues . . . had to attract participants by the grant of franchises, freedoms and privileges. . . . They had to persuade them to come. . . . [T]he initiative came from below, and this too was an essentially European pattern. Implicit in it was a sense of rights and contract—the right to negotiate as well as petition—with gains to the freedom and security of economic activity."[125] Note that according to Landes, "the initiative came from below"; that is, from the bottom, the common people, suddenly able to negotiate with and petition those holding power above them. That is why Landes can assert that "Europe's great good fortune lay in the fall of Rome and the weakness and division that ensued. . . . [F]ragmentation was the strongest brake on willful, oppressive behavior. Political rivalry and the right of exit made all the difference."[126]

The favorable local circumstances allowed the residents of the major Italian cities to pursue their self-interest; and as the resulting rise in economic activity enlarged the class of tradesmen and rich merchants, they sought to enlarge the freedom they needed to operate their businesses as they saw fit. Once a middle class gains economic success, they can demand and get enhanced political freedom. As Mancur Olson reminds us, the demands were not always polite: "In Venice, after a doge who attempted to make himself autocrat was beheaded for his offense, subsequent doges were followed in official processions by a sword-bearing symbolic executioner as a reminder of the punishment intended for any leader who attempted to assume dictatorial power. . . . The same city states also tended to have more elaborate courts, contracts, and property rights than most of the European kingdoms of that time. As is well known, these city-states also created the most advanced economies in Europe, not to mention the culture of the Renaissance."[127]

Contemporaries also meditated on these achievements. Marsiglio of Padua (1275-1342) wrote *Defensor Pacis*, a treatise describing the political activities of the period that helped perfect the mechanics of representative government. Recorded 400 years after Iceland's Althing, and only a century after the Magna Carta, these "democratic" principles became part of the literature documenting the successful striving of common men throughout Europe. Marsiglio was a friend and contemporary of William of Ockham (1285-1347), one of the Oxford-based Franciscan monks that were challenging the Pope's positions on faith and property. The two men argued that "ultimate sovereignty resides in the majority of the people. . . . General Councils are to be formed by popular election. . . . Councils alone should lay down standards of orthodoxy, and the Church is not to meddle in affairs of state."[128] These fourteenth-century thinkers and writers documented the ongoing battle for free elections of representatives as well as the need to separate church from state, the religious from the secular, thereby sowing the seeds of the Reformation three hundred years later. For obvious reasons, both Occam and Marsiglio were excommunicated in 1328 and barely escaped from Avignon to find protection in Munich under Emperor Louis.[129]

Such were the rebellious acts and ideas that fueled the growing independence of the people in Florence, Venice, and the other independent cities of Europe. Notably, no such ideas were being publicly promulgated anywhere else on the planet. Indeed, at this very time, the Mongol empire was disintegrating, and the newly established Ming dynasty was restoring traditional Taoist and Confucian thought and traditions: "[T]he new rulers burned their ocean going vessels, banned foreign travel for Chinese, and spent a large portion of gross national product on building massive new walls to lock foreigners out and Chinese in."[130] Like most central-government projects, China's great walls represented a massive confiscation of food, labor, and opportunity from the common people—all to a harmful end: the closing of the Oriental mind.

Things were different within the fractured principalities of Europe. The flowering of a few free societies toward the end of the Middle Ages was rooted in a deep respect for the individual. There were no millions of slave laborers forced to build massive stone walls. Instead, there was a growing demand and respect for each person's rights. These demands emerged from an individualism informed by Christianity and classical antiquity, an individualism which was "first fully developed during the Renaissance and has since grown and spread into what we know as Western Civilization" and whose essential features include "respect for the individual man, that is, the recognition of his own views and tastes as supreme in his own sphere . . . and that it is desirable that men should develop their own individual gifts and bents."[131]

The foundation for this humanism had emerged many years earlier as the Dark Ages gave way to efforts to regain the classical greatness of Imperial Rome. Paul Johnson explains how the first universities built in the twelfth century emerged from the scholarly work that had been done within the church to recover the works of antiquity. As early as the tenth and eleventh century, this recovery and translation was supported by the copying and disseminating of manuscripts, and it led to an explosion of literacy and scientific thought. "Aristotle's writings on logic began to circulate in the West from the ninth century, though they were not available in full until 1130. . . . Because of the transmission through Islam, Aristotle remained suspect in the church's eyes as a possible source of heresy, but that did not stop the great thirteenth century philosophers Albertus Magnus and Thomas Aquinas from constructing their summae on an Aristotelian basis."[132]

Credit must be given to the Dominican order of monks who led the way for scientific and rational thought in the new universities springing up in the twelfth century in Germany, England, Italy, and France. Albert the Great was drawn to the University of Padua by the Blessed Jordan of Saxony, a Domincan who travelled among all the major European universities, encouraging the best young men to study science, chemistry, logic, and the traditional classic subjects. Roger Bacon and Thomas Aquinas learned their love of scientific observation and experiment from such earlier teachers as Albert and Robert Grosseteste. The latter, coming from a poor family in Suffolk, managed to become a "master" at Oxford not later than 1192 or 1193 A.D. These members of the Catholic Church, by their firm scientific outlook, paved the way for science co-existing with faith in Western Europe, a major tipping point. And they did it long before the Renaissance, in the early Middle Ages.

These positive developments were firmly in place in the thirteenth century, but it took another century for the Renaissance to gain momentum. Johnson gives two reasons for the slow but ultimately unprecedented achievements of the Renaissance. The ancient world had been built on what Johnson calls "muscle power," the surfeit of slaves and cheap labor. Such civilizations had no incentive to replace human engines in galley boats or turnstiles. But in Medieval Europe, under the impact of Christianity, slavery declined. "By the time of the Domesday Book (1086 A.D.) the number of slaves listed in England was tiny."[133] The Black Death in the mid-fourteenth century further reduced the population of western Europe, by 25 to 30 percent, resulting in a demand for increased productivity. This need was met by individual artisans and workers who created labor saving devices— things as simple as the wheel barrow, horse collars, and swiveling front axles, to wind and water mills, to modern sailing ships. With these innovations, "internal and external trade in Europe doubled with each generation. . . . At the same time the expansion of trade produced ancillary practices, such as insurance and banking, on an ever-growing scale, aided by the invention of techniques such as double-entry bookkeeping. Thus in the later Middle Ages, wealth was being produced in greater quantities than ever before in history, concentrated in cities specializing in the new occupations of large-scale commerce and banking, like Venice and Florence. Such cities were chiefly to be found in the Low Countries, the Rhine Valley, and Northern and Central Italy."[134]

While these locales flourished, much of France, Spain, and Germany remained mired in feudal land systems with the peasants held down by aristocrats and restrictive class structures. In Poland and Russia, the oppression was even more thorough and smothering. Thus, it was not Western Europe as a whole that progressed. Innovation occurred in the places the common man enjoyed the greatest amount of economic freedom. As wealth accumulated in these cities, lavish patronage of literature and the arts encouraged widespread efforts to pursue literate and artistic vocations. This in turn was accelerated by the two most significant forms of "intermediate technology" developed during the period: the printing press and the paper-making industries, which coalesced in 1450 and spread rapidly throughout Europe. "The speed at which printing spread, the quality and quantity of the production, and the extraordinary mechanical ingenuity displayed together constituted a kind of industrial revolution."[135]

Thus the economic bounty derived from free business activity and the new labor-saving devices, along with continued safety from external invasion, allowed the Renaissance to blossom into the fourteenth century. And, obviously, all this was the work of individuals: of artisans, bankers, tradesmen, printers. Johnson, too, stresses that the supreme accomplishments of the Renaissance were "the work of individuals," by which he means the creative geniuses such as Dante (b. 1265), Boccaccio (b. 1313), Petrarch (b.1304), and Bruni (b. 1369), whom he calls the first humanists. These were outsiders, non-academics critical of the universities and their pedagogy. "They associated universities with the kind of closed-shop trade unionism also found in the craft guilds. Universities, in their view, stamped on individualism and innovation."[136] The outsiders salvaged many of the classical texts, traveling to Constantinople and bringing home manuscripts to be saved and copied. The final glut of classical documents arrived with the refugees escaping from the Turks after the fall of Constantinople in 1453 as the forces of Islam began their two-hundred-year invasion and occupation of Eastern Europe. This dramatic shift of learning, literature, and scientific methods from the Middle East to Western Europe constituted another major divergence in historical development. Islam rejected new inquiry even as the Christian West and its freer people welcomed it and employed the new ways and means with extraordinary success.

Empowered by freedom, emboldened by financial success, the humanists, technical innovators, and the businessmen of the Renaissance had an enlightened vision. They self-confidently and freely questioned the world about them, and looked for ways to improve their lot. A major irritant was the rigid hold of the established church, its vast landholdings, the ostentatious lifestyle of its clerisy, and its constant taking of money from the parishes throughout Europe. Those closest to the center of the Catholic Church were least in awe of its leadership. The eventual revolt of the Protestant Reformation was encouraged by the spirited Lorenzo Valla (b. 1407), a lecturer in Padua, Rome, and Naples who also held high posts in government. His scholarly work included discussion of the rediscovered works of the second-century Roman critic Marcion, who had subjected the canonical texts of the New Testament to careful examination, accepting some and rejecting others as forgeries.[137] A revolution in critical thought was underway that challenged both academia and the church. By the second half of the sixteenth century, this criticism spread to German speaking central Europe, "with books pouring from the presses in ever growing numbers. . . ."[138] "It is notable that both Valla and Erasmus referred to their opponents as barbarians, and . . . as humanism spread, its language became more vituperative, provoking in turn harsh language from those thus classified, who held leading positions in the Church."[139]

This legacy of the Renaissance, this new reliance on the individual and reason, reached Northern Europe just in time to take root before the decline and fall of the Italian city-states. By the early 1500s, the primacy of the cities of Italy was over, as was the Renaissance itself, crushed by the recurring invasions of the super powers of Europe. Spain ended up in control of most of Italy, and creative men languished under the new oppression.

However, the next hundred years would see a new growth of freedom in Holland that would finally throw off the shackles of Imperial Spain. The advance of Western civilization was never of one piece. The common people had to regularly leap-frog from one enabling locale to another.

Holland: Bourgeois Burghers at Work

A hundred years before Jefferson helped write the American Declaration of Independence, the people of Holland, lost amid the maze of European power politics, had a rare opportunity to throw off foreign oppression. To achieve this goal, they waged a war of independence against Spain from 1568 to 1648. The result was the Golden Age of Holland, made possible by the independent spirit and industriousness of her citizens. During this period of ferment and revolt, the Dutch were ruled from afar by a King of Spain who could not maintain the usual high degree of oppression normally favored by Europe's ruling monarchs. Worst of all, from the King's perspective, was the rapid adoption in Holland of the successful business practices of the northern city-states of Italy, and the critical ways of thinking inspired by Martin Luther's revolt against the Catholic Church. These refreshingly assertive attitudes demonstrated the breadth of thought and expression that finds a way to percolate upward when societies are not stifled.

The Dutch, like the Phoenicians, occupied an undesirable, marshy strip of coastline envied by none of the surrounding monarchies. Much of it was literally under the sea. There was no aristocracy in these parts of Holland, and the ragged seamen who manned the fishing boats used to battle the King's fleet of warships were derided as "Sea Beggars." As Barbara Tuchman writes, these seasoned and salty sailors loved the name, and proudly proclaimed that, beggars or not, they would triumph—and they did.

During this period, the Dutch were especially receptive to the Protestant Reformation and challenges to the religious authority of Rome and its Popes. Inspired by the revolutionary new spirit of religious freedom, they gave shelter to refugees from all over Europe. Holland's isolation and relative freedom from oppression allowed her citizens to establish Holland as a major ship-building and textile-manufacturing nation. By 1648, the Dutch were the major seafaring nation in the world, having wrested the lead first from Spain, then England. Thus "within one generation of autonomy [the Dutch] had transformed themselves into the greatest trading nation in the world, holding the commercial center and financial heartbeat of Europe, and resting on a seaborne empire that stretched from the Indian Ocean to the Hudson River."[140]

Thanks to innovations in the methods of doing business, larger commercial ventures became possible. The widespread ownership of stock companies, assisted by laws granting limited liability for companies, met a growing need of small entrepreneurs. The Dutch East India Company was chartered in 1602, before the first settlers came to America. Twenty years later, the Dutch West Indies Company was created, and with ample capital would go on to engage in worldwide trade.

The new financial tools, including security trading institutions and banking organizations, were developed by tradesman—not intellectuals. By allowing rapid expansion of economic growth and improvements in productivity, they multiplied the benefits of the Industrial Revolution in Holland. Mancur Olson observes that if a society is to realize "all the gains from trade, there has to be a legal system and political order that enforces contracts, protects property rights, carries out mortgage agreements, provides for limited liability corporations, and facilitates a lasting and widely used capital market that makes the investments and loans more liquid than they would otherwise be."[141] These were the mechanics that helped create prosperity—subjects rarely touched on by the philosophers, who busied themselves trying to recap the main principles put in place by those "beneath" them.

The Dutch economic miracle was accomplished over four hundred years ago. The sources of it are plain enough, but most of the world still doesn't get it. As we will see in the following chapters, the fanatical devotion of many Western intellectuals to socialism, and even communism, has helped prevent a few simple contract- and property-protecting rules from being employed to eliminate the poverty and famines that plague many Third World nations.

Like the American colonists, the Dutch were settling a new land, one they had reclaimed from the sea, in an area of little importance to the rest of the world. Their progress was not hampered by the rigidities of established social classes and landed gentry. Barbara Tuchman makes the point well: "England's captains were limited by the nature of their society, which assumed that a gentlemanly land ownership, unspoiled by manual or commercial work, was the highest and purest ideal of social life. English sea captains were likely to be volunteers of the nobility with narrow practical experience, if any, while Dutch captains and admirals were more often the sons of salt-sea sailors who had grown up handling the ropes. Dutch Admiral de Ruyter, hero of the 17th century navy, astonished a French officer by taking up a broom to clean his cabin and afterward going out to feed his chickens."[142] The hands of such a common man usually show the signs of constructive involvement—scars, calluses, even manure—signs rarely seen on the hands of intellectuals.

Even as it chafed under the excesses of the Catholic church, this plain Dutch society provided a tolerant haven for the religious of all faiths, including those Pilgrims who would eventually leave their safe haven to land in Plymouth, Massachusetts, and build a new world. In Tuchman's words, "The Revolt of the Netherlands was not a movement of national sentiment, which hardly existed, nor of political ideology. . . . The motivating sentiment in the Netherlands was hatred of Spanish tyranny. Forces and events in the eighty-year struggle were a turmoil of infighting among sects and parties, of deals and overtures to foreign states, of mounting oppression by the Spanish rulers that augmented popular hatred to a frenzy and, in a deeply fragmented state, linked the fragments together in a common will for independence."[143]

This same spirit of independence inspired strong support of the Protestant Reformation. Calvinism, one of the most fiercely independent offshoots of the Reformation, found a ready home with the Dutch. This rebellious spirit led to the Resolution in 1581, called the Oath of Abjuration, issued by the Hague's only local assembly. The Oath stated that Philip II, King of Spain, had violated the obligation of a ruler to be fair to his subjects, and it claimed for the subjects the fundamental right "to withdraw their allegiance and to depose an oppressive and tyrannical sovereign, since no other means remained to them of preserving their liberties."[144]

The delegates in the Hague thus anticipated the words of Thomas Jefferson almost two hundred years before he set pen to parchment. They also anticipated Hobbes, Montesquieu, and Locke, none yet born. Thus, these delegates in the Hague, without any guidance from intellectuals, simply stated their seemingly obvious and fundamental rights, and demanded their liberty. They didn't write five hundred page treatises, nor did they analyze and debate abstract theories. They simply demanded freedom—it was really no more complicated than that. And they were only repeating arguments used before, in the cities of Italy, to claim the right of every man to freedom. And yet, Locke and Hobbes, who wrote voluminously on the pros and cons of freedom and democracy hundreds of years later, gave little or no credit to the ordinary mortals who preceded them.

This demand for human rights, claimed in 1581 in this small enclave hemmed in by huge European monarchies, demonstrates just how "men's instinct for liberty, and belief in the people's right to depose a leader, a ruler who has governed unjustly, travels in deep common channels."[145] They had no philosopher on hand to explain the natural human passion for liberty to them. Instead they just felt the passion, made it happen, showed how it was done. All the modern intellectual writers on political science after 1581 have done no more than "report" and "analyze" what was already a known and established fact.

Commenting on the outpouring of great art in seventeenth-century Holland, Kenneth Clark asks what sort of society was responsible for this financial and artistic success. He finds the answer in the numerous group portraits of the Dutch masters: "[S]omething does emerge which has a bearing on civilization; these are individuals who are prepared to join in a corporate effort for the public good. For the most part they are solid, commonplace people, as they would be today, and they are portrayed by commonplace artists; but from this. . . . There arose one of the summits of European painting, Rembrandt's 'Staalmeesters.' . . . One can't imagine groups like this being produced in Spain or seventeenth century Italy, even in Venice. They are the first visual evidence of bourgeois democracy. Dreadful words—so debased by propaganda that I hesitate to use them. Yet in the context of civilization they really have a meaning. They mean that a group of individuals can come together and take corporate responsibility; that they can afford to do so because they have some leisure; and that they have some leisure because they have money in the bank. . . . They might be of meetings of local government committees or hospital governors today. They represent the practical, social application of the philosophy that things must be made to work."[146]

Once again, we see common people doing the work that needs to be done, providing the stepping stones of human progress—when they are free to do so.

More than a century later, the people of Holland would not fail to recognize kindred aspirations in the new world. Barbara W. Tuchman describes how the "first salute" by another nation recognizing the independence of the new American government was sounded as an American warship entered the Caribbean harbor of Eustatia on November 16, 1776. The Declaration of Independence was only a few months old, and the ancien regimes of Europe were skeptical at the impudence of the signers. But the Dutch who controlled the island were mindful of their own recent struggle for independence: "The guns of Fort Orange were returning the ritual salute on entering a foreign port of an American vessel, the Andrea Doria, as she came up the roadstead, flying at her mast the red-and-white striped flag of the Continental Congress. . . . In its responding salute, the small voice of Eustatia was the first officially to greet the largest event of the century—the entry into the society of nations of a new Atlantic state destined to change the direction of history."[147] The Dutch had struggled long and hard for their own freedom, and their hearts were with the Americans.

Johannes de Graaf, appointed Governor of Eustatia by the Dutch in 1776, had been in office nine weeks when the Andrea Doria sailed into the harbor seeking guns and ammunition for the colonists' war. Despite pressure from the British to blockade American shipping, de Graaf declared the port open to the Americans without reservation, and personally invited the captain and officers of the Andrea Doria to dinner. Ironically, the ship was named for the famous Admiral of Genoa who in 1528 fought the French for the freedom of his city. Thus, the successful struggles for freedom of Holland and Genoa in the sixteenth century laid a groundwork for the American colonies quest in the eighteenth century.

Scotland: The Protestant Reformation Realized

In the mid-sixteenth century, a cultural revolution began that would upset the rigid structure of Scottish society. John Knox arrived out of nowhere "and single-handedly inspired, intimidated, and bullied Scotland's nobility and urban classes into overthrowing the Catholic Church."[148]

Knox had spent his early years "in exile, imprisonment and even penal servitude chained to a rowing bench in the King's galleys." After arriving in Scotland in 1559, he preached the new Protestantism, and the Scots embraced it. They accepted its harsh rules because it promised direct access to God for every congregant, and created a united community with each individual honored yet bound together. "'God loveth us,' John Knox had written, 'because we are His own handiwork.'"[149] This dedication to the Almighty served very well to subordinate any obedience to other authority, whether that of the King, the nobles, or the established Churches.

The common people liked his message and after massive protests and bloody battles, they and Knox prevailed. "He and his followers scoured away not only Scottish Catholicism but all its physical manifestations, from monasteries and bishops and clerical vestments to holy relics and market square crosses. They smashed stained-glass windows and saints' statues, ripped out choir stalls and roodscreens, and overturned altars. . . . In any case, the idols disappeared from southern Scotland, and the Scottish Kirk rose up to take its place."[150]

In the 1570s, just a few years prior to the Dutch Oath of Abjuration, Knox spoke of how all political power was vested in the common people, not in Kings, nobles, or even clergy. Although Scotland never gained a widespread electorate, Knox had made another baby step that would eventually lead, in the United States, to universal suffrage. He declared that it was the duty of every man to defend his rights and power against tyranny from any source. Doing just that, in 1638 the citizenry forced their leaders to sign a National Covenant that ensured democratic elections and legal protections for the citizens. Scotland thus anticipated the Glorious Revolution in England some thirty years later. Later philosophers would write complex treatises about the rights thus defended, but give no credit to Knox. The liberating impact that Knox brought to Scottish culture illustrates how good ideas flow, not from the top down, but from the bottom up—quite the opposite of what intellectuals would like to believe. And, ironically, if there was any ideological element or philosophy in Knox's teaching, it was based on the religious precepts of Protestantism with its support for the freedom of man from any earthbound tyranny.

As in other enclaves where the common man emerged with rights and freedom from oppression, good things began to happen. "The effect of this egalitarian democratic spirit on the Scottish culture would be profound and long-lasting," writes Arthur Herman. "When Englishman Gilbert Burnet visited western Scotland in the 1660s, he had never seen anything like it. 'We were indeed amazed to see a poor commonality so capable to argue upon the points of government, and on the bounds to be set to the power of princes. . . . This measure of knowledge was spread even amongst the meanest of them, their cottagers and servants.' Robert Burns framed it more memorably."[151] Herman quotes the poet:

> What though on hamely fare we dine,
> Wear hodden-gray, an' a' that;
> Gie fools their silks, and knaves their wine,
> A man's a man for a' that.
> For a' that, an' a' that,
> Their tinsel show, an' a' that;
> The honest man, though e'er sae poor,
> Is king o' men for a' that. [152]

The Scots brought the same homespun style and simple honesty to their work. With the growth of literacy and schools, Scotland enjoyed its own Renaissance and, for a while, led Europe in learning, medicine, engineering, and trade. Glasgow's merchants prospered, and an affluent merchant class created a vibrant economy. Edinburgh society was more literary than Glasgow, and the university attracted many scholars. But both cities were more democratic than London and Paris, more open and boisterous, and equally fond of good food and drink.

But the glory of Scotland was short-lived. The nation's prosperity created a new elite, especially among the academics in Edinburgh, who forgot the humble origins of their prosperity: "The closes and wynds of Edinburgh flowed with alcohol. Drinking . . . 'engrossed the leisure hours of all professional men'. . . . Half the bench of the Court of Sessions . . . were well-oiled before they met in the morning. . . . A gentleman or writer would be routinely identified as a 'two-' or 'three-bottle man,' depending on how much claret he consumed at a meal or single sitting."[153] Numerous social clubs sprang up in Edinburgh, most notably the Select Society, founded in 1754, a gathering place for Edinburgh's elite. In the two hundred years since Knox arrived in Scotland, the country had grown rich from the new ways of thinking and the growth of enterprise. With these new comforts and affluence, common among mature societies, came an unfortunate parallel growth of intellectuals, who arrived to feed off the successes of the common man. The Select Society's members were quite different from the men in Burn's poem, definitely preferring fancy silks to the plain "hodden-gray."

Scotland's new intelligentsia still believed in Christianity, still believed that it nourished men's souls and refined their manners. But in the 1750s, progressive clergymen such as William Robertson took it upon themselves to bring the church into what they considered the modern world. They called themselves the Moderates. Although not wholly endorsing David Hume's denial of an Almighty, they fought for a more enlightened and compassionate Presbyterianism. Among them were virtually the entire elite of the well-soused intellectuals meeting in Edinburgh's social clubs. One Evangelical response came from the East Lothian minister John Witherspoon, who satirized the Moderates in a literary jab entitled "Ecclesiastical Characteristics." This humorous and widely circulated essay offered the following mock advice on how to write a sermon to the clergyman aspiring to the mantle of enlightenment:

1. All his subjects must be confined to social duties—as opposed to religious doctrines.

2. There must be no reference to an afterlife.

3. His authorities must be drawn from pagan writers, and none, or as few as possible, from Holy Scripture.

4. He must be very unacceptable to the common people.[154]

Robertson and his friends in the social clubs of Edinburgh represented "a new kind of cultural elitism. Yet the very fact that the Moderate's most formidable opponent had to resort to a secular literary genre, the satire, to score his points showed who was really winning, and who was losing, the overall battle."[155] Armed with intellectual cleverness and well-honed literary skills, the intellectuals, unable to contribute directly to the improvement of the nation, contributed instead their ideas and theories on how to make it more ideal. Lacking practical suggestions that may have actually helped, they confined themselves to the kind of questions that Plato had played with two thousand years earlier—Is there a God? What is his nature? How do you define justice and reason? What is the essence of man's relationships to the universe and to one another?

When Benjamin Rush arrived in Scotland in 1767 from the colonies to study medicine, bearing letters of introduction from Benjamin Franklin, he shared Witherspoon's unhappiness with the moral relativism of the intellectuals who had taken over Scottish universities. Meeting David Hume at a dinner party, he found him to be "rather ungentle and clumsy." Worse, "Hume's evident religious skepticism, and the relaxed attitude about religion generally among Hume's Moderate friends, disturbed the young Benjamin Rush, suffused as he was with the ardent afterglow of the Great Awakening."[156] In contrast to the secular philosopher Hume, Witherspoon belonged to the ordinary people, and subscribed to the evangelical spirit so popular with American Scots. Witherspoon was a linear descendent of John Knox and shared the latter's love of freedom, as well as his loyalty to his faith.

This sort of forthright democratic attitude had made him known in the frontier of America, and especially among the leaders of the great religious revival, the Great Awakening. In fact, Benjamin Rush was in Scotland primarily to persuade Witherspoon to become the new president of Princeton University. Witherspoon agreed and his departure in 1768 marked the triumph of the Edinburgh Moderates— an ascendancy that portended the end of Scotland's golden age. Like

Plato in Periclean Athens, the "enlightened" intellectuals of 1750 Edinburgh marked not the pinnacle of their society, but the beginning of the end. Scotland's renaissance and ascendancy had been created by hardier and simpler men, men who eschewed the fine wines and silks of the Select Society.

Many leading Scots agreed with Witherspoon that righteousness, not birth or membership in drinking clubs, should establish the order of men; that democracy must be open to everyone; and that the new "overly enlightened" church leaders in Scotland had gone astray. Many of these foes of the new Scottish order had indeed already fled to America, led by the Lowlanders and merchants: "By 1707, Glasgow families such as the Bogles had been doing business in the middle colonies for nearly three decades, much of it through illegal smuggling."[157] Other Scots followed. "Scots and Ulster Scots immigrants had created the first American frontier along the slopes of the Appalachians and Alleghenies. After the American Revolution, their descendents helped to extend and govern the result—Andrew Jackson, John C. Calhoun, James K. Polk, Jim Bowie, Daniel Boone, William Clark (of the Lewis and Clark Expedition), Sam Houston, and General Winfield Scott, whose grandfather had fought at Culloden."[158] A popular Scottish ditty expressed the mood of those who rebelled at the growing secularism, the lingering restrictions on their freedom, and the growth of the intellectuals in Scottish society:

> To the West, to the West, to the land of the free;
> Where the mighty Missouri rolls down to the sea;
> Where the man is a man even though he must toil,
> And the poorest may gather the fruits of his toil.[159]

In 1775, when King George called on Parliament to send troops to Boston to enforce obedience, he argued that the colonists should "see the light and recognize 'that to be a subject of Great Britain, with all its consequences, is to be the freest member of any civil society in the known world.'"[160] There was some truth in what the King said.

However, he apparently had not noticed that for the past 150 years, millions of his subjects were leaving England and Scotland because they did not consider it to be quite free enough. The Scots wanted more freedom. The lure of America was strong, and when you add the fact that the new and rising intelligentsia in the major cities of Scotland looked down on the working man and denigrated his religious faith, the natural consequence was a flood of emigration—a brain drain of colossal proportions.

Edward Gibbon was a Scottish intellectual who did not leave. As a member of the House of Commons and a supporter of the King and Lord North, he voted against accommodation of the American rebels, writing that "The conquest of America is a great work."[161] Ironically, Gibbon was just completing the first volume of his masterpiece, *History of the Decline and Fall of the Roman Empire*. His observations therein should be accorded considerable skepticism in light of the fact that it was his vote that day which endorsed one of the first steps in the dismantling of the British Empire. The rising influence of such "great thinkers" and their escalating attacks on religion drove many a good man and woman to leave Scotland and devote their genius to the New World.

The Scottish example shows how a vibrant society, when taken over by its intellectuals and philosophers, can lose its faith and unity. "Between 1717 and 1776, perhaps a quarter of a million Ulstermen came to America, 100,000 of them as indentured servants. They did not remain servants for very long, as colonists soon discovered that Ulster Scots were not born to be obedient."[162] The Highlanders were next to go. The flight of so many of Scotland's most original thinkers and doers helped one stepping stone of freedom to crumble while fortifying a new one across the ocean.

In 1848, a thirteen-year-old Scot named Andrew Carnegie came to America. Starting out as a bobbin-boy in a textile mill near Pittsburgh for a dollar twenty a week, he eventually created for his new land the prototype of the modern industrial corporation—one that by 1892 was "producing steel equal to one-half of the entire production of Great Britain."[163] And so the country that had dominated the steel industry for over a century lost the lead to a family whose motto was "Death to Privilege." Rather than try and buck the closed system of their homeland, the Carnegies had sought the opportunities of an open and upwardly mobile society, and thus helped create the next stepping stone of economic progress.

As all this was transpiring in America, progress in Scotland was slowing down. Even so, its people were still far better off than, for example, those of Spain, Russia, and Germany. Scotland in its mature years has suffered less than those countries simply because its intellectuals and philosophers weren't nearly as bad as theirs. But that is a story for Chapters 11 and 13.

England: A Thousand Years
of Persistence by the Common People

In most civilizations, back to antiquity, men instituted some system of courts and judges to mediate the disputes that naturally arose when many people lived together. King Solomon was renowned for his ability, though an autocrat, to adjudicate disputes fairly and equitably. The Phoenician traders and merchants established adjudicative boards to handle trade disputes. The Greek city-states had more advanced legal systems, as did the Romans. There were courts and judges in the Italian city states, and in Holland as it emerged from Spanish rule. In England, the people developed a unique judicial system based on case law and precedent. Although occurring slowly over a very long time, this gradual development of the rule of law played a vital role in establishing rights and legal protection for the people. The process was slow because, of necessity, it required limiting the power of a well entrenched King and his nobles.

As an island fortress, England was relatively safe from attack. It was successfully invaded only twice in history—by Julius Caesar in 65 A.D., and by William the Conquerer in 1066. This stability helped allow each advance in freedom to persist so that it could be built on year after year, century after century, until something close to a representative government could be attained. It would also permit the cumulative build-up of infrastructures so important in creating wealth for the ordinary citizens. The trim and fertile pastures lying between straight walls and hedgerows in the English countryside date back for centuries.

The English people showed remarkable persistence in demanding from their kings and queens a recognition of basic human rights. It took over half a millennia to achieve any kind of success. But gradually, over the decades and centuries, the people achieved many steps toward greater freedom. The history of England illustrates how, even when basic safety is assured, the common man's struggle for rights can be slowed to a crawl by the machinations of big government, big church, and grasping aristocrats.

But it also illustrates how freedom can nonetheless be achieved—not by any grand ideological design, but by determined grappling with problems at hand: "[T]he dominant fact about the economic institutions that emerged in Europe with the decline of feudalism is their wholly pragmatic character and their lack of ideological commitment to any economic principle other than economic effectiveness and survivability. The system that generated Western economic growth evolved before it was recognized as a system or advocated as an ideology."[164] First the common man created, then came the ideologues; and, finally, the philosophers claimed credit with elaborate expositions that rarely gave credit to the people who had accomplished the breakthroughs.

It was this irrepressible persistence of English entrepreneurs, lawyers, and farmers that created the micro-level practices that we ultimately inherited under the name of laissez-faire capitalism. "It was 1776 before Adam Smith first produced the systematic rationale that furnished the basis of a laissez-faire ideology, and by then the Western economic institutions were in place and economic growth was well under way."[165] Adam Smith described the obvious beneficial results that had emerged from capitalism, stock companies, patents, and the division of labor that had been developing sequentially for over 500 years in Florence, Holland, and England. His father had been a customs official, so he was acutely aware of the effectiveness of smugglers and illegal manufacturers, and how they could out-hustle the state-protected monopolies.

From the Magna Carta onward, the early struggles for freedom were devoted to declaring the basic rights of citizens and gaining legislative and judicial systems independent of the King. Once Parliament approached equal status with the King in 1688, its members wanted to get in on the lucrative practice of licensing businesses. The result was that "a number of measures gradually transferred decision-making power from the state to private citizens. The country very gradually rid itself of the authoritarian powers of abusive redistribution, absurd regulations, privileges and excessive controls. . . . Parliament, in an attempt to compete with the King for the same sources of income, decided that it too would grant the privilege of establishing an enterprise, in return for credits and bribes. . . . By the end of the nineteenth century, almost the entire population had free access to property and to business activity."[166] The mercantilist system was on the way out, for regulated business could not compete with small entrepreneurs unleashed to act individually for their own profit. Ordinary citizens once again moved mountains, overturning the entire economic system to establish free enterprise and capitalism.

They made these gains by claiming the same rights to negotiate and petition that had been used so effectively by the citizens of Florence and Holland. The opportunities generated by unencumbered trade and technical-mechanical innovation were so great that enterprising individuals were willing to risk their lives to gain these rights. David S. Landes describes it this way: "The economic expansion of medieval Europe was thus promoted by a succession of organizational innovations and adaptations, most of them initiated from below and diffused by example. The rulers, even local seigneurs, scrambled to keep pace . . . to attract enterprise and the revenues it generated. . . . In these centuries a whole new array of commercial instruments came into use. . . . Almost all of this 'commercial revolution' came from the mercantile community, bypassing where necessary the rules of this or that city or state . . . creating in short a world of its own like an overlay on the convoluted, inconvenient mosaic of political units. . . . It was the world of Adam Smith, already taking shape five hundred years before his time."[167]

England thus benefited from the gradual steps forced on its leaders over these years and was ultimately transformed into a modern market economy. In France, Spain, and Russia, where the autocratic governments maintained a much tighter grip, the common people were ultimately obliged to resort to violent revolutions. As de Soto observes, the terrible thing about such violent transitions is that "the possibility of controlling its outcome democratically and peacefully is lost."[168] The atrocities and chaos flowing from the revolutionary fervor in those other countries led to the ascendancy of such undesirable rulers as Franco, Lenin, Stalin, Robespierre, Fouche, and Napoleon.

The example of England is unique and exemplary. Nothing like it had ever happened on such a large scale. If other nations had simply followed the path to success so vividly demonstrated, they could have achieved the same advances without all the bloodshed. Here are some of the steps of that path:

c. 1190   The Court of Common Pleas, the origin of common law and a legal system to settle civil disputes, is established.

1215   King John signs the Magna Carta, after his taxes have provoked rebellion among his nobles. They demand rights that even the King must respect.

c. 1315   Court of the King's Bench established, along with circuit justices, to administer "the common law of England, grown out of custom and judges' decisions (case law), and occasional acts of legislation. . . ."[169]

1496   Trade treaties end embargo on trade with the Netherlands. King Henry VII assists the efforts of cloth merchants to break into European, Italian, and Danish markets. Assisted business and expanded the middle class.

Henry VIII—Split with the Pope to marry Anne Boleyn

1529   Thomas Cromwell, serving under Henry VIII, initiates the use of parliament and its statute-making authority to reform constitutional monarchy. Cromwell, a common lawyer, respects medieval law and encouraged judges to obey statutes, "leading up to the modern principle that judicial interpretation means the strict application of the act, not an arbitrary explanation roughly within its limits."[170] His statutes end the Pope's authority in England, reform the Church of England, and enable Henry VIII to marry Anne Boleyn.[171]

1540-1570s John Knox and George Buchanan campaign to empower all political authority in the people, not in kings, nobles, or clergy, setting forth "a full-fledged doctrine of political sovereignty [that is] the sort of view we are used to ascribing to John Locke; in fact, it belongs to a Presbyterian Scot from Stirlingshire writing more than a hundred years earlier."[172] Later Reformation-era statutes establish the state as a limited monarchy with law-making authority residing in the Assembly of king, lords, and commons.

1559   Queen Elizabeth provides military assistance to John Knox in Scotland, who is fighting for freedom from the French and the Catholic Church. Leads to Treaty of Edinburgh in 1560 to restore parliament and complete the Protestant Reformation.

1603   After Tudor Queen Elizabeth dies, the Stuarts regain the throne under James I. His discriminatory policies drive the Pilgrims to Holland, then to Plymouth, Massachusetts. After his death in 1625, the persecution of non-conformists in England continues under his son, Charles I, who fights with Parliament for revenue to finance costly wars with France and Spain.

1627   Five Knights' Case unites Puritan barristers to defy Charles I and enforce clause 29 of Magna Carta against unjust imprisonment of MP's. They argue that the King's "special command" lacks the status of "law" and therefore is insufficient basis for indefinite detention. Over the next twenty years, lawyers develop the legal basis and courtroom process that ends in the King's execution for tyranny against his subjects.[173]

1628   Edward Coke drafts The Petition of Right. Parliament asserts its rights against the king, "denying his right to levy charges upon, or to imprison, or punish anyone, or to quarter soldiers on the people, without due process of law."[174] Charles dismisses Parliament, exacts illegal levies on the people, and flouts their authority.

1635   Peak of emigration from England to the American colonies. Charles I and Archbishop Laud oppose wholesale migration and impose restrictions on departures. "In 1637, eight ships were about to start, when they were forcibly detained. Oliver Cromwell was one of the passengers. . . . It would have been better for Charles, and the head on his kingly shoulders, had he permitted that ship to have gone upon its way."[175]

1640   The Long Parliament. Prosecution of the King's chief ministers, beheading of the Earl of Strafford. Civil War breaks out and Oliver Cromwell emerges as the leader of the New Model Army to win major victories over the King's forces. This "new" army is democratized, with officers and soldiers drawn from all classes. "England discovered a new force, The Ironsides . . . in which footmen, draymen, and ships captains held high command, side by side with men of family."[176]

1647-1649   The New Model Army declares its obligation to defend the peoples' just rights and liberties. The House of Commons, with loyal monarchists physically driven out, reverberated with speeches about how "the People are, under God, the original of all just power [and] have the supreme power in this nation." The rump parliament puts the King on trial "as a tyrant, traitor, murderer, and enemy of his country."[177] The ultimate "commoner," John Cooke, leads the prosecution and wins the case.

1649   Charles I beheaded. The Stuart kings fail to usurp power and the people reassert the right to try a king for malfeasance—a right underscored in Venetian processions hundreds of years earlier, in which a symbolic executioner marched with the doge as a reminder not to assume dictatorial powers.

1660	The landed nobility side with Charles II to restore the monarchy. Those who had worked to convict Charles I are tried, found guilty of regicide, and executed. Cooke faces gruesome execution reserved for commoners with courage and defiance: "Death is nothing to me, let them quarter my body none so much. God will bring all the pieces together."[178]

1688   The Glorious Revolution. James II replaced by Protestants William and Mary in a bloodless reform. Bill of rights established; rule of law is made supreme. Judges become independent, as appointments cannot be revoked and are made only by Parliament.

1689-90   John Locke's *Two Treatises on Government*, arguing against the divine right of kings and for a division of power between the king and parliament. "Politically, Locke's theories were a summary of the kind of thing that was in fact being practiced in England."[179] Indeed, these "things" had been practiced in England and elsewhere long before Locke's birth. The first Cromwell had thrown off the yoke of the Church and the second Cromwell had demolished monarchical authority.

1695   Establishment of rules to protect the press from censorship.

1698   Stock exchange opens in London.

1721   Robert Walpole installed as prime minister, making 10 Downing Street his official home. Long before Adam Smith and the French Physiocrats, he argued that the economy would prosper with a minimum of state regulation, advocated free trade, reduced taxes, and removed restraints on trade. He knew few books, his son Horace acknowledged. "He knew mankind, not their writings; he consulted their interests, not their systems."[180]

1733   John Kay invents the "flying shuttle," beginning a flood of mechanical labor-saving inventions and inaugurating the Industrial Revolution. Parliament grants patent rights for fourteen years.

1700s   Presbyterian Church in Scotland develops the most extensive system of education in Europe, enabling middle class youth to achieve positions of leadership. Medicine flourishes, and Scotland's doctors spread across the world.[181]

1807   Parliament bans international slave trade.

1832   Reform Act establishes popular vote for election of members of Parliament.

1833   Formal emancipation of slaves in Great Britain.

1833   Parliament authorizes anyone to open a business in London; regulated monopolies begin to give way to free markets.

1862   Parliament authorizes any registered business to become a limited-liability stock company, thus freeing entrepreneurs to grow and compete. By the end of century, almost the entire population of Great Britain gains free access to property and the right to engage in business activity.

1873   British warships anchored off Zanzibar force the closure of the slave market; expansion of European imperialism to Asia and Africa brings slavery under pressure around the world.[182]

Many of these political and economic reforms happened only because bands of citizens took up arms. Their insurrections were only partly successful, because the aristocracy, allied with shrewd kings and queens, tended to grudgingly give only half a loaf—just enough to placate. This clinging to power by the beneficiaries of the ancien regime explains why the march to freedom took almost a thousand years in England, as compared to a single century in sixteenth-century Holland.

Still, the constant pressure from the bottom did gradually gain additional rights for the common man. As Thomas Sowell put it, "Freedom must be distinguished from democracy, with which it is often confused. The British people had many rights that were lacking in much of Europe, and in most of the rest of the world, long before they acquired the franchise with which to control government."[183] And economic freedom is more important to the average person than political freedom.

Over this 600-year period, then, the development of a common law and a strengthening parliament gave commoners expanded rights and a chance for fair hearings. The right to be judged by a jury of one's peers emerged through negotiations and established customs at local levels. A Parliament (of Lords) reduced the arbitrary power of the King, and eventually the commoners got a second legislative body as well—to wit, the House of Commons. Progress was slow, eked out over many years by ordinary working compromises, but it was steady. "The uneven, uncertain, and inconsistent evolution of the institutions and traditions of freedom in Britain followed no blueprint or elaborated doctrine. Out of this apparent chaos, however, emerged institutions, traditions, and landmarks on the road to human freedom in general, as well as for the British themselves."[184] Such work at the grassroots level would later be enshrined, albeit in a garbled manner, by the writings of philosophers that followed.

The United States: The Ultimate Stepping Stone

In colonial America of the late 1700s, a unique system of government emerged that embodied what men had sought for centuries—a republic, based on democratic principles, with enough central power to function as a nation, but balanced by a legislative and judicial branch and by a federalist principle that reserved substantial rights to the states. For good measure, a Bill of Rights was added to protect each individual from the abuses of tyranny. The creators of this document were provincials, marginal, borderland people—rustics, farmers, lawyers, merchants, and tradesmen.[185] The system was not imposed from on high, nor adopted from a genius-designed blueprint. Instead it was negotiated—hammered out in a tough political process by ordinary citizens.

During the past two and a quarter centuries, the nation founded on this conception of freedom has met and overcome a continuing series of crises. The American Dream has survived every challenge; through it all, the words of Emma Lazarus carved on the Statue of Liberty have served as a beacon to people from all over the world with the courage to pack up and vote with their feet:

> "Keep, ancient lands, your storied pomp," cries she
> With silent lips, "Give me your tired, your poor,
> your huddled masses yearning to breathe free. . . ."

Millions of ordinary people bid goodbye to the pompous aristocracies, closed economies, and rigid religious orthodoxies of their mother countries. The word spread fast, and people came from every continent, eager to gain a fresh start in a New World of freedom and opportunity. And they loved what they found. They settled in, learned the language, got jobs, and built a great nation. There is still a waiting list, and many just pour in illegally.

This flight to freedom and opportunity has been going on for 400 years—a depressing but unmistakable sign of the continuing failure of most other nations to provide their citizens with comparable benefits. Such a long-standing failure is a remarkable testament to societal inertia—the inability to reform institutions even when the solutions have been clearly established. This inertia has dogged mankind's advance throughout history. It is that failure almost everywhere else on the planet that makes America's extraordinary track record of success so remarkable.

The huge gap between America and the rest should not be downplayed—there has to be vitally important reasons for the disparity, reasons that explain how Americans built such an impressive lead over everyone else. Further, since modern large national economies and cultures do not spring out of thin air, but develop slowly, and gradually build momentum, the reasons for America's success must lie in what was happening during the past couple hundred years.

The modern media and much of the public today are excessively concerned over current events, as if anything done in the past few decades had anything to do with the world we were born into. America's critics ignore that fact that its number one position in the world didn't just happen—it resulted from the energy of its people as unleashed within the nurturing cultural mores of the past 400 years. Because those centuries witnessed an unprecedented advance in the well-being of its citizens, the institutions and customs common to that period should be modified only with the greatest of care. There is considerably less reason for making drastic changes in one's course when you are far ahead than when you are way behind.

The American Revolution and the subsequent establishment of the Constitution and Bill of Rights were major milestones in world history. Whether or not the Americans fully realized the global import of what they had done, the rest of the civilized world was fascinated by it. That the rag-tag militias of the former British colonies had won the war was impressive, even shocking, in itself. And that the Americans had enunciated their bold demand for freedom as "self-evident," and claimed the support of God for their right to liberty, certainly had a refreshing impact on the effete and worldly courts of Europe. Of course, they should not have been surprised—a similar process had occurred in isolated pockets within Europe itself for millenniums. But the incredible conceit of the European elites, still enjoying their privileges of inherited rank, had blinded them to the greater realities of freedom that were blossoming around them.

Even more startling to the European elite than the Americans' stated principles of freedom was the character of the individuals sent to Europe to represent the new nation. In Paris, the austere and scholarly John Adams made a solemn counterpoint to the charming Benjamin Franklin in his fur hat and homespun clothes. Both men brought with them the extraordinary personal strength and uncompromising independence characteristic of those who had tamed the American frontier. Franklin, especially, "had a high old time. The septuagenarian played the French like a pianoforte, and they delighted to be played by him."[186] Thomas Jefferson, succeeding Franklin in 1785, had mostly criticism for the country. He wrote that France was "loaded with misery, by kings, nobles, and priests, and by them alone."[187] They were followed in 1789 by Thomas Paine, who stayed on to engage in intrigue and encourage the French Revolution.

During this period, copies of the American documents proclaiming the right to establish a new free nation were widely circulated throughout Europe. "By mid-1777, only a year after American independence had been declared, the state constitutions and bills of right had begun to appear in Europe. [By 1778, these included] the texts of the constitutions of all the new American states—documents, LaRochefoucauld declared, that were 'the finest monuments of human wisdom. They constitute the purest democracy which has ever existed. . . .'"[188]

Although monarchies of the most lavish and oppressive form still ruled most of Europe, the more liberal leaders and intellectuals were extremely interested in the revolutionary character that founded the United States of America. Translations were made of the Declaration of Independence, the Constitution, the Federalist papers, etc., "all of which were read, Franklin reported, 'with rapture,' and which nourished intense discussions among the French intelligentsia and liberal politicians, on the constitutional principles of ideal states and the possibilities of reform."[189] These uniquely American documents were studied and discussed throughout Europe. But that's all the elites did—just talk about them. Unfortunately, the American example of a free and peaceful republic has been rarely emulated elsewhere in the world; and even when it was, it was rarely done as well as the original.

In *The Ideological Origins of the American Revolution*, Bernard Bailyn suggests these ideas and documents arose from "a massive seemingly random eclecticism."[190] In spite of references to theoretical arguments, the main impetus was probably simple hatred of King George and Parliament's oppressive rules and taxation. However, the colonists "liked to display authorities for their arguments. . . . But this display of classical authors is deceptive. . . . Often the citations appear to have been dragged in as window dressing. So Jonathan Mayhew casually lumped Plato with Demosthenes and Cicero as the ancients who had initiated him 'in the doctrines of civil liberty.' Oxenbridge Thatcher too thought Plato had been a liberty-loving revolutionary, while Jefferson, who actually read the Dialogues, discovered in them only 'the sophisms, futilities and incomprehensibilities of a foggy mind.'"[191]

One of the key figures at the Constitutional Convention was a lawyer from Scotland who had settled in Carlisle, Pennsylvania. James Wilson spoke at virtually every session and brought the common sense wisdom of a Scottish minister, Thomas Reid, to bear on all constitutional questions. Reid, initially a minister, taught at King's College in Aberdeen and considered Hume's theories "pretentious nonsense." Reid maintained that man is born with an innate common sense that needs no proof for questions of moral truth and the reality of the earth he is born into. Reid "democratized the intellect, by insisting that the ordinary man could be as certain of his judgments as the philosopher was."[192]

Benjamin Rush was also familiar with Reid's "commonsense philosophy" and advised Tom Paine to use Reid's phrase as the title of his famous book, *Common Sense*, that so emphatically presented the case for American independence. Thus, a common lawyer helped bring both the passion for liberty and a confidence in the common people to America. But, back in Scotland, Thomas Reid's "Scottish School," that

Thomas Reid (b.1710) Scottish preacher and teacher. His maxim: "I despise philosophy and renounce its guidance; let my soul dwell in common sense."

espoused a philosophy of common sense, lost out to Hume's skepticism and moral relativism. Intellectuals of the subsequent two hundred and fifty years ignore Reid and extol Hume because they by nature prefer the complex concepts that justify their being, and are unwilling to present any argument that the common people are as wise as the intelligentsias.

The framers of America's new government relied, not on philosophical theories or abstract reasoning, but on practical sense, their immediate needs, and the common history of free institutions. They relied on "precedent and to an unbroken tradition evolving from time immemorial. . . . And they assumed [that] the accumulation of the ages, the burden of inherited custom, contained within it greater wisdom than any man or group of men could devise by the power of reason. . . ."[193] The miracle of America's creation—the Declaration of Independence, the revolution, victory, and the writing and implementation of the Constitution—was that it happened so fast. In the last twenty-five years of the eighteenth century, the Americans managed to recapitulate and perfect all the steps of mankind's 3,000-year struggle to find a better way to order society. In workmanlike fashion, they took all the building blocks from the past successes in Athens, Rome, Florence, Holland, and England, and put them together, adding custom features to suit American conditions.

The American form of government proved to be both excellent and flexible, able to undergo constant adaptation and improvement ever since. It was accomplished by the concerted effort of many ordinary people, although a few displayed uncommon skills in writing and oratory. The most commonly cited man to be crowned as America's "first intellectual," Ralph Waldo Emerson, was not to write his first book until half a century later. And his writings gained recognition largely for his assertions regarding the importance of self-reliance, simplicity, and independence—the very characteristics epitomized by the ten generations of Americans that had preceded him and that had established the conveniences of Emerson's comfortable home in Concord, Massachusetts.

In the ensuing 200 years, only a handful of countries have been able to duplicate the American achievement in free governance. The European nations, sharing a similar knowledge and background, struggled endlessly, with but little success. Tyranny, revolution, and war marked the Continent's nineteenth century; and in the twentieth century, the twin monsters of Nazism and Communism engulfed the Continent, slaughtered millions, and subjected more millions to enslavement and concentration camps that displayed an inhumanity unprecedented in history. Twice within thirty years, America and Great Britain had to come to the rescue to restore a semblance of order out of the chaos ravaging Europe.

The first signs of failure in Europe could be witnessed on the Thursday afternoon of "October 26, 1775, [when] His Royal Majesty

George III, King of England, rode in royal splendor from St. James's Palace to the Palace of Westminster, there to address the opening of Parliament on the increasingly distressing issue of war in America."[194] Earlier that year the events at Lexington Green and Bunker Hill had highlighted the growing tensions between the King's forces and the colonists. "The boom of cannon saluted His Majesty's arrival at Westminster, and with the traditional welcoming ceremonies performed, the King assumed his place on the throne at the head of the House of Lords, flanked by the peers in their crimson robes."[195] Speaking for twenty minutes, his majesty proposed that it was the better part of wisdom "to put a speedy end" to such disorders, then returned to St. James's Palace. Lord North had already arranged for the hiring of German mercenaries and ordered an expanded military and fleet to impose the force of steel on the protesting Americans.

Far from traveling from palace to palace in a splendid carriage, John Adams at the time was making trips on horseback from Massachusetts to Philadelphia to serve as a member of Congress, which was meeting to discuss greater freedom for the colonists. It was a 300-mile trip in the dead of winter that took two weeks. Adams had "the hands of a man accustomed to pruning his own trees, cutting his own hay, and splitting his own firewood."[196] He "enjoyed no social standing. He was an

John Adams, husband of Abigail, went to London to visit the King.

awkward dancer and poor at cards. . . . There was no money in his background"[197]; but "he had emerged as one of the most 'sensible and forcible' figures in the whole patriot cause."[198] A commoner, his deeds were already matching those of the King—except for the small difference that Adams proposed to escalate the disorders that the King wanted to quell.

Ten years later, the victor, John Adams would arrive in London as the new American minister to the Court of St. James, representing a free America. One of his first diplomatic duties was to speak at a private audience with King George. Adams stood before the King and formally asked for "your Majesty's royal benevolence, and of restoring an entire esteem, confidence, and affection . . . between people who, though separated by an ocean and under different governments, have the same language, a similar religion, and kindred blood."[199] With excellent manners and grace on both sides, the appeal of the rebel, lawyer, and farmer was accorded official acceptance by the royal tyrant who had ordered the colonists' subjugation. It was, all in all, one of the really big days for the common men and women of the world.

Since those momentous times, the governance of the new nation has drawn on a larger base of its people than had any prior society. And prosperity and leisure has been afforded to a wider proportion of its people than was attained in any prior society. Jean-Francois Revel observes that "The American Dream is not simply a matter of how to become a millionaire; it has more to do with the osmosis between the working and middle classes that was achieved much earlier and more extensively than in Europe . . . and is much more conducive to upward mobility."[200]

Across the ocean, the European social and economic structures retained a rigidity that, despite six hundred years of reform, still did not provide enough opportunity for their people. Millions of Europeans packed up their belongings and left to go where opportunity was greater. And they did not go to the Middle East, Africa, or Asian nations. For the past 400 years, freedom seekers throughout the world demonstrated this "common wisdom" by voting with their feet, which took them to America. The influx created an ever-growing pool of talent and energy. In England, Ben Franklin's grandfather was a blacksmith, but feeling hampered by its socio-economic rigidity, he moved to America. In England, George Washington's grandfather was a common laborer. When he left, England lost a worker, but America gained a great general and its first president. These families were held back in England, unable to fully exercise their talent for themselves or for their country. In America, they were empowered.

Mark Steyn has applied population statistics to the analysis of history to consider why English has emerged as the language of global business, and why a quarter of the world's population belongs to the British Commonwealth. His answer: "Because in the early nineteenth century the first nation to conquer infant mortality was England. . . . By 1820 medical progress and improvements in basic hygiene had so transformed British life that half the population was under the age of fifteen."[201] This created a young and vibrant population, ready and able to work and care for the smaller older generation. Plus, the surplus manpower emigrated to settle North America, Australia, New Zealand, and to provide administrators and businessmen throughout the West Indies, Africa, India, and the Pacific. Fortunately, these emigrants took with them the very useful English systems of law, property rights, and principles of personal liberty that enriched all who received them. The rapidly expanding population produced, not shortages, as eco-doomsayers are wont to predict, but economic growth and strength. It is a recurring fact that most successful nations experiencing solid economic growth and rising income per capita did so in periods of rapid population growth. This was a source of strength to both America and European nations of the eighteenth and nineteenth century when increasing populations provided an abundance of what Julian Simon calls the "ultimate resource."

The transfer of world authority to the United States is consistent with history, which shows the freer communities growing and thriving, then finally declining after having passed on their innovations to another free society. As the torch of freedom and prosperity was passed from Florentine, Italy, to Holland, to England, to Scotland, and finally to America; each new recipient nation flourished, even as the strength and fortunes declined of the nation that had passed that torch. Individual European countries still grew, albeit slowly and sporadically, but they never escaped the burden of their rigid class systems. To make matters worse, at a certain level of affluence and maturity, the intellectuals arrived to retard the growth of freedom, undermine culture, promote bureaucratization and socialism, and, often, spew philosophies of hate and rage that helped spread the horrors of war. As the last straw, the peoples of such excessively "enlightened" nations have now even lost the urge to procreate and currently suffer the consequences of rapidly declining birth rates. In another generation or two it will be both a lonely and scary world for almost every young European growing up—he or she will have no siblings, no uncles or aunts, no cousins—no family. But there will be a Big Brother—the government in Brussels, to rule over them.

Sooner or later, the flawed vision of Europe's elites was bound to precipitate the decline of old Europe—which thus, almost by default, handed the lead to America.

Chapter 6
Why the West Won

"There was conflict after conflict between individual kings and their bishops. . . . Such struggles bred opportunities which helped to keep a civilization open to new developments, alive and dynamic.
—J. M. Roberts

THE SISTER-IN-LAW OF Osama Bin Laden, Carmen Bin Laden, has published a vivid portrait of life in Muslim cultures. She was raised in the West but married into the Bedouin culture of Saudi Arabia. "I was impetuous, impulsive—I longed to be free." But she discovered the rigid conventions of life in the Middle East, "where clan rules are more important than personality. In the Middle East, you never develop as an individual. People may manage to escape their traditions for a short while, but then these rules catch up to them."202

Western societies escaped this ancient oppression three thousand years ago, when the first Greek classics depicted heroes most definitely exerting their individuality. Ever since the Greek and Roman pantheon was replaced by Christ, the men and women of the West have fought and argued with their God, pleaded with Him and railed at Him, criticized Him and denounced Him, and, when they felt it necessary, established new religions—all under the undoubtedly pleased gaze of their Almighty Father. Like the rebellious teenagers of a strict but loving family, Western men and women in this way became adults. They accepted the burden of free will, the attendant personal responsibility, and the obligation to lead constructive and purposeful lives. And in spite of their piety, they retained their rights to explore science rationally; to improve their laws, government, and material lives; and to develop their individual potential to the fullest.

Somehow, most of these people found a way to separate their secular lives from their spiritual lives, to separate church and state, and thereby avoid the suffocating theocracies that have suppressed almost all other peoples. Jeffrey Hart has referred to the resulting productive tension between the classical and biblical strains in Western civilization. He suggests that this tension added to the restlessness and energy of Western people, leading to their relative advance over other cultures.[203] Others have called this cultural dichotomy the antagonism between Athens (knowing) and Jerusalem (believing), which gave Western men that added questing attitude that spelled success. In any event, this mental separation of church and state was a major turning point in man's history, for it retained the comfort and support of faith while releasing the secular world from the oppressiveness of dogma. Every man's mind was thus liberated to explore, shape, and improve the world he lived in. Those individuals could have done the same thing anywhere on the planet if only given the chance.

Why "Attitude" Matters

As we have seen in previous chapters, when a new and open society was sufficiently secure and free, its people had the rare opportunity to develop the traditions, values, and culture that allowed them free expression of their initiative and talents. These opportunities generally arose in small enclaves at the edges of the fractured and competing states of Europe. The question may be asked: Was this the only place on earth that these opportunities arose or was there something unique about the people of these Western enclaves? The Radzewicz Rule states that all people will advance if given some security and little oppression. However, it appears that their advance may be more rapid and grander if they are strengthened by a certain intangible—some form of empowering attitude or faith. In history's stepping stones of progress, the indigenous people that carved out advances had one common denominator—they considered themselves to be free and independent agents; they demanded such freedom, and fought for it; and their self confidence was consequently buoyed by a loyalty to their nation, their faith, and their families.

Rose Wilder Lane spelled out this crucial role of "attitude" in 1943. In *The Discovery of Freedom*, she wrote, "A time comes when every normal man is a responsible human being. His energy creates a part of the whole human world of his time. He is free; he is self-controlling and responsible because he generates his energy and controls it. No one and nothing else can control it. Nevertheless, during some six thousand years of the Old World's history, a majority of men have believed that some Authority controlled them."[204] This mistaken notion that some Authority ruled over men explains the snail-like development of freedom and prosperity over those millenniums. It also explains the uniqueness of those few enclaves where the populace would not accept that stifling condition, but flexed their muscles as free men and women. Now, one might ask, would not every human being placed in such an enclave, no matter where they were transported from, manifest that same militant attitude demanding a free expression of their personal ambitions?

Followers of some Eastern faiths are taught that if they resist the class and cultural strictures they are born into, or basically "rock the boat," they will be punished in their next life by being dumped, reincarnated, into an even lower class of beings. This grim prospect must certainly dampen their attitudes and any inclination to improve their life or conditions. Of course, that Hindu belief is just another form of oppression because it restricts the potentialities of its followers. An individual who was unable to shed that belief would never be completely free of oppression no matter where you placed him or her. Further, most individuals are primarily the product of their upbringing, and are helped if a spirit of independence is ingrained in childhood—it may take a generation or two to inculcate the beliefs and values that have characterized Western man. That may explain the inertia that held back so many societies—their people never had a sufficient opportunity to develop the independent attitude needed to sustain freedom.

Quite differently, where there is a culture and faith that exalts man and endows him with free will and responsibility, he is emancipated from any mind-set that might retard individual action. As Professor George F. Thomas writes, "The aim of duty is not only to fulfill the needs of persons but also to help them realize possibilities of value in their lives."[205] The Greek-Christian culture is widely believed to have given Western people a predisposition to exert their will in the search for new possibilities.

Ivan P. Hall, with a lifetime of experience in Japan, has deplored the insularity of its leaders and written about how their cultural censorship was and remains an obstacle to innovation. He tells about how in the 1890s Westerners were called in to create the first university. "During the first two decades of the Meiji period (1868-1912) . . . they brought the entire corpus of Western higher education and learning to Japan at a time when the Japanese had neither the trained scholars nor the translated texts to do so by themselves."[206] The cultural lack of imaginative attitude is illustrated by Hall's description of the Japanese efforts to catch up with the West: Erwin Baelz, a German physician, served from 1876 to 1902 as chief advisor in establishing Japan's first medical school and hospital, located at the newly created Tokyo University. However, he became more and more disenchanted with his hosts as he saw many of his Western compatriots dismissed and sent home after their brains had been picked. "The Japanese, Baelz suggested, often seemed not to understand the true source and nature of Western science, mistaking it for a sort of machine that could be carted off to new places and made to perform the same work, rather than seeing it as an organism requiring a carefully nurturing atmosphere."[207] In contrast, the extraordinary freedom of thought and enterprise in America allowed a multitude of individuals to develop new and better ways of doing things. The Japanese wanted to pick the plums of Western technology "without seeking to appropriate the spirit that had nourished the tree."[208]

It is essential, however, to note that the "nurturing" Hall mentions is not something the government does from on high—rather it a by-product of each individual's learned knowledge that he or she is free from governmental direction and responsible for their own actions. It is that free spirit of the common man that enhances creativity, and it must emerge spontaneously—it can never be forced from on high. An independent spirit and rebelliousness allows, on the dark side, a raw, uneducated teenager to call the president an idiot or a crook, or even burn his country's flag, but on the bright side, allows such an otherwise despicable youngster to develop a new software program to revolutionize telecommunications, create new miracles of the Internet, or whatever. The common man in America is often brash and irreverent, and sometimes coarse and vulgar, but his mind is not shackled by too many niceties and proprieties, and that permits the innovative breakthroughs fueling our economy.

Making Use of Human Energy

Since men first organized into social groupings they have endeavored to increase their well-being by cooperative action. This application of group action, to be successful, had to work under some direction or control. As a general rule, that authority was too controlling. Ms Lane laments 6,000 years of inertia in man's history because the Old World thinkers all believed that some form of Authority had to direct any society of men. "Look at any available records of any peoples, living anywhere at any time in the whole history of the Old World. They revolt against their King, and replace him by another King. . . . For generations or centuries, they revolt and change these rulers; then they revolt against that kind of Authority, and set up another kind."[209] The mistake is looking for any Authority to rule. The founders of the American Republic, when they wrote the Constitution, recognized the inadequacies of Old World attempts at free societies. They also knew of the occasional successes and looked to their examples for useful governing mechanisms. Thus armed, they proceeded to diffuse the new nation's central powers to such an extent that there would be minimal authority from above to interfere with the citizens' freedom of action.

It has always been the great thinkers of history that have been the most ardent advocates of Authority. Plato "worked out in monstrous detail an ideal system, a totalitarian State (which he called a Republic) in which every human impulse is absolutely controlled by a few philosophers."[210] Spengler pulls out of history's jumble a series of civilizations that somehow spontaneously rise and fall. It is not clear why or how this happens, and the role of individuals is not considered. "This view of human life is supported by an erudite analysis of all past history and by a host of Spengler's intellectual followers. Of course, any American who is not an intellectual knows that this world is not inhabited by gigantic, invisible creatures called Civilizations. He knows that ordinary men and women, using their energies, make a civilization and keep on making it, every day, every hour, and that nothing but their constant, individual efforts can make a civilization and keep it existing."[211] Thus, Rose Wilder Lane confirms that it was just such ordinary people that created the stepping stones to progress during the past few millenniums. And it follows that such progress was most rapid and extensive when the people were free of the mental restrictions imposed by aristocracies and intellectuals. An atmosphere of freedom brought out the best in people, enhancing their activity with both a sense of responsibility and a desire for creative achievement.

Since the days of Homer, these empowering examples of free and responsible men were respected and widely known throughout much of the world. But they gained little foothold in the Eastern empires and many of the Western monarchies. It is arguable that it was mental and spiritual oppression more than physical oppression that held back most societies. Johan Norberg has touched on this in praising the role of heroes and their beneficial impact on national attitudes and mores: "We need heroes, because they say something about what our values are, what is good, what is great, what is bad, what we should strive for, and what we should try and avoid."[212] This is refreshing stuff—all about values and absolute moral differences—that allows people to strive to be better, to achieve things, to even be a winner! Some of today's intellectuals don't even want to keep score lest they hurt the sensitive "feelings" of the losers!

Unfortunately, the egalitarian follies of moral relativism, cultural diversity, and affirmative action, the latest "new ideas" rigorously imposed on our students by today's intelligentsia, is replacing heroes with victims. This loss of attitude, if continued, may serve as a model for what happens when a nation's people lose their grit. For it is only through the application of guts, grit, and common sense that individuals can employ their energies to improve their lot in life. No one else can do it for them.

"In the human world there is no entity but the individual person. There is no force but individual energy. In actual human life the only real Society is every living person's contact with everyone he meets."[213] This gets to the original fundamental cause of all historical progress—individual action. All supporting factors like education, the scientific method, representative governments, and free markets, were simply creations of ordinary people finding ways to magnify their action. Such systems that advanced productivity and freedom are often mistakenly cited by historians as the reasons that advances were made—which is like saying that people are living longer because of good medicines and surgical procedures. But those medicines and procedures did not just happen—they were the product of individual human action. And that action had nothing to do with the armchair abstractions of soft-scientists—the advances were the product of individuals working in laboratories and operating rooms; individuals who had mastered Organic Chemistry and Molecular Biology; and devoted years of concerted effort to attain the medical expertise to contribute to society.

Innovations by such uncommon men and women became the hallmark of Western culture. In the following sections we will look at more of those effective mechanisms that free people in the West have engineered to advance their well-being. But, note that the mechanisms are not what created the advances—it was the individuals who tried them, tested them, then modified them, and fine tuned them to make them effective.

Empowering Everyone

The people of the West have long been characterized by robust striving for self-fulfillment and personal gain. Ayn Rand has described this vigorous and active approach to life as an expression of personal "religion"; Douglas North as an expression of "social psychology"; Vernon William as the underlying force of "experimental economics"; Hernando de Soto as the key to "empowering the illegals." Whatever one calls such individual effort, its satisfaction does result in progress, often rapid and astonishing progress. Many hands make light work. The elites are too few, too comfortable, and too deficient in the common practical knowledge of the masses. Vast stretches of the globe lost the race to freedom and prosperity because the powers that be refused to make room for the personal fulfillment of the hopes and dreams of those multitudes at the bottom.

David Landes asks why the Chinese failed to reach their potential and for an answer consults Elvin's *Pattern of the Chinese Past*, in which Elvin observes that "Almost every element usually regarded by historians as a major contributory cause to the Industrial revolution in north-western Europe was also present in China. . . . Had the Chinese possessed, or developed, the seventeenth century European mania for tinkering and improving, they could have made an efficient spinning machine out of the primitive model described by Wang Chen. . . . The crucial point is that nobody tried."[214] The more crucial point is that nobody was allowed to try. The absence of a free market sustained by strong property rights has always deterred economic activity, and the rulers of the Heavenly Kingdom were always interfering, manipulating prices, prohibiting various activities, exacting bribes, and curtailing private enrichment.

Another deterrent in the East was "the quasi-confinement of women to the home," by which half the population was prevented from contributing to society.[215] In Japan and the West, women may not have had full voting rights but they had access to the public space, could man the textile machinery and the cottage industries, and were expected to contribute income to the family. While Western traditions did place women in a subordinate role, the "suppression" was relatively minor compared to other cultures, and, more importantly, it has been gradually but regularly lessened over time. The concept of chivalry and romantic love found its greatest expression in European culture; ever since Chaucer, much of Western literature has catered to the Gothic romance tastes of European women. And Western women, though only recently approaching full equality, have always enjoyed considerably more influence than those of the Middle East. Perhaps the pillow talk of a spouse is both more constructive and influential than the cooing of a concubine.

Sinologist Etienne Balasz finds that sexist deterrents preventing Eastern women's full participation were symptoms of massive and monolithic-totalitarian control: "Chinese society was highly totalitarian. . . . There is to begin with a whole array of state monopolies, which comprise the great consumption staples: salt, iron, tea, alcohol, foreign trade. There is a monopoly of education, jealously guarded. . . . [A]nything written unofficially, that escapes the censorship, has little hope of reaching the public. But the reach of the Moloch-State, the omnipotence of the bureaucracy, goes much further. There are clothing regulations, a regulation of public and private construction . . . the colors one wears, the music one hears, the festivals—all are regulated. . . . [T]he providential State watches minutely over every step of its subjects, from cradle to grave. It is a regime of paper work and harassment. . . . It is the State that kills technological progress in China. . . . The atmosphere . . . is unfavorable to the spirit of free inquiry."[216] Thus the far-flung authority of the Imperial Court exerted a crushing physical as well as a mental control over its peoples, and when it came to tinkering, pleading, innovating, "no one tried." The elite had everything they wanted, the peasants had nothing to gain.

The causes of the East's fate should raise warning flags in the West. In our democracies, the newly arrived intellectuals, who love to prescribe and administer, are increasingly burdening their nations with just such centralized programs—even as China's leaders have begun to see the light and to encourage extraordinary industrial and business enterprise. This reversal, by which the West is now introducing the very policies that held back progress in the Orient, could represent a historical tipping point—unfortunately, unlike most of the divergences of the past three millennium, it would be one that tips the future in favor of the Orient and against the Western democracies.

The year 2005 marks the 600th anniversary of one of history's legendary explorers, and its celebration in Beijing raises the question of whether man can learn from history. Admiral Zheng He, a Muslim eunuch from Central Asia, rose to great heights in the Imperial navy of Ming emperor, Zhu Di. The Chinese navy at that time enjoyed the strength and prestige created during the preceding century under the recently ousted Mongol rulers, the Khans. Between 1405 and 1433, emperor Zhu Di continued the Khan's expansionist policies and financed the most costly and far-reaching expeditions of Eastern history; the journeys of Zhu Di's commander, Zheng He, took him as far as India and the east coast of Africa. Zheng's ships were much bigger than anything the Europeans could build at the time. He or his successors may have sailed around the Cape of Good Hope before the Portuguese did in the opposite direction almost a hundred years later. But Zheng's seventh voyage was his last and marked the end of Chinese naval exploration. Ming rulers had never favored the Khan's international ambitions and so withdrew inside their vast landmass. The emperor closed the door—and the minds of his subjects. "China had embarked on a long period of isolation like that imposed on Japan by the Tokugawa shogun late in the 17th century."[217]

Such extraordinary shutting down of enterprise was repeated throughout Oriental history. There was very little opportunity for independence, rebelliousness, and competition, there were few men like Martin Luther or Oliver Cromwell, or women like Abigail Adams, Clara Barton, or Joan of Ark. *The Economist* calls this one of the great might-have-beens in history: "Might China have avoided decline? Or was, instead, the recall of the fleet a symptom of a deeper malaise in Chinese society? In competing Europe, after all, Columbus was able to flit from court to court until he finally found a backer for his expedition of 1492. For Zheng it was the emperor or no one." But "a deeper malaise" was already present in China. And even today, it is likely that "China's heavy-handed officials, as intolerant of non-conformity now as under the Ming, will once more contrive to scuttle the ships of its visionaries."[218] In China it has always been thus. The example of China shows how a nation's progress is destroyed when the awe-inspiring potential of its people is suppressed by autocratic ways, or when the good habits of independent and enquiring minds stifled.

The Psychology of Success

E. L. Jones asserts that economic growth "is the means of solving the dire human problems caused by want, and it does matter desperately."[219] Throughout history, most people have had to constantly struggle to obtain even minimal shelter and safety for themselves and their families. Most of the world's people still struggle in this hand-to-mouth fashion; widespread relief has been found only in a few advanced nations, and to a significant degree only during the past few centuries. A fortunate few enjoy material comforts, the free practice of religious faith, relative peace of mind, and time for aesthetic, recreational and spiritual pursuits. There may be a synergy here, for we can see intimate connections between the work needed to attain improved economic and political freedom, and the mental-spiritual side of life. Although Westerners have successfully separated secular activities from their spiritual beliefs, they nonetheless buttress each other.

Dr. Nathaniel Branden believes that self-responsibility "is not an onerous burden but a source of joy and personal power. . . ."[220] Western man succeeded in no small part because the culture he shaped gave meaning and encouragement to self-reliance and constructive action. Every human requires the personal satisfaction gained from some form of accomplishment; the disciplined effort expended toward such a goal adds purpose and resolve to individuals, and contributes to a stronger more vital nation. We will see in a subsequent chapter how after the Protestant Reformation there was a burst of just such creative effort as new religions not only opened men's thinking but encouraged enterprise, thrift, and personal accomplishment.

In a recent interview Maya Angelou was asked what was the biggest issue facing women today and in her reply she stressed the need for self-esteem. No amount of enabling legislation will advance women's roles in society unless they believe in their own self-worth and are prepared to exert themselves by seizing each and every opportunity. Just as a society cannot defend itself unless its people love the country and believe it is worth defending, neither can an individual work toward accomplishments unless they feel able, worthy, and deserving of the goal. It is only complete self respect and attitude that creates the can-do feeling and empowering motivation that ensures success. Homer's male heroes inspired this approach to life, and men had to fight for millenniums to establish the few locales where it could function. As that attitude is adopted by more and more women, their societies will be strengthened by their unleashed talents. Accomplishment feeds personal satisfaction, just as success fuels success, and thus Western values and beliefs served to empower individual activity. Submission and obedience have never been the hallmark of Western people.

> *Western civilization, it seems to me, stands by two great heritages. One is the scientific spirit of adventure . . . humility of the intellect. The other great heritage is Christian ethics . . . humility of the spirit. These two heritages are logically, thoroughly consistent.*
>
> —Richard P. Feynman

Mortimer Adler recognizes the importance of a citizenry's self esteem—normally achieved through sound habits, unity, and a solid work ethic. Such cultural influences must both encourage and restrain a people for a nation to succeed. He approaches the subject via philosophical analysis of moral values. First, he decries the ancient Epicureans as well as the modern self-avowed hedonists like John Stuart Mill and Spinoza, who argue that whatever you desire is good, pleasure is whatever you like, and there are no absolute moral values—everything is relative. David Hume examined this issue and also found few absolutes, and thus "is responsible for the skepticism about the objective truth of moral philosophy that is prevalent in the twentieth century."[221]

These flawed philosophies of the great writers contributed to today's moral relativism and its emphasis on "feeling good" and instant gratification. Today's academics, intellectual hostages to such demented philosophers, teach that it is impossible to make any distinction between cultures—that we cannot determine which are better and which are worse. Then, with their customary flawed logic, they proceed to explain how America is the worst society. Of course, many students will quickly recognize this as nonsense, especially the foreign students who have actually lived in other cultures and struggled to get to America. But many swallow this destructive message. To the extent that they allow their hopes and ambitions to be squelched by it, these youth lose the positive attitude needed to capitalize on the opportunities that are available. These students are today's real victims. With their potentialities undermined by their teachers, they are excluded from the satisfactions of participating, competing, and succeeding, which can only work to their own detriment and to that of their country.

It is alarming to see how these ideas of the intelligentsia are harmful to their own nation and to their fellow countrymen. The burden of their bad ideas comes from not seeing what matters— historians and economists have always emphasized such factors as iron deposits, climate, soil fertility, and navigable rivers rather than looking to the motivation of the individuals who located and made use of such assets or found substitutes for them. It is the natural arrogance of intellectuals to ignore the real people doing things, and instead look to abstract forces or generalized concepts to explain what was happening. But why do those people, many with high intellect, have such a faulty view of reality? Professor Sowell has said it's a "vision" thing.[222] A very similar answer was given many years ago by the great satirist Jonathan Swift, who's classic *Gulliver's Travels*, deals with a fictional race of Lilliputians. Like the intellectuals of Swift's era, as well as the intelligentsia of today, the Lilliputians loved fine distinctions and abstract concepts. Unfortunately, however, these people also had a vision problem—they could "'see with great exactness, but at no great distance.' They suffer from a lack of perspective. It is not their fault; that is the way they are built."[223]

The Power of Private Property

Successful cultures may differ widely in exactly how they encourage the individual to prosper. But the most successful approaches rely on the maintenance of legal and financial security of individuals that allows them to keep the fruits of their labor and to readily own and trade property. The individual economic gains that result not only foster a growing general prosperity, but also the self-confidence of the individual, fueling further efforts and further success. Unless such innate motivational characteristics of people are recognized, a vibrant economic-political structure cannot function. Over the past four centuries, such exuberant activity and personal self-confidence became a particularly American characteristic. In *Cowboy Capitalism*, Olaf Gersemann, a reporter for Germany's largest economic and business weekly, analyzes the beneficial results of American self-confidence and suggests that modern Europeans who disparage the "cowboy mentality" might do better to emulate it. He argues that the greater market freedoms in the United States create a more flexible and prosperous system than is possible in rigid and over-regulated Europe.

In Chapter 8, the unfortunate plight of people living in underdeveloped nations is attributed in large part to their inability to own and transfer property. The majority of would-be homeowners and entrepreneurs throughout the world are forced to live as squatters and operate businesses illegally because of inadequate property laws in those nations. Much of the energy unleashed in England and America has been the result of deeds of title and financial instruments that were created during the past 1,000 years by merchants and traders in the enclaves distinguished by free enterprise activity. These mechanics of private property helped determine success versus failure for their people. Unbelievably, deficiencies in the ability to obtain legal title to property remains a major obstacle to progress in most countries—the people mired in poverty throughout the Third World sit on but can't use a vast wealth of assets that dwarfs all the aid given to their governments during the past fifty years by the central planning intellectuals "managing" the IMF, World Bank, and related foreign aid programs.[224] These gifts of trillions of dollars, to people who can't even use what they already have, is evidence of the economic ignorance of the elites running the large international agencies. It also indicates an intellectual arrogance because they simply don't comprehend that those suffering people would prefer to help themselves if just given the opportunity.

Nature Versus Nurture

Some commentators have regarded the persistent failure of some societies as built-in, the consequence of a permanent racial inferiority. Thus, it has been argued that American Indians, or the Australian Aborigines, or the remote tribes in the heart of Africa, had less intelligence, or less innate gumption and initiative, or less of something else vital to progress, than did the peoples of China or Greece. However, it has been fairly well established in the past century that such genetic or racial differences as do exist are marginal in importance. Thomas Sowell, for example, has analyzed many of the measurements and tests conducted to determine such differences. He concludes that while there are sometimes big differences in knowledge between racial and ethnic groups, there are no significant differences in innate intelligence or native abilities.[225]

Differences in general level of accomplishment arise only when one society over an extended period of time has provided basic safety, ennobling values, and sufficient individual freedom for its citizens to capitalize on these advantages. The cumulative acquired knowledge, skills, and attitude of a graduate student of astrophysics at MIT can be contrasted sharply with that of a young Australian aborigine growing up in the remote bush. The large differences between them are the result of the slow but consistent development of knowledge and attitude in the West over thousands of years. All the advantages of the

MIT student are attributable to his being steeped in, and having access to, countless discoveries and civil advances made by enterprising individuals who seized the opportunities offered during history's various stepping stones to progress. A modern college graduate can take pride in his learning, but he should never lose sight of the fact that his opportunities rest on the hard-won accomplishments of predecessors. Americans are wealthy today simply because they have inherited the priceless values, customs, and institutions passed on by common people of the past. Without that head start, we would all be aborigines.

The MIT student must have had the kind of childhood in which all those previous human accomplishments could inform his mind and character. Typically, he was born into a relatively stable middle-class or lower-class family that valued work and discipline. He finished high school, never joined a gang, avoided heavy drug use, acquired no criminal record, and had no children before going off to college. Another youngster, growing up in a nearby community but without the same cultural and familial advantages, might be little better off than the Australian aborigine. Good parenting is thus a vital ingredient of both personal success and societal success.

An individual needs training, education, a positive attitude, a constructive optimism, and ennobling values if he is to reach his full potential. But the ideas of the intellectuals usually exert an adverse affect on such childhood development. Can anyone doubt that exposing children to moral relativism, multiculturalism, illegitimacy, atheism, defeatism, contempt for country, or a victim mentality will surely erode rather than reinforce the foundations of character they need to help their neighborhood or build a satisfying life?

Much, often disciplined direction is necessary to raise mature civilized adults. Such training and spiritual-cultural conditioning has in its varied forms always created marked differences in the individuals making up different societies. Some cultures have been especially successful in rearing citizens of exceptional competencies. Remember that while all humans may have the same basic intelligence and abilities, there can be wide differences in the knowledge and skills imparted to the youth of differing cultures. Some cultures built a cumulative and escalating competency that they handed down from each generation to the next. Such acquired knowledge obviously accelerates progress in a nation. Throughout history strong and united families have first reared and then contributed children prepared to play a vital role in safeguarding and advancing their country. It took generations of patient parenting effort supported by an affirmative culture to produce that MIT graduate referred to above. That student illustrates how the unique and varied mix of secular and religious principles that underlie Western cultures and their strong family units found a way to multiply both the capacity and the energy of its people. Nurturing and encouraging those capabilities and attitudes represent "the secret weapon" of Western civilization.

Colonialism and Conquest

E. L. Jones dismisses European imperialism as an explanation for the failure of other societies to keep pace with the West: "A different imperialism is to be indicted. This was the command economics imposed by dynasties from the steppes of central Asia: Ottoman, Mughal and Manchu, all of them latter-day models of the Mongol onslaught. It was this, not the hydraulic agriculture of a timeless Asian Mode of Production, nor Western trade or conquest, that determined the fate of the East. Steppe imperialism was what made the difference, by clamping in its selfish grasp the customary agricultures and nascent trade sectors of the 'early modern' Islamic Middle East, India and China."[226] In concert with deterministic philosophies and religions, these societies imposed the most rigid mercantilist systems imaginable, never allowing their downtrodden subjects an opportunity to break through the system.

The Oriental despots were superior to their European counterparts in one crucial respect: no one ever suppressed the peasants as effectively as they did, which was one reason their societies were unable to defend themselves and quickly succumbed to European colonization. Mercantilism in Europe did over-regulate, did restrict trade to favored monopolies and guilds, and many entrepreneurs were hung for breaking legal restrictions. But these barriers and sanctions did not totally suppress individual business activity, whereas the Eastern dynasties' rigid control and restriction of education to the elite destroyed any chance for innovative thinking at the bottom levels of society.

The accumulation of colonies has been characteristic of all powerful nations. The Phoenicians established colonies throughout the Mediterranean world. Then the Greeks pushed them aside and established their own colonies. Eastern Europe was held hostage by the Ottoman Empire for hundreds of years and served as a source of raw materials and slaves to enrich the homeland. Every large civilization throughout history raided neighboring societies for loot and slaves— or worse: The Caribs on the island of Guadeloupe would regularly raid surrounding islands to capture women as slaves and men to eat. Female slaves that escaped their captors in the late fifteenth century would appeal to Columbus' men to take them away, "rather than remain amongst those who had eaten their husbands and children."[227]

The establishment of colonies and dependencies did facilitate trade and return riches to the conqueror. But these exactions were not the cause of the conqueror's success, but were the result of existing superiority. The very fact that one nation subdued another nation established that one was already more powerful than the other. As much as pacifists would like to hide from it, physical dominance has always and still plays a pivotal role in national affairs. Colonies, like slavery, always existed wherever people were not strong enough to resist them.

There is also the fact that colonies by themselves were not necessarily of value. Discoveries are of little use if people are not in a position to exploit them. Jones points out that "Cheng Ho's distant voyages had not transformed Ming China, neither had the Malagasys or Polynesians, famous voyagers, transformed their homelands, nor, come to that, had the adventurous Vikings transformed an earlier Europe by crossing the North Atlantic. Responsive commercialism had emerged in medieval Europe, and it was that which made the discoveries effective."[228]

One stepping stone briefly empowered the masses in the Orient; and, had it been more than a flicker, it might have led to Eastern supremacy. This advance illustrates one of the benefits of widespread conquest and colonization. The Great Khan, Genghis, gained control over vast areas spanning Asia and Europe and for a barbarian showed greater sense than all his more cultured "betters." Genghis upset the settled and rigid behavior of all the Eurasians he conquered and introduced new and better ways of doing and thinking. He tolerated all faiths, established local councils for peasant self-rule throughout his realms, promoted education, expanded rights for women, pioneered the use of Chinese engineers and explosives to lay siege to and destroy Muslim fortifications, permitted no aristocracy except that of merit, and established a new code of law based on just and pragmatic principles that created order within the sprawling and diverse empire he controlled.[229] His empire drew upon every region and every class for a wealth of new ideas, a process of cross-fertilization often seen in times of historical progress.

But this open and progressive society, created so suddenly, did not last. There was no underlying heritage or faith to support the Khan's policies, and no time for them to take root. The philosophies and religions of the rival kingdoms pasted together did not support the new laws and social structure being imposed. Moreover, the succeeding Mongol government under Tamerlane did not share the democratic and tolerant beliefs of the founder; and the successor rulers were not so interested in maintaining the empire as they were in the mystical and openly erotic practices of splinter religious groups from Tibet, diversions that could only serve to weaken their control. Mongol society clearly lost the initial unity and drive that had made the Mongols the supreme power on earth for more than a hundred years.

The Khan's great conquests helped transfer Oriental science and inventions to the West, where they were improved and capitalized upon. It was another case in which the conquered benefited more than the conquerors. In sharp contrast, the Chinese, Indian, and Islamic leaders were just waiting for the collapse of the Khans in order to re-impose their theocratic stranglehold on their subjects. They weren't interested in emulating the ideas of others. Throughout history, much of the transfer of improved systems and mechanics from advanced cultures to less advanced cultures was accomplished by conquest. As a result, colonization was a two way street, with the conquered absorbing the desirable ways of the invaders, and vice versa.

Thanks to conquest and trade, few locales were ignorant of the advances of other societies. India, which is succeeding in the new Global economy, owes much to the contributions it gleaned from British colonials who transplanted some of the better English practices during their occupation. What hurt the Arab Sultans and Islamic states was not ignorance of but failure to learn from the Mongols, the Italian traders, the Greeks, the Phoenicians, and all the societies that had demonstrated the advantages of free and open societies.

The Middle East was exposed to the entire world's colonial activities both as an aggressor that overran its neighbors, and as a culture invaded by others. The benefits of such transfusions flickered only briefly, around the turn of the first millennium. The refusal of most countries in the region to absorb or adopt successful governing and educational systems from other nations was caused by the rigid fundamentalism of its religious and intellectual leaders. Without the benefits from a separation of church and state power, this monolithic culture ended by holding the entire society in permanent immobility.

The Impact of Education

Level of literacy is another societal difference that affects success. The publication of books and the spread of literacy among a historically huge part of the population in Western Europe was unmatched anywhere else in the world. In the fifteenth century Gutenberg introduced movable type and the printing press to the Western world. Within fifteen years of his death there were printing presses throughout Europe. "By 1500 there were 1,700 at work, in a total of 300 towns. The number of titles being printed annually was over 2,000 by 1600. . . . Cheap stores of technical knowledge moved outwards to the men of action and affairs, the military, the administration, the landowners."[230] Once again we see grassroots empowerment of the common man propelling huge growth in social capital. The added capacity for innovation through increased knowledge proves to be just as critical, if not more so, than the possession of natural resources or navigable rivers.

The benefits from innovative developments in paper and printing might also have been attained in the Chinese Empire. They discovered these processes and initially displayed the same level of technical skill, but the books that were printed were restricted to the elite members of the Imperial palace. "The Chinese literati were too well assured of the success of Chinese institutions and too firmly convinced of the self-sufficiency of their own cultural world to spare time and attention for the pursuit of barbarian trifles."[231] This failure to capitalize on new technology was firmly rooted in Asia's past.

Ruled by autocrats who feared that their subjects might gain knowledge of the outside world, China was insular, and that insularity prevented progress. The culture's seemingly rich literary and artistic heritage disguised the general backwardness of scientific thought, which remained handcuffed by tradition. There was indeed plenty of intellectual thought, but it was often routine, summarizing, and official, rather than fresh and exploratory: "Scholarship continued to flourish under the Manchus on a massive scale. Vast compilations, systematizations, and summaries of earlier knowledge were completed under official patronage. Carefully edited texts and authoritative commentaries crystallized the long tradition of Chinese learning. . . ."[232] This is the kind of "erudition" that Richard Feynman called "the disease of the intellectuals" as he speaks of Islamic scholars who wrote not only commentaries, but commentaries on commentaries. "They described what each other wrote about each other. They just kept writing these commentaries."[233] They concentrated on their past with detailed reviews—a national preoccupation with the same kind of superficial theses common in today's American soft-science doctoral programs. China's "high" culture, mired in such traditional scholarship, simply failed to apply or even see the potential applications of new technology. And when they did, the leaders forbade any change, for fear it would reduce their power.

The same lapses afflicted the Ottoman Empire. "Constantinople acquired a press in 1726 but closed it down from 1730 to 1780 and again in 1800. Between 1726 and 1815 that press brought out only sixty-three titles. . . . The literacy gap between Europe and Turkey was the difference between fifty percent and five percent, a ten-fold difference, while the difference between publication rates was a factor of ten thousand."[234] These examples show how the fear of change within an authoritarian government, coupled with a rigidly orthodox philosophy or religion, can resist all progress. Literacy was one casualty.

In summary, it was not the absence of new technology that made the difference between civilizations. The difference arose because the common people of Europe were free to use new technology—to talk about it, apply it, develop it further. And they enjoyed that freedom because the Europeans did not suffer from religious and intellectual orthodoxy to the same extent as the denizens of the East. Nor was the common man crushed by the steep social pyramid and oppressive centralized structure common throughout the great Middle Eastern and Oriental Empires. Almost everyone has conceded these cultural differences, but argued about their importance. Once one recognizes that all progress comes from the bottom, from empowerment of the common man, it becomes clear how and why those cultural differences caused one society to lag, another to advance. Under Imperial and autocratic regimes, the ordinary man was never afforded the opportunity to achieve. Instead he suffered, and the economies of such regimes suffered. Even today, many of their rulers are still wondering how to catch up.

Innovation Versus Invention

We have seen how in shipping, printing, and publishing the West was uniquely receptive to new ideas and quick to apply new approaches to daily activities. It was not, however, "the West" as some kind of amorphous social blob or "cultural force" that made these applications and adaptations. Beginning in the Middle Ages, it was the ordinary workers in hundreds of small towns in the Western European nations who built and operated the presses. Their hands-on efforts created the mechanical innovations that sparked the rapidly increasing efficiency and expanded production seen so markedly for the first time in Western Europe. They were motivated by self-interest; they were enabled by their freedom; and, they were rewarded by being able to keep the fruit of their labor.

Francis Bacon (1561-1626) once listed "the three greatest inventions known to man—the compass, gunpowder and the printing press—all derived from China. Yet it was Europe that brought them to improved design, employed them on a wide scale, and generally in technology and science came to surpass its mentors. Europe's application of improved mechanics stretched back to the horse-collar, horseshoe, water-wheel, crossbow, and wheel barrel, all introduced in the Dark Ages."[235] Major new inventions did not by themselves help the society in which the discovery was made. They had to be used. For centuries, the Arabs abandoned use of the wheel, chose not to build roads, and relied instead on camels, pack animals, and tribal nomadic life. Talk about roads not taken!

The Chinese printing press was never adapted to mass production and only minimally served the elite in China. In contrast, Gutenberg and many later innovators constantly improved the presses that multiplied throughout Europe. From medieval times, European history was a record of ceaseless small advances, wrought by the imagination of ordinary souls working to make production easier, quicker, and cheaper. "Given the long-standing mechanical background of even benighted rural areas [of Europe], where there were water mills with complicated gearing, and given the inquisitive practicality of many who in other societies seem to have spent their leisure single-mindedly in pursuit of pleasure or at best in impractical philosophizing, the persistent advance is not so surprising."[236]

The Rise of the Common Man

Each of the factors described above helped to advance the economic well-being of Western nations, but they were not the primal cause. Schools, tools, and democracy were not the cause of progress but the results of progress. All advances came from freedom and human energy. It was finding a free setting in which to function that allowed individuals to work unobstructed by coercive authority. The rest flowed from their hard work and common genius. When united by a loyalty to their secure and open community and buttressed by a comforting faith they were motivated to nurture their families, establish schools, cooperate in mutual efforts, and develop a culture and attitude that gave free rein to their native talents. By protecting their turf against aggressors, and establishing legal systems to protect their lives and property, they created just and democratic society. Working from such strength they were able to travel, trade, learn from other cultures, and establish colonies to support their enterprises. It came down to simply getting rid of authority at the top and empowering the many at the bottom.

This blueprint of how societies function best was demonstrated in the Greek and Phoenician seed-beds of freedom. Their example was followed wherever and whenever a people could establish free and open societies. Such opportunities occasionally arose along the edges of Western Europe as outlined in Chapter 5. Such enclaves were helped by the fracturing of power among the states and church, a growing tradition of individual reasoning, and new religious alternatives. In those few isolated regions relatively free of oppression, the common men and women gained personal independence and power and a measure of freedom to pursue their goals as they saw fit. They got the chance to try. If half the battle in life is just showing up, the other half is swinging the bat once you reach the plate. But in most non-Western cultures, the common people were never allowed to even get on deck, let alone take a swing.

The ennobling Western action to end slavery shows the influence that the common men of the West had gained. It also reflects an advantage of Western Europe in its quest for freedom and prosperity. The "little people" had a voice, and their religious and ethical principles moved them to create change and thereby to improve society. In contrast, "Among the Islamic nations of North Africa, and the Middle East, the abolition of slavery came especially late, with Saudi Arabia, Mauritania, and the Sudan continuing to hold slaves on past the middle of the twentieth century. Mauritania officially abolished slavery on July 5, 1980—though its own officials admitted the practice continued after the ban."[237] Abolition was part of a democratic process unique in the

*Rosa Parks: Only in America—
a black woman got it done!*

West to end the practice of human bondage that had blighted almost all societies since the beginning of time.

It is only an extraordinary ignorance of history that allows some critics of Western civilization to fault the West in particular for having once allowed slavery when it was the free Western nations that ended first the traffic in slaves and finally the practice itself. The abolitionist movement was part and parcel of the democratization process extending suffrage to a broader group of citizens that emerged in Western societies as a stepping stone to modern freedom. There were very few such stepping stones in Oriental and Middle Eastern societies. The abolitionist movement was even more fundamentally a reflection of respect for the individual that implied the equal rights of every man and woman. When women did ultimately receive the right to vote, representational government in the West finally embraced all citizens. It is self-evident that America has benefited greatly from the additional talents and energy that minorities and women have brought to the nation.

Other cultures and religions that still keep women and entire castes of people in subordinate roles demonstrate that multiculturists are wrong. Societies guilty of such exclusionary practices cannot be regarded as equals until they abandon such gross discrimination. It is a sign of the quagmire in academic thinking that many professors still blithely instruct their charges that it is the West in particular that is racist and sexist, while passing over in silence the much worse, glaring, and firmly institutionalized racism and sexism in other nations. In many Middle Eastern nations, women are suppressed, scholars and dissidents silenced, minorities ostracized. Officials stage public executions in stadiums, and the specter of a vengeful God is enlisted to preach violence and urge suicide bombing of innocents. No amount of political correctness can cloak such pervasive contempt for the sacredness of each individual life in these nations. As Ms. Manji says, "Through our screaming self-pity and our conspicuous silences, we Muslims are conspiring against ourselves. We're in a crisis and we're dragging the rest of the world with us. If ever there was a moment for an Islamic reformation, it's now. For the love of God, what are we doing about it?"[238]

The sharply different religious and ethical beliefs of the West may well have contributed to its extraordinary success. As a minimum, the positive influence in some societies of general respect for all people, men and women, must be considered in any analysis of economic history. To the extent that the potentates of the East prevented appropriate conceptions of individual rights, respect for life, and rational debate from emerging and gaining sway, they may justly be blamed for the failure of their societies to keep pace, and for the obvious misery and unhappiness of their peoples.

Chapter 7
Defining Historical Progress

The real story of America is the unprecedented wealth of the ordinary citizen.
—Ben Stein and Phil De Muth

WHAT CONSTITUTES PROGRESS? Of all the patterns in history, the most ever-present and widespread characteristic of human society is one of oppression. Ever since men first organized socially, the strong have dominated the weak. Throughout the past 3,000 years, societies have persisted in every part of the world that allowed privilege and luxury only to the few, while imposing virtual slavery and poverty on the many. Historians have mistakenly lavished praise on the high cultural achievements of Imperial China, the French royalty at Versailles, Tsarist Russia, the Egyptian Dynasties, and the rich lifestyle of Islamic Sultans. These autocratic regimes accumulated great wealth by subjecting their people to lives of virtual slavery—the Egyptian pyramids and the Great Wall of China were massive governmental projects, erected on the bodies of countless common men and women who perished on the job.

The opulence to be found in authoritarian civilizations was enjoyed by only a small circle of a favored elite within their imperial courts. The achievements of such cultures never went much beyond spectacular culinary feats, formal accouterments and elaborate dress, the splendor of their palaces and gardens, the extravagance of their leaders' burial vaults, and the adoring poetry and drawings of favored artists. Their harems and concubines were without equal; bureaucrats scoured the countryside and invaded neighboring regions to procure the prettiest girls. Although such "high" cultures of the Orient and the Middle East have impressed many an intellectual scholar, they are more apt to disgust a sensible and modest common man. The upwardly mobile society of Genghis Khan—open to all religious beliefs and offering opportunity to all individuals of merit, sharing the duties of administration with women, and organizing local councils to govern remote areas—was in many ways more distinguished by real progress than any of the exclusive and haughty imperial courts.

The emperors of Imperial China and the sultanates of the Islamic world were steeped in the shallow opulence worshiped by modern intellectuals—fancy clothes, formal dinners on fine china, fawning literature, a leisurely and indulgent lifestyle reserved for a select few at the top. That is why we sometimes hear that such

Selim II, "the Sot,"
son of Suleiman the Magnificent,
lost the battle of Lepanto, 1571

civilizations represent pinnacles of human development. Granted, there have been periods of social stability within such societies, and some of them provided peace and at least minimum rations for the populace. But all such eras operated only through a suffocating control that restricted personal achievement, prevented technical progress, and denied freedom of action and any expression of individuality.

In New England, only the first generation or two of settlers had to spend their lives hacking at the soil with primitive hand tools, walking behind their oxen to plow the virgin land, housed in primitive dwellings. The peasants of China and India have had to live like this for millennia. It is more bad reporting by the intellectuals to excessively praise what can only be described as "achievements for the few" within these tyrannical empires.

Meaningful historical progress entails improvement in the lives of a broad spectrum of humanity, with liberty widely enjoyed and each person free to strive for personal happiness and achievement. That type of measure lies at the heart of Abraham Lincoln's call for "a nation of the people, for the people and by the people." Such a standard was enshrined in the American Declaration of Independence, which proclaimed the right of everyone to "Life, Liberty, and the Pursuit of Happiness." It was the provision of such rights to ordinary people that represents historical progress. Let's look at the record—and how this progress was made.

The Rights of Man—An Ancient Principle

Professor Alan Dershowitz has recently applied his considerable legal acumen to the question: What is the source of the "human rights" that form the bedrock law of most free nations? He attacks the claim that rights come from God—those unalienable God-given rights that America's founding fathers cited. He also denies that rights are derived from nature and would thus possess the immutable characteristic of scientific laws of physics and astronomy. His own view supports the thesis of this book: "For those, like me, who believe that human beings design—invent—rights to prevent the recurrence of wrongs, there is a special obligation to advocate and encourage others to accept the centrality of rights in a democratic society."[239] That sounds as if it was just ordinary lawyers and merchants tinkering with the legal system who "invented" our common law and the enumerated rights of citizens, a process that went on for centuries in England from the time of the Magna Carta to the present.

Dershowitz adds that our understanding of human rights emerges "not from some theory of perfect justice but from its opposite: from the bottom up, from trial and error, and from our collective experience of injustice."[240] While Dershowitz denies that rights come from God or nature, he does concede that he thereby suffers "a heavier burden of persuasion." Jefferson wrote his material a couple hundred years ago (and pre-ACLU) and consciously or unconsciously reduced his "burden of persuasion" by ringing references to the self-evident nature and justice of each man's God given-rights to freedom.

Whatever the justification of rights, when the Founding Fathers hammered out the Constitution and Bill of Rights, they did exactly what Dershowitz posits—they worked out rights based on their collective experience and common sense. However, this was all done with the benefit of knowledge developed during three thousand years of prior innovation by fellow rebels and entrepreneurs. The gradual establishment and expansion of English legal practices over six hundred years was recognized as real world examples of mechanisms that worked favorably for the people. This historical laboratory of evidence—actual case studies, not philosophical treatises—is what inspired the handiwork of the Founding Fathers.

And even that centuries-old tradition had antecedents. In the dim first steps along the path to freedom, the Judeo-Christian traditions asserted the special dignity and inviolability of each man and woman. The Old Testament is full of practical commandments concerning the ethical conduct of life.[241] These religious precepts outlined basic and useful rules about justice and the good and virtuous life long before Plato's time. They established the rights of individuals to fair treatment, honest impartial judges, and the protection of their property; and undoubtedly played a part in giving future generations in the Western world the conviction that human rights are unalienable and worth fighting for.

Unfortunately, these ancient principles had to be repeatedly fought for and that took true grit. Remember that the original peasants who sought leniency or justice, whether in China or England, were often armed with hoes and shovels and were faced down by a King in his robes of gold and his cavalry bristling with steel. The peasants' individualistic traditions and the belief that God was on their side may both have been essential to buttress their simple hatred of the oppressors and carry the day. Even recently, in the battle over Apartheid in South Africa, Bishop Tutu relied on his bible and cassock for strength and protection whenever he marched for reform. The motivation of most people is stronger when backed by a faith. The common man has often needed all the help he could get to fortify his extraordinary acts of sacrifice and courage; the many steps from oppression to freedom were not carved out from the safety of a warm and cozy office in Harvard Yard. In fact, pure logic and reasoning would never have sufficed as the sole armaments in the common man's fight for his rights over the ages.

Measuring Progressive Solutions

Students of history have on occasion speculated on the overall flow of history, to seek explanations and ultimately tie everything up into a neat solution. In the hard sciences, mathematical inquiry and careful experimentation has led to remarkable discoveries. Primitive man thought illness was connected to evil spirits or the whims of the gods; medicine men practiced chants, incense burning, and even human sacrifice to gain good luck, improve the weather, or cure disease. But because many doctors investigated how the body actually works, doctors today can perform triple bypass surgery and kidney transplants, and insert artificial knees. The scientific method, using precise measurements and experiments, fueled these advances. Such logical and clear reasoning has been the hallmark of progress in the hard sciences.

Not so in the soft sciences. Because political-economic and religious matters do not lend themselves to exact quantitative measurement and testing, it is hard to prove beyond question what works and what doesn't. Although common sense can generally separate the best ideas from the worst, the soft-science fields have proven particularly divisive, and its thinkers have generally preferred the realm of conceptual theory at the expense of practical applications. The problem is exacerbated by two stubborn facts: First, our social, political, and religious affairs can never be improved beyond the very real limits dictated by the varied and imperfect behavior of mankind. Second, it has proven especially difficult for soft science theorists to objectively distinguish the ideal they seek from what is actually attainable. Consequently, most writers have too often debated lofty concepts beyond the understanding of ordinary men, and proposed systems and institutions that ordinary men could never live with. When Solon established a form of democracy in Athens, long before the time of Plato, he never claimed to have given them an ideal system, but rather the best they might find workable. Most scholars ever since have failed to comprehend his point—they just keep criticizing systems that work because they are not perfect, and then go on to prescribe perfect systems that do not work!

In nature, we know that the sun and tides will rise and fall when they are destined to by the laws of nature; we can compute such events to the nearest minute, and are powerless in any way to change them. They are immutable. But in society, there is no clear law governing who should vote, how much a society owes the indigent, nor to what degree we can take away a property owner's rights for the good of society. This lack of certainty or proof on such questions is compounded by the fact that most leaders, the aggressive individuals who usually get to the top, are primarily interested in staying at the top, so do everything they can to confuse and bewilder those under them. When such leaders have access to the media, control the major aristocratic subgroups under them by dispensing favors to them, and have armies, police forces, and SWAT teams to enforce their goals, it has been very hard for the masses to get a straight answer on what is best for them or their country. The autocrats and demagogues, constantly present and under every form of government, are always finding new and better ways to fool those at the bottom.

The programs and reforms that such leaders promise to enact, often cobbled together from the recommendations of "experts" and the latest notions of intellectuals, are designed primarily to win votes. Thus politicians try to convince the people that their intentions are noble and their policies will cure all problems. Like the patent medicine huckster who claims his potion will cure all ailments, they rely on the gullibility of the people. Naturally, such campaign promises are rarely fulfilled, or if they are, the results usually disappoint.

But the situation is not intractable, because we can still look back and determine which forms of governance have actually worked best.

Then the issues are confined to reality—the actual past practices—and the historical record will reveal how they worked. Practiced dispassionately, this approach is more like the scientific method employed by physical scientists. And yet, even then, there is little consensus, measurements are inexact, and biases swamp the debate. Many investigators of history cannot see beyond the optimum model that, in their view, should eventually prevail. Indeed, the unrealistic dreams of the intelligentsia render every reality unacceptable, so that they are constitutionally unable to honestly assess the evidence. Since everything they see, past or present, fails to mirror their dreams—i.e., of a utopia, with experts like them calling the shots—they feel impelled to condemn it outright, no matter how beneficent it may have been compared to the available alternatives. Thus, they denounce the ancient Greeks and America's Founding Fathers for having slaves, or for not giving women the vote. Or they distort or downplay the beneficial role of free enterprise because to acknowledge it means to relinquish their utopian and socialistic fantasies. The student of history is confronted with a variety of interpretations of history, and must not simply memorize a particular faddish version as one might master the multiplication tables. One must instead weigh and evaluate the clashing interpretations and come to one's own conclusions.

The socialist and communist systems imposed over the past 100 years in dozens of countries have failed time after time. But the legal and market mechanisms that actually work have been installed in a growing number of nations, with measurable benefits. Within the pages of this book we cite the works of dozens of economists and historians who confirm the all-important role of the individual in creating economic progress, and how security and freedom combine to give every individual a chance at prosperity. In a few isolated regions, the happy confluence of appropriate conditions allowed ordinary people to initiate dynamic prosperous free economies. These freer societies were, admittedly, located in areas conducive to trade and maritime activity; but this happy circumstance cannot have been a sufficient condition, for there were hundreds of such locations. In the handful of societies that achieved success, they only achieved it by allowing individuals to function freely and in safety; these were the so-called "laboratory societies," as Jean-Francois Revel calls them; the societies "where civilization's great inventions are tested. Not all are necessarily blessings, but they irresistibly prevail. . . . Athens, Rome, Renaissance Italy, eighteenth century England and France—all were societies of this type, not as a result of some abstract 'process,' but because of human deeds. In the twentieth century it was the turn of the United States."[242]

Revel, though an intellectual (and a French intellectual, to boot), clearly ranks human deeds over abstract theory, thereby casting doubt on any blanket condemnation of intellectuals. Broad generalizations do tend to suffer this comeuppance (though, on the other hand, deviations from a norm hardly gainsay the existence of the norm). We examined in earlier chapters the "experimental societies" that Revel refers to. One might also call them seed beds, for in these labs, the havens of many years of painstaking progress, the seeds of economic and political freedom grew, were transplanted, and, in the eighteenth century, flourished as never before in the United States. These under-lying systems of economic freedom have since spread to a number of other countries, to achieve similar results regardless of climate or geography and in spite of differences in constitutional structure. The correlations of the annual Economic Freedom of the World Indices support the direct relation between the institutions supportive of economic freedom and a resultant prosperity.

Denying the Evidence

With the collapse of communist Russia, some observers believed that any uncertainty about choice in governments was settled. Joseph J. Ellis writes, "Though it seems somewhat extreme to declare, as one contemporary political philosopher has phrased it, that 'the end of history' is now at hand, it is true that all alternative forms of political organization appear to be fighting a futile rearguard action against the liberal institutions and ideas first established in the United States in the late eighteenth century. At least it is safe to say that some form of representative government based on the principle of popular sovereignty and some form of market economy fueled by the energies of individual citizens have become the commonly accepted ingredients for national success throughout the world."[243] That says it all in a sentence—popular sovereignty, a market economy, plus an acknowledgement that it is the energy and effort of individuals that create progress.

If reasonable consideration of the mounting evidence is decisive, Francis Fukuyama and Professor Ellis are correct to imply that the debate over fundamentally different ways of organizing society is over, and that representative government and capitalism have won. Fukuyama calls it "the end of history," but it is not over quite yet. Indeed, a totally different and wholly incorrect conclusion is being taught in schools and universities. The professors and award-winning book authors are falling all over themselves to echo the current politically correct line that the good fortune of the West has all been just a matter of luck, or of the weather. Any suggestion that some groups actually did better than others is virtually verboten in today's bastions of learning.

This distortion of reality has a sinister purpose. Its promulgators are not being kind to spare the feelings of backward societies. Rather, the most radical of the intelligentsia are so religiously enthralled by their utopian imaginings that they are bent on destroying the best society that exists today—it's blocking their brave new world. It's true: a cadre of radicals is dedicated to the goal of destroying America. They demonstrate the convoluted thinking process that characterizes the dishonesty of today's academics, and illustrate why the advent of intellectuals so often marks the turning point in a society—the prelude to decline and collapse.

What Works? What Creates Progress?

The prescriptions of such men as Hernando de Soto and Mancur Olson, while not as precise or foolproof as penicillin in stamping out disease, do offer a proven answer to the plight of the Third World. Not every technical detail of what constitutes good government can be mathematically proved, but there has been enough experimental data gathered to draw sound general conclusions about what makes for a robust economy and what does not. But first one must ignore utopian notions of what "should" be, and accept what realistically can be. And the track record of the most successful societies teaches us what can be. Rather than try to tear down the few rare examples of systems that best enabled freedom and prosperity, it makes sense to apply those systems to all the other locales that are still far behind. Vast numbers of peoples can be helped by raising them to the levels of the most successful societies. And despite the endless arguments among academics, we know which systems have worked best.

William McNeill asserts that "cultural pluralism and differentiation is a dominating feature of human history; yet beneath and behind that pluralism there is also an important commonality. That commonality found expression in the rise of a world system that transcended political and cultural boundaries because human beings desired to have the results of the operation of that system."[244] That system was "the enrichment that market exchanges helped to provoke and sustain by rewarding efficient producers." People wanted "access to rare and valuable goods that could not be found close at hand." This is why trading is found in every society, and it has enabled innovations to be borrowed by all societies. McNeill indicates that this borrowing is "one of the clearest patterns in world history. . . . Any geographical displacement of world leadership must be prefaced by successful borrowing from previously established centers of the highest prevailing skills."[245] As we have seen, among the earliest beneficiaries of trade and cultural exchange were the Phoenician and Greek cities that gradually developed an original basis for free prosperous societies. Today's global economy, though much larger, is still fashioned after those pioneering models from antiquity.

Tom Bethel has written how traditional trade and market exchanges grew exponentially with the advent of modern property law. In *The Noblest Triumph*, he praises the unique mechanics that were developed in the West to provide secure property rights—which is what enabled the free operation of trade and market exchanges. He points out that secure rights to property are also essential to the personal freedom of citizens. Property provides the store of value that ensures independence. Eighty years of Communist experience demonstrated the folly of intellectuals who believed that centrally directed economies and nationalized industries, with bureaucrats making the trades, could match the decision-making genius of millions of property owners working on their own behalf. For the common people to prosper, the "S" in the Radzewicz Rule involves both their physical security from attack as well as secure ownership of their accumulated savings. The rare enabling societies that led to modern prosperity did so only by providing both of those essential forms of security.

Over the millennia, the small steps forward that common people have taken when allowed to take them have been few and far between. The perennial obstacles to the achievement of freedom are still with us, and threaten our liberties today. All great societies have eventually crumbled into ruins, but by drawing the appropriate lessons from their fate, we can yet delay or prevent the ruin of the American one— conceivably even help reverse the decline of Europe—and continue the upward trajectory of the Western experiment.

Chapter 8
How Developing Nations Can Develop

Capitalist apartheid will inevitably continue until we all come to terms with the critical flaw in many countries' legal and political systems that prevents the majority from entering the formal property system.

—Hernando de Soto

How much money must be thrown down the drain before we realize money is being thrown down the drain? How many generations of starving Third World children must we see before we realize that so-called humanitarian and development grants only prolong the misery and poverty within recipient nations?

Abundant statistical evidence indicates that over the past five decades the average income of most impoverished nations has either declined or, at best, remained constant, despite huge grants and programs designed to help them lift their economies and alleviate poverty and starvation. Most of the torrents of aid given by the major Western nations over that period has been either stolen or squandered—or worse. In *Africa Betrayed*, George B. Ayittey documents how such aid failed to spur economic growth and has even, in the words of Dr. Rony Brauman, a head of Doctors without Borders "unwittingly fuelled—and are continuing to fuel—an operation that will be described in hindsight . . . as one of the greatest slaughters of our time."[246] By helping to fund dictators, the Overseas Development Assistance underwrote genocide.

In *The Market for Aid*, authors Klein and Harford admit that "we are still in the dark about which donors, or which projects, are achieving the best results."[247] Their book analyzes what they call "the international aid industry," an appellation reflecting the size and scope of the vested interests engaged in "helping the poor." They report that thanks to fifty years with dubious results, researchers are "paying growing attention to the quality of aid given." So, after a delay spanning three generations of victims, the "researchers" are beginning to wonder if the aid works! No wonder intellectuals never get anything done. But, it gets worse. There is an obstacle confronting these researchers: for "before measuring the average quality or effectiveness of aid, we need to know what makes aid high quality or effective. We have only a vague idea of this, and tentative early research has revealed little except the paucity of the data."[248]

What is needed, then? They prescribe further research: "The real value of this embryonic work on aid quality is to highlight the importance of the issue and the scale of our ignorance."[249] Such determined agnosticism about and even acceptance of failed results shows the mind of the intellectual at work. The evident failure of the nostrums is irrelevant—the urgency of the problems is irrelevant—in their role as experts their only "solution" is to keep gathering data as billions more dollars are wasted and millions more people starve to death.

At some point the data-gatherers should read the newspapers. Continued violence and civil disorder makes progress in some of these nations impossible, whether they receive aid or not, and no matter how wisely they use it. The first prerequisite of progress is a certain minimum level of physical security. Peacekeepers from the United Nations have consistently failed to maintain order in the dozens of country where they are deployed. Coalitions of African armies have also failed. Indeed, the unrealistic expectation that the United Nations might bring security has only deferred more feasible solutions. And giving aid to the leaders in such countries encourages only further strife as new leaders emerge to scramble for the foreign largesse.

Klein and Harford even suggest that aid harms the recipient nation. Consulting several research studies, they note that "aid flows . . . are significantly correlated with a worsening of political risks for external investors, implying a deterioration in economic institutions. . . . Cases since the 1960s illustrate the effect. The ten biggest deteriorations in democratic institutions are associated with large aid inflows in the previous year. . . ."[250] The authors explain this by reference to the paradox of "the resource curse," which dictates that "countries with abundant natural resources grow more slowly than those without."[251] But anyone familiar with how people react understands that wealth based solely on gifts will kill initiative, motivation, and effort. Charity, if it is to have a long-term beneficial effect, must be modest and directed to those who can develop micro-businesses to build the country from the bottom up.

That is why, even when they enjoy a degree of stability and order, most of the less developed countries (LDCs) have failed to achieve economic growth. The foreign funds have typically gone to those at the top, not those at the bottom. This ongoing blunder is the direct result of the centrist theories of Western economists and government planners, who believe that only government programs can create prosperity. Their notions are reinforced by ideologues who will go to any lengths to pretend capitalism does not work—and that their social-communal dreams are the wave of the future.

Such misdirected aid has usually been directed into the construction of large administrative and bureaucratic agencies, which cannot create wealth but only suffocate the activity of the individuals who do create wealth. Additional amounts were funneled into the secret bank accounts of corrupt leaders. If there was any left over, it was plowed into grand macro-economic projects that may well look impressive, but do nothing to lower or eliminate the restrictive laws of these nations, or bolster their inadequate protections of property rights. Without appropriate enabling institutions, free enterprise cannot exist, or is at least greatly hampered, and the common people cannot exercise their entrepreneurial skills. Even when the leaders and planners of these countries claim to support business, and create governmental programs designed to encourage business and investment, they are usually only adding to the regulatory skein that strangles the vital economic activity of ordinary people.

The market reforms needed to create prosperity require careful adherence to the specific free market mechanisms developed in Western democracies. Edgardo Buscaglia and William Ratliff point out that "market systems involve much more than giving the private sector the power to allocate resources. Most of the legal and judicial frameworks in developing countries . . . reflect a past reality that has not adapted to modern organizational and technological innovations. . . . Today, legal reforms are being considered or are in some degree under way around the developing world, though they still lag far behind economic reforms."[252] The magnitude of the task facing these developing nations underscores the huge achievement of those few Western democracies that originally developed the intricate systems of government, legal processes, and economic freedom that led to modern prosperity. These specific and detailed mechanical systems and institutions that helped Western societies progress were rarely the subject of the great philosophers' writings. The philosophers concerned themselves with generalities about freedom, the rights of man, equality, the justification for representative governments, the need for legislatures and judiciaries—all the relatively obvious devices that had already been instituted by ordinary people. Thus they recapitulated past principles and ignored the "how" of improved implementation. Just as a gas engine needs, not just a fuel pump and a few pistons, but also all the bells and whistles that make it run smoothly, so a nation requires the judicial and legal framework that can support vibrant economic activity.

> *The ultimate resource is people—skilled, spirited, and hopeful people who will exert their wills and imaginations for their own benefit, and so, inevitably, for the benefit of us all.*
>
> —Julian L. Simon

The Failure of Central Planning

A report on world hunger issued by the Rome-based UN Food and Agriculture Organization reveals the failure of UN efforts. The headline tells us that "hunger, malnutrition kill 6 million kids a year." We learn that the numbers of those starving to death have increased over the past decade. A member of the intelligentsia would conclude: "Let's have some Hollywood celebrities run a benefit concert to send over more food." The benefit concert would be held and all parties involved would feel really good about it. On the other hand, a person of common sense would conclude: "Whatever the UN and Hollywood celebrities have been doing these past fifty years has failed. Let's do something different."

In fact, there has been an emergency situation for at least fifty years, and the United Nations has failed to alleviate it despite the trillions of dollars expended on attempted solutions. It is important to note the time period—the tragic parents we currently see in the photos from sub-Saharan Africa, clutching their dying babies, are the survivors among the similar children depicted in the pictures we saw twenty years ago, whose parents were the children of the malnourished babies photographed forty years ago, and so forth. None of the handouts and none of the Hollywood fundraisers has helped. Neither have the World Bank and IMF programs, nor the CARE packages, or the "adopt a child" programs. Everything that has been tried has failed to address the underlying causes of poverty. They are band-aid solutions that only temporarily lessen the misery or extend the lives of the few who receive the food or medicines doled out. These band-aids will not prevent the same misfortune from visiting the children and grandchildren of today's victims. But the apparent satisfaction of providing such brief respites has armed those employed in "the international aid industry" with renewed zeal only to bestow more band-aids, rather than tackle the enduring causes of the poverty.

Klein and Harford very appropriately contrast such seemingly irremediable conditions with the results in Taiwan and the Republic of Korea after the United States stopped aid to those nations in the 1960s. After the aid ended, necessary reforms followed. "Aid-dependent governments are accountable to donors, not to their population."[253]

Unbeknownst to the United Nations, their own report makes clear why they have failed: Incredibly, it states that "hunger and malnutrition are among the main causes of poverty, illiteracy, disease and deaths." Think about that sentence. Learn to question such fine sounding and glib assertions. In fact, the opposite is the case. It is the poverty, illiteracy, and disease that cause hunger, not the other way around; otherwise CARE packages alone would have solved the problems! This completely backwards way of looking at the problem is why trillions of dollars of food sent to Africa over the past fifty years has only added to hunger and malnutrition.

This distinction between cause and effect is not just a matter of semantics or word games—it is matter of life and death. The flagrant reversal highlights the irrational vision of the intellectual elite that dominate foreign policy and aid programs. Any sound solution requires a correct understanding of economic history. Remedial action must come from the bottom—individual activity—not from the administrators at the top with their hand-outs and fatuous advice. Those who teach a theory of how some nations do better than others based on climate, luck, or geography only help perpetuate the misery by obscuring the solution.

The "huddled masses" that arrived in America, or Iceland, were often undernourished and hungry. But they did not have to await foreign aid to find their next meal. They planted crops, built homes and farms, and established businesses or found employment with those who did. They did it from scratch—out of a wilderness, starting with no infrastructure, no aid, no grants or loans. They gradually developed the land and escaped poverty, learned to read and write, or at least made sure their children learned to, so that after a generation or two they were no longer living in privation. By contrast, the United Nations and the wealthy nations have been tossing programs at African hunger for three generations, with zero net progress.

The cause of such persistent hunger is a government that does not allow its citizens to earn a living, live in safety, or go to school; that regulates economic activity so that only the elites can participate and get rich; that allows looting and genocide. A society in which free economic activity can flourish will soon see an end to hunger. People will work for food—if they can. If only they could live in freedom and security, the people of Africa would need but a generation of effort to emerge from poverty. It calls for simply more "S" and less "O" to make the Radzewicz Rule operate its economic magic.

Hernando de Soto has called for a new set of commitments to make capitalism work; lip service to free markets is not enough, he suggests. "It makes no sense continuing to call for open economies without facing the fact that the economic reforms underway open the doors only for small and globalized elites and leave out most of humanity."[254] What is required is to allow the common genius of those at the bottom to create, innovate, accumulate wealth, and invest for the future. No amount of central planning or government investment can ever match the unfettered energy and activity that can come from the efforts of the multitudes at the bottom. But they must be granted full and easy access to commercial activity and must be assured the safe and ready transferability of their assets.

These conclusions underlie de Soto's efforts to allow the "illegals" access to the restricted economic space in Peru and other LDCs. He has worked to create property rights and systems of financing so that all the individuals holding assets that are currently non-transferable can engage in the economic activity required for prosperity. So called economic reforms are not effective until they get down to the nitty-gritty details of recorded deeds, transferable mortgages, financial instruments, and effective legal-judicial practices. These solutions are further documented by dozens of authors cited in this book in addition to de Soto and Mancur Olsen.

> *If the United States were to hike its foreign-aid budget to the level recommended by the United Nations—0.7 percent of national income—it would take the richest country on earth more than 150 years to transfer to the world's poor resources equal to those they already possess.*
>
> —Hernando de Soto

And yet, predictably, there is still a constant demand for increased financial aid to solve the problems of LDCs. These demands come not so much from the denizens of those less-developed countries as from the intellectual elites of the West, and the UN bureaucrats who want to oversee the planning and disbursements. These kinds of people would never admit the failure of central planning despite the bloody and abysmal seventy-year track record of the communist and socialist governments they championed. When these elites have a grand conceptual plan they don't want to be confused by facts. Should the West pursue those same high-spending programs for another fifty years, more likely than not, these LDCs will still be just as poor as they are now, and another two or three generations of people will remain sunk in the direst poverty.

Pouring good money after bad only makes it less likely that the populations of these strife-ridden countries will institute the reforms they so desperately need. If aid is to be continued, it should be used solely to reward those nations that have established basic security for their people and have demonstrated the ability to empower members of their lowest economic groups to operate freely—to own their homes and businesses, to mortgage and sell them with simple but legal deeds of title, and to open and operate business ventures with a minimum of red tape and no burdensome licensing requirements.

The Folly of Partial Solutions

Some intellectuals admit the need to modify these failed aid programs. Unfortunately, the minor modifications they propose—strengthening of international organizations or extending the jurisdiction of international courts—will not address the fundamental problems. Naturally, these ideas typically come from the very "thinkers" who expect to administer them from on high. In essence, it's just more-of-the-same, and more-of-the-same is still going to fail, despite any slight differences in the packaging.

Most of those addressing the problem propose solutions that will only turn back the clock on human freedom. Anne Marie Slaughter, for example, rightly points out some of the problems confronting us, but her solution argues for an increasingly complex, global web of "government networks." She believes that such entities as the World Bank and the G-8 "frequently make good things happen." She suggests that these organizations can help nations to "participate in global regulatory processes," and "promote convergence, compliance with international agreements, and improved cooperation among nations on a wide range of regulatory and judicial issues."[255] Now, there's another phrase to ponder: How will any of those prescriptive regulations help the people at the bottom?

Slaughter's praise for international regulatory agencies is not universal. In the anthology, *The International Monetary Fund: Financial Medic to the World?*, over a dozen writers deplore the actions of the IMF, and many of them urge its abolition. Milton Friedman echoes the opinion of George Shultz, William Simon, and Walter Wriston that it "is ineffective, unnecessary, and obsolete. We do not need another IMF" and "should abolish the one we have." According to Friedman, centralized planning "works no better on the global than on the national level."[256]

The words "regulatory" and "compliance" appear way too often in Ms. Slaughter's prescription to be accidental. Tellingly, she never mentions the need to empower the individual and, in fact, to liberate him from the regulatory excess that has been keeping so many of the world's poor permanently locked in poverty. Moreover, she ignores the half century of failure by the World Bank and IMF to help underdeveloped nations actually advance. Thus her proposals suffer from the Platonic sin of expecting solutions from the top to be passed down to those

> ### Micro-Vs Macro Economics, or Gandhi vs Slaughter
>
> *I will give you a talisman. Whenever you are in doubt, apply the following test. Recall the face of the poorest and the weakest man or woman whom you may have seen, and ask yourself, if the step you contemplate is going to be of any use to him or her. Will he or she gain anything by it? Will it restore him or her to a control over his or her own life and destiny? In other words, will it lead to swaraj (freedom) for the hungry and spiritually starved millions? Then you will find your doubts and your self melt away.*
>
> —Mahatma Gandhi
> (Last Phase, Vol. II, 1958, 65)

at the bottom. It would be wiser to insist first on radical revision or even abolition of the international agencies that are now either ineffective or outright harmful because of their bloated bureaucracies, toleration of corruption, and eagerness to impose harmful policies on the nations they pretend to help. Such international institutions would require many reforms, a new transparency, well-defined and measurable goals, and a clear audit trail before they could begin to work positively without encouraging the oppression that undermines those goals. The people of the Third World are restricted and regulated enough by their own nations without having to suffer yet another layer in the form of a global spider web of international agencies.

Help at the Bottom

A much more successful approach to assisting the people of Less Developed Nations has been pursued by the Women's World Banking (WWB) organization, conceived during the first UN World Conference on Women held in Mexico City in 1975. Ten visionary women from five continents shared one belief: that simply increasing economic access for poor women could change the way the world works. The key was to empower poor women around the world by opening access to finance, improving micro-finance institutions, and providing support to make change possible. These policies were pure de Soto—the idea of removing obstacles so individuals can help themselves. No million-dollar loans or grants, no central plans, no humongous programs—just helping an aspiring woman open a hairdressing salon, sandwich shop, or cleaning establishment. Once set up in business, the path cleared, these small businesswomen did the rest.

WWB recently had twenty-four affiliates in nineteen countries, each one independent, governed and managed by local leaders. As of the end of 2002, affiliates were reaching over 815,000 clients, 77 percent of whom then lived below the poverty line. Loan sizes averaged $356, with an aggregate outstanding portfolio in excess of $120 million. In addition, WWB supported leading micro finance institutions through its WWB Associates program. At the end of 2002, these Associates reached over 2.8 million micro-borrowers, with an aggregate outstanding portfolio of $196 million, and an average loan of $275. As a result of the WWB effort, millions of women have been enabled to build a business and accumulate assets, allowing them to improve their living conditions, keep their families well fed, educate their children, and develop respect at home and in the community.

In Ms. Slaughter's book, though, as in many similar volumes, we find no reference to the WWB or any such entrepreneurial activity. Nor any reference to Hernando de Soto's work in Peru opening doors for thousands of small business people. Too many of the elite will never recognize how loans averaging as little as $200 to $400 can make a difference. They don't understand how businesses operate, have never established or operated a business of their own, and are wedded to grand theories and government plans administered from large office suites far removed from the real world. The only place they themselves are able or willing to find employment is within bureaucratic empires funded by governments, universities, and foundations—the only institutions, by no coincidence, which do not keep track of whether given actions and programs actually work, and are not obliged by the realities of competition and the marketplace to scuttle the ones that fail.

Esther Ocloo, the first Chairperson of WWB, wanted to know why women were so often spoken of "as victims, or as passive beneficiaries of social services? Poor women are the world's farmers, traders, informal industrialists. Women need access to financial services—not charity, not subsidies."[257] Esther knew what she was talking about, having begun her own business career selling a few jars of marmalade before moving on to become one of Ghana's leading agribusiness industrialists. Her successors at WWB have written that government programs based on a social welfare, subsidy approach nearly always end up as vehicles for political patronage, with extremely low repayments, market distortions, and an eventual reduction of services. What poor people need are opportunities to participate as homeowners, innovators, and entrepreneurs in their economies. Micro-business financing helps them to increase their assets and living standards, and to shape their societies for the better.

Operating on a parallel course, the Grameen Bank provides loans and guidance to entrepreneurs in Third World nations. Founded by Professor Muhammad Yunus, this organization reflects its founders' discovery that "the world's worst social and economic problems are unwittingly created in the classroom, because they shape the young people's minds too rigidly, or without enough warning that our knowledge in social sciences is only tentative. . . ."[258] His organizations have sought to provide individuals throughout the world the opportunity that microcredit provides to realize their potential: "My work in Grameen has given me a faith; an unshakable faith in the creativity of human beings. That leads me to believe that human beings are not born to suffer the misery of hunger and poverty. They have much more important things to do than struggle for physical survival. They suffer because we have trained our mind to accept the fact that nobody can do anything about poverty except offer charity."[259] The professor's mission has proven remarkable. Starting in 1976, they soon reached milestones: a hundred thousand borrowers, $1 billion lent, two million borrowers. "It was thought that the poor would not be able to repay: in fact, repayment rates reached 97 percent. . . . By the end of 1998, the number of branches in operation was 1,128, with 2.34 million members (2.24 million of them women) in 38,957 villages. . . . It is estimated that the average household income of Grameen Bank members is about 50 percent higher than the target group in the control village, and 25 percent higher than the target group non-members in Grameen Bank villages. The landless have benefited most, followed by marginal landowners. This has resulted in a sharp reduction in the number of Grameen Bank members living below the poverty line, 20 percent compared to 56 percent for comparable non-Grameen Bank members."[260]

The grassroots operations of both the WWB and Grameen initiatives provide direct support to individuals who seek to better their lot in life. Both organizations demand personal responsibility from their members, strict repayment, and an attitude of trust and cooperation; and they encourage socially responsible business practices. As unabashedly free-enterprise capitalists, their members respect the creativity and good intentions of every human being. As Professor Yunus told the BYU graduating class, "The market place is open for everyone, even for those who are not interested in personal gain, such as people who get inspired by the prospect of social changes for betterment. . . . Economics must incorporate within itself that the market place is not an exclusive playground for the blood-thirsty profit seekers, it is a challenging field for all good people who want to set the world in the right course." This is a faith for all those idealistic youth who seek to improve the world by actually helping others. It is not as glamorous as dictating policy from international board meetings luxuriating in plush conference rooms in the capitals of the world. But it works.

In short, the best solution is to recreate in every nation the kind of safe and open environments—what Mancur Olsen calls "market enabling" systems—that have made possible all of mankind's advances in economic freedom and prosperity over the past 3,000 years.

The Appeal of Free Enterprise

The Grameen programs and Women's World Banking are not operating alone. Despite the wrongheaded preachments of the intellectuals and social engineers, we are seeing a growing recognition that economic freedom fosters prosperity. An index of economic freedom similar to that of the Heritage Foundation is published by the Fraser Institute, and the findings show remarkably similar results. Fraser's *2004 Annual Report of Economic Freedom of the World* measures the extent to which 123 countries allow a free market. The publishers, assisted by eighty institutes from many nations, are in general agreement "that free choice of informed individuals is the foundation for an equitable, prosperous and free society." The editors assess each nation with respect to a number of factors that help or hinder the economic activity of individuals. Their studies demonstrate that "when low income countries adopt and maintain policies and institutions consistent with economic freedom, they are able to attract more investment and achieve substantially higher growth rates than other economies."[261]

The advances in economic and legal systems that were forged by enterprising individuals in rare historical periods developed over thousands of years are now summarized by the practical economists compiling both the Fraser and Heritage Foundation Indices. When such conditions are re-created it is then the empowered individuals who will create the progress desired. In the 2005 Heritage Foundation *Index of Economic Freedom*, the eight primary institutional factors used to measure economic freedom (or the lack thereof) were listed as follows:

1. Corruption in the judiciary, customs service, and government bureaucracy
2. Non-tariff barriers to trade, such as import bans, quotas, strict labeling and licensing requirements
3. The burden of taxation and trends in government spending as a percent of output
4. Efficiency within the judiciary and the ability to enforce laws.
5. Regulatory burdens on business such as health, safety, and environmental regulations and reporting requirements
6. Restrictions on banks and financial services
7. Labor regulations such as established work weeks and mandatory separation pay
8. Informal markets such as smuggling, piracy of intellectual property, and underground provision of labor and other services[262]

Each of these factors is divided into sub-categories whereby the investigators can collect data to measure the over-all burden of government on the economic activity of its people. In the aggregate they are very simple: every factor concerns either whether the government provides the minimal services needed for its people to conduct business securely; or, whether the government provides so much regulation that its functions are oppressive. Just as the Radzewicz Formula dictates, a free economy needs just enough Security—but not too much, and minimal oppression in the form of mercantile interference with businesses.

The importance of freeing up the economic activity of common people from legal and bureaucratic restriction has rarely been better documented than in the work of Hernando de Soto. He sees the world's poorest people not as a proletariat itching to topple the market, but as budding entrepreneurs eager to join it. He has demonstrated that the way to beat terrorism and totalitarian regimes was to remove their recruits—the desperate, impoverished, and oppressed people who see no other escape. And the way to do that is to empower them with economic freedom, the right to buy and sell their homes and businesses, to operate their businesses free of arbitrary restriction, and so forth.

De Soto correctly faults both the so-called democratic Left and the Right wing parties. He points out that they both "are primarily mercantilist and thus have more in common than they imagine. . . . Both intervened directly in the economy and promoted the expansion of state activities. Both strengthened the role of the government's bureaucracy until they made it the main obstacle, rather then the main incentive, to progress. . . . There are of course differences between the right-wing mercantilism and left-wing mercantilism: the former will govern to serve foreign investors or national business interests, while the latter will do so to redistribute well-being to the neediest groups. Both, however, will do so with bad laws which explicitly benefit some and harm others. Although their aims may seem to differ, the result is that in Peru one wins or loses by political decisions. Of course, there is a big difference between a fox and a wolf but, for the rabbit, it is the similarity that counts."[263] Both the political Left and the political Right have forgotten the power of the basic financial and legal tools that were developed in the West and that made those nations employing them supreme in the world.

When entrepreneurs can't function legally, they go underground. In 1990, de Soto noted that "the underground market now accounts for 50 percent of GDP in Russia and Ukraine and a whopping 62 percent in Georgia. The International Labour Organization reports that since 1990, 85 percent of all new jobs in Latin America and the

Caribbean have been created in the extralegal sector."[264] Unfortunately, this underground activity is held in check by its very illegality—so that operators are denied credit, have no property deeds on file, and can transfer virtually none of their assets. "And yet most of the poor already possess the assets they need to make a success of capitalism. Even in the poorest countries, the poor save. The value of savings among the poor is, in fact, immense—forty times all the foreign aid received throughout the world since 1945. In Egypt, for instance, the wealth that the poor have accumulated is worth fifty-five times as much as the sum of all direct foreign investment ever recorded there, including the Suez Canal and the Aswan Dam. . . . If the United States were to hike its foreign-aid budget to the level recommended by the United Nations—0.7 percent of national income—it would take the richest country on earth more than 150 years to transfer to the world's poor resources equal to those they already possess. But these resources are held in defective form. . . . They have houses but not titles; crops but not deeds; businesses but not statutes of incorporation. It is the unavailability of these essential representations that explains why people who have adopted every other Western invention, from the paper clip to the nuclear reactor, have not been able to produce sufficient capital to make their domestic capitalism work."[265] Why should the United States spend the next 150 years giving them what they already have? Instead, the governments of those lands should follow de Soto's blueprint and liberate those assets now—assets the poor already possess, but which are sunk in regulatory quagmires.

Hernando de Soto is not devoted to capitalism per se in the way that a modern liberal is devoted to socialism. He recognizes the detailed mechanics of each, the failure of socialism, and the need to perfect the operation of capitalism. But he appreciates what capitalism can do when allowed to function properly. In fact he writes that, "Much more important to me are freedom, compassion for the poor, respect for the social contract, and equal opportunity. . . . For the moment, to achieve these goals, capitalism is the only game in town. It is the only system we know that provides us with the tools to create massive surplus value."[266] The phrase "free enterprise" is apt—it describes the system that demands freedom and encourages enterprise.

Some skeptics contend that free enterprise is not for everyone, that Westerners are superior to the residents of poverty-stricken countries—have a better brain, or work ethic, or culture, and that such are the reasons the West is so much richer. Those who live in privileged areas may enjoy feeling superior. If so, their arrogance lies in forgetting that they inherited all the advanced infrastructure of the West, a cultural and institutional infrastructure developed painfully over many centuries, and which many in the current generation—with the exception of hard scientists, soldiers, and workers—have done little to advance.

There is abundant evidence that all people would like to enjoy the economic freedom pioneered in the West. A flood of immigrants continues to seek access to Western democracies. A number of nations have been adopting the trappings of capitalism. The safety of good law, property and personal rights, and freedom from regulation "empowers individuals in any culture," argues de Soto. And "Vietnamese, Cuban, and Indian immigrants have clearly had few problems adapting to U.S. property law."[267] Nations as diverse as Japan, Hong Kong, Chile, Singapore, Bahrain, and members of the former communist bloc have instituted many of the protections that liberate the energy of their people, and as a result have seen an immediate and favorable impact on their economies.

The United Arab Emirates provides an excellent case study on how to achieve rapid economic growth by adopting free market principles. "Dubai erupted from an idea or 'vision,' as it is referred to by government officials there, of Sheik Mohammed bin Rashid Maktoum, the ruler of Dubai and now also Prime Minister of the United Arab Emirates."[268] His vision was to remove all restraints on business activity. Although not a democracy, the enlightened leaders transformed the country—from what "was pretty much a barren desert twenty years ago, Dubai has become the commercial capital of the Middle East despite having virtually no oil money of its own."[269] The vision put in place meant that regulation is minimal, businesses can be easily and quickly started, red tape is avoided, liquor is served, "and the feel of the place is somewhere between Palm Beach and New York."[270] From 1995 to 2004, GDP rose at a compound rate of 21 percent, building and manufacturing is booming, and it already has one-quarter as many hotel rooms as New York City. These advances were accomplished in no small measure because part of the leaders' "vision" was "to make business easy to conduct and thereby gain an advantage over a country like India, which has a clear population advantage but a poorly developed infrastructure and an overdeveloped regulatory framework."[271] What Maktoum gave his people was more Security and less Oppression. They apparently had the Attitude to take that empowering environment and create a new financial and vacation Mecca for all the world to see. There was no need for natural resources, foreign aid, IMF policies, instruction from the World Bank, or other such top-down coercion.

One of the problems with top-down aid programs directed by bureaucracies is that it ignores the intense feelings of inequality and resentment common in many Third World countries. Samuel Z. Stone has collected a number of popular tales common within the native populations of Central America that illustrate the complexity of these attitudes. A common theme in these stories "has to do with how Indian resentment either remains tacit or is expressed as resistance to whites and how that reaction has affected the quest for equality."[272] Stone's tales reveal

Mahatma Gandhi combined Hindu non-violence and a London law degree to "invent" peaceful protests and spoke-up against India's caste system.

the century old discrimination and resentments among the races and how this prompts many individuals to resist interference and "push back" in every possible way to preserve their dignity. Obviously, that attitude, which varies with each nation, must be cautiously accommodated in order for a helping hand to be accepted. Indeed, it should be anticipated that "help" administered by expert outsiders will be resisted, which is why the micro-finance techniques such as used by Grameen and the WWB can be so effective.

Based on a recent trip to Tanzania, Merrie Cave reports a similar situation in Africa where their hosts "constantly repeat their favorite mantra: only Africans themselves can make a real difference in their nations."[273] They also report that until rural poverty is reduced there can be no progress. But since the people have limited land rights and no access to finance they are powerless; and their activities are restricted to an informal underground economy. This situation appears to be an almost universal impediment to progress, documented by many astute observers, and indicates that simply encouraging micro-economic opportunity should be the most important element of assistance programs. And yet, coming out of such eminent institutions as the Woodrow Wilson School at Princeton, we hear that we need an improved world order, where, "States still acting as unitary actors will realize that some problems cannot be effectively addressed without delegating actual sovereign power to a limited number of supranational government officials, such as judges, and arbitrators in the WTO, NAFTA, and the ICC."[274] This new master plan is called "macroeconomic cooperation" and typifies the type of solution that intellectuals dream up while holding forth in their ivy covered towers. And the "cooperation" suggested in the "new master plan" doesn't sound too voluntary for the proposed international agreements "will be directly enforced through vertical government networks."[275] That type of thinking is so far removed from the simple needs of the potential Indian, mestizo, and landino entrepreneur in Guatemala that a sensible observer can only say, "My Goodness." The WWB has shown that progress is built by $300 loans made directly to such proud and determined people at the bottom who only ask for the way to be cleared so they can utilize their own energies to improve their lives.

All men and women want the opportunity to get ahead, provide more for themselves and their families, and to raise their standard of living. "You cannot walk through a Middle Eastern market, hike up to a Latin American village, or climb into a taxicab in Moscow without someone trying to make a deal with you. The inhabitants of these countries possess talent, enthusiasm, and an astonishing ability to wring a profit out of practically nothing. They can grasp and use modern technology."[276]

These people will never benefit from vast aid programs administered by bureaucrats. They need the open economic opportunities that can only be achieved by a massive reduction in centralized controls. Until such de facto freedom of action is provided to every citizen, and the corruption of government officials is ended, there will be no progress in reducing the poverty of Third World Nations. If the total withdrawal of aid that worked so well in Taiwan and Korea is too tough a medicine, then, at a minimum, aid should be restricted to the micro-practices advanced by organizations like Grameen and the Women's World Bank.

Chapter 9
Mercantilism, Smuggling & Illegal Immigration

*It was the very completeness and rigidity of the
feudal system that made heresy and rebellion
necessary ingredients of change, and maritime trade
was surely a prolific source of both ingredients.*
—Nathan Rosenberg and L. E. Birdzell

THE COMMON DENOMINATOR seen in those rare and isolated locales
where free enterprise developed was that fishermen, merchants, and
artisans were allowed to act unburdened by an aristocratic class,
academics, intellectuals, or an overpowering central political authority. Such situations unleashed the genius of the inhabitants. All such
locales witnessed an escalation of prosperity for a relatively wide class
of citizens.

The leaders of Europe's large and autocratic nations noted the
phenomenon and tried to echo the success in their own countries by
encouraging entrepreneurs and skilled manufacturers. But they could
not bring themselves to fully allow "free" enterprise. To keep control
they usually tacked on licensing requirements, regulations, and restrictions. In later days they sought to control currency conversion,
balances of trade, and gold stocks, and to tinker with fiscal and
monetary policy in pursuit of centralized ends.

This semi-adaptation to free enterprise became known as "mercantilism," a national economic system that attempted to control,
direct, or channel all business activity within a nation state. These
attempts to recreate the energy seen in free regions met with only
limited success because they did not allow full and open freedom for
the people. "To achieve its objectives," writes Hernando de Soto, "the
mercantilist state granted privileges to favored producers and consumers by means of regulations, subsidies, taxes, and licenses. . . . [W]ell

being and order were conceivable only if individuals and their organizations were regulated by the state and subordinated to its highest interests."[277] Today's administrators of foreign aid have by their centrist policies resurrected the evils of the mercantilism that a couple hundred years ago the West largely escaped.

The effect of mercantilism has always been exclusionary—the little guys are denied the opportunities granted to the big guys. Unfortunately, mercantilism still lives, even in the so-called capitalist nations. It is seen whenever politicians, bureaucrats, businessmen, or trade unions collaborate to stack the deck for or against another group. De Soto criticizes capitalism as practiced today because too often it operates as "a private club, open only to a privileged few, and enrages the billions standing outside looking in. This capitalist apartheid will inevitably continue until we all come to terms with the critical flaw in many countries' legal and political systems that prevents the majority from entering the formal property system."[278] The only recourse for enterprising entrepreneurs is to engage in business illegally, which inhibits any significant success.

A Bad Day Fishing Is Still Better Than a Good Day Working

Since the time of the most primitive societies, men have sought economic independence and well-being by going to sea—to fish and trade. The transient and individualistic nature of these employments, combined with their isolation from direct supervision, made them relatively free from the oppressive control of authorities. To this day, fishing remains one of man's best escapes from the hurly-burly of social and hierarchical life. Ships can enter and leave a nation from many small harbors. They can to do so in the fog and in the dark of night. Those who man such ships, like all good fishermen, reveal few secrets. Thus whenever societies were established by the sea and in favorable geographical locations for trade, a window of economic freedom was cracked open, enabling residents to at least partially escape the control of their superiors. Such tastes of liberty fostered the realization that this was the way men should live—free and empowered, relying on oneself, with adventure and profit at every turn.

These employments played a role in economic history by revealing the essence of opportunity. Hunting and gathering certainly also laid a foundation; but on the high seas, the sky's the limit. As scholars and academics sat in their cloistered halls pondering the uncertainties of life, the real actors went out and discovered the real world, leading to an irrepressible growth in commerce. Mark Kurlansky, in his remarkable history of the lowly cod fish, observes that Adam Smith "singled out the New England fishery for praise in his seminal work on capitalism, *The Wealth of Nations*. To Smith, the fishery was an exciting example of how an economy could flourish if individuals were given an unrestricted commercial environment. The British Crown had never intended to grant such freedom, and now it had a colony that no longer needed it—a dangerous precedent in the midst of the empire."[279] The early settlers in America developed a thriving fishing industry that led to shipbuilding, trading, and a prosperous merchant class. Remarkably, they had accomplished this within fifty years after the Pilgrims landed in Plymouth. And this vibrant economic activity was not restricted to the sea. It was evident in all spheres of colonial business affairs due to an almost total absence of regulation, aristocrats, restrictions, and intellectuals. The individuals in every village and town were free to set up shop and respond to every industrial and commercial opportunity.

In Europe, when merchants and traders had achieved financial success, royal authorities found it in their interest to establish a "partnership" with the rising merchant classes. This beneficial arrangement was advocated in 1515 by Machiavelli in his *Discourses*, in which he advises that a ruler's firm hand be moderated enough to avoid the hatred of his subjects, "for making himself hated never turns out to be for the good of a prince. The way to avoid it is to leave your subjects' property alone."[280] It was also evident that letting the merchants and entrepreneurs operate their businesses created ever-rising revenues to tax. For these reasons, a few of the habitually autocratic rulers of Europe had the sense to lighten the reins on their subjects. In practice, however, at least by modern capitalist standards, the rein was lightened only slightly. The Crown typically granted monopoly powers to selected merchant groups, and in return, the merchants allowed the Crown to regulate and tax their enterprises. The King favored monopolies because he didn't want his resident companies competing against each other for export business. He mistakenly believed that with just one exporter the companies could charge more, thereby produce more taxes, and be easier to oversee.

The mercantilist system proved temporary, at least in parts of Western Europe and America, because it had two major fundamental flaws. First, businesses over-regulated by a central government become inefficient. Second, any monopoly system, by excluding eager competitors, loses the talent, energy and innovation that emerges from open rough and tumble competition. In short, the incestuous relation between the government and the favored businessmen invariably bred corruption and sloth. Meanwhile, the less-favored businessmen were waiting in the wings to show up the insiders, often by smuggling and other means of skirting the regulations—which was easier to get away with in England than in France, one reason mercantilism faded faster in the former.

And the degree of restraint and oppression was only relative. In France, worthy entrepreneurs, attempting to compete against unfair monopolies granted for bribes to the chosen few, and thereby "forced" to operate illegally, were hung by the hundreds. The Brits were a little less vigilant in upholding the power of the monopolists, and only hung offenders by the score. This difference, probably unwitting, gave the advantage to the Brits as they reaped the efficiency of less restricted competition. But think of the persistence of the common men, risking the gallows for the opportunity to make a living. What we have today was won by such lowly and indomitable individuals, but it was not won easily!

Among the common men there will always be a number who, by dint of native talent and motivation, prove superior to those at the top and who therefore fuel the constant upward mobility of free societies. That is why free, open competition, capitalism, will always beat any other system. Given a chance, the Davids usually slay the Goliaths. And so the mercantilist era ended.

Yet it wasn't until 1833 that the British Parliament enacted laws limiting monopoly powers and allowing anyone to open up a business in London. By then, European businessmen in the New World had been enjoying for over two centuries a level of economic freedom undreamed of on the continent. Thus, even Western Europeans, the creators of the Industrial Revolution, ended up lagging thanks to their vestigial mercantilism and go-slow approach to political and economic freedom. Just as Western Europe had outpaced the rest of the world, America now outpaced Europe.

Divergences and Tipping Points

Professor Pomerantz pinpoints 1850 as the point of divergence for "the West," the year that England supposedly pulled ahead of China due to a "lucky" discovery of coal.[281] We've noted earlier the untenability of this thesis, which ignores, among many factors, the sporadic dynamism that created the actual historic steps to freedom and prosperity. But a very real divergence had occurred a hundred years earlier, one China had nothing to do with: it happened when America pulled ahead of England.

That earlier divergence occurred when Europe commenced its decline to second-place status and America began its advance to the top. This switch of leadership occurred because in the New World the common people enjoyed more freedom than they had been allowed in Europe. How could a mother lode of coal found in the England of 1850 have been critical in determining East-West hegemony, when this was the very year the Carnegies left Scotland for Pittsburgh to eventually help create the biggest and best coal and steel industry in the world? The West would have surpassed China even if England had sunk into the ocean.

This divergence, and all the stepping stones before it, illustrates that we should not embrace a "Euro-centric" theory of history. The term is misleading. One could refer equally well to a Phoenician-centric, Greek-centric, or Italian-centric theory. Why stop at the second-to-last stepping stone? America has been the setting of the fullest expression of modern prosperity for centuries, and it has been a truly culturally diverse achievement. Instead we should call it a "liberty-centric" theory of history, for it was only liberty—not ethnicity—that allowed common people to make it happen.

The situation in the American colonies during the 1600s was unique in human history. There was an almost total absence of regulation. At first, there were separate French, Dutch, and English settlements but these were gradually intermixed, divided, or enriched and diversified by the arrival of new groups. The English who were unhappy in Massachusetts' theocracy split off to Rhode Island to create a separate state open to all religions. There were no regulations or zoning or licensing boards to contend with. Best of all, virtually all the Lords and Ladies of European aristocracy had been left behind in Europe. American colonists by this new start made their escape from mercantilism complete. The unprecedented economic success that resulted demonstrated for all to see how simply liberating the common man from central authorities created rapid increases in economic prosperity.

Under mercantilism, outsiders were forced to the sidelines, denied licenses to operate legally, and were thus obliged to resort to the fine art of smuggling and to illegal manufacture in outlying locales. The authorities resisted these evasions and sought by innumerable Acts to tax and control shipping and unlicensed manufacture. On most continents and in most countries they succeeded only too well. But Western culture rarely made for a passive citizenry. Imagine the anger and frustration of Rhode Island importers, suddenly ordered by the king to place all their purchases of molasses with just a few English-controlled ports in the Caribbean—when nearby French and Dutch ports offered the same or better product for less money. That form of state regulation reduced choice, inflated prices, and might have bankrupted the traders. But the Rhode Island merchants found a solution. In 1772, when the British warship, the *Gaspe*, too vigorously enforced these trade restrictions, the Newport merchants boarded her, ordered the crew ashore, and torched the boat, which promptly sank to the bottom of Newport harbor.

The average merchant believed it was entirely reasonable to circumvent oppressive and "unfair" laws by smuggling, freebooting, and black markets: "Smuggling was of particular importance in Britain's American colonies. Beginning in 1660, Britain adopted Navigation Acts which restricted British coastwise and colonial trade to vessels owned and manned by British subjects   . The enforcement of the Navigation Acts had been lax up until 1763, and a prosperous American merchant marine had developed, much of it illegally." After 1763, as the British sought new revenue to pay the debts of the Seven Years' War and to support the continued presence of the redcoats in the colonies, they stepped up enforcement of the Acts.[282] They were followed by the Molasses Act, the Stamp Tax, and finally, in 1773, the Tea Tax, all of which inflamed the colonists and provoked the sinking of the Gaspe and a couple years later the Boston Tea Party. Unable to control the smugglers, rioters, and protestors, the king made the unwise decision to crush the Liberty Boys of New England. He sent in troops and the shooting began. It is noteworthy that the freedom the rebels fought for was economic freedom, the ability to trade openly and freely, without government restriction. Political freedom was only a secondary catalyst of the Declaration of Independence.

Many attempts to assign causes to the ebb and flow of history have resorted to theories of economic determinism. Thus, many people say the Civil War or the American Revolution were fought over "mere" economic interests, as if the principals involved fought the wars just for personal monetary gain. It is true, however, that in almost all major military or political conflicts a large economic factor has always motivated the primary actors. Indeed, the thesis of this book is that man's three-thousand-year struggle against tyranny has been primarily a struggle to gain affluence through economic freedom.

That battle for freedom of action, in defense of the right of individuals to earn a living and provide well for their family, unburdened by excessive taxation and bureaucratic restrictions, has been quite rightly the justification for armed conflict. And isn't economic freedom a much nobler reason for strife than Napoleon's dream of glory, or Hitler's dream of racial purity, or Stalin's nightmarish Marxian ideology of communal ownership and State control, or the French revolutionaries' disastrous and bloody search for "equality"? So-called "economic determinism," i.e. the desire to make an honest living, should be welcomed as a beneficent mover of historical events. And when people worked to obtain their own economic freedom they were also gaining political freedom for all.

Are Law Breakers Smarter Than Law Makers?

In America, a substantial underground economy goes unrecorded, untaxed, and unregulated, but it's still relatively small compared with the open and regulated economy. In many less developed countries, though, such operations account for a majority of the business activity. Rather than condemn such illegal activity, however, it might be wiser to condemn the laws. Both in the United States and these other countries, going underground is, for many people, the only answer to excessive regulation and taxation. Smuggling represents, throughout history, for any enterprising individual, the only logical recourse to onerous trade regulations and taxes. If one constructs a simple line graph, with the vertical axis being the "percentage of population breaking the law," and the horizontal axis representing "the stupidity or unenforcibility of the law," the line will show a steep ascension to the right, reflecting the average person's reaction—the stupider the law, the more justified its violation.

The unfortunate experiment in the 1930s to end consumption of alcoholic beverages, "Prohibition," would appear well to the right on such a chart. It was one of the first instances where the nation's elites gave in to demands to "Mother" its citizenry. Subsequent centrist programs to hand out substantial benefits without rigorous proof of need would also be well to the right. (Is there anyone who doesn't know of someone collecting disability checks for a relatively minor or non-existent ailment?) An outstanding current example is the rapid growth in illegal immigrants. These wily lawbreakers are incentivized in two ways. First, it is worth the risk, not only for employment opportunities but to gain the excessively compassionate welfare and hospital emergency room services freely offered to them; and second, the risk is minimal because the anti-illegal immigration laws are not seriously enforced. Thus, the illegals are proving to be smarter than the Washington elite, and by their ease in skirting the laws, proving the stupidity and unfairness of both the welfare and immigration policies.

Just as smugglers brought down mercantilism, these illegals will destroy America's welfare and medical practices. The difference to be aware of is that when smugglers broke mercantilism, it helped the economy, but when today's illegals break the welfare system, it may bankrupt the nation. While the people at the top may not understand reality, those at the bottom do. And can one blame a poor uneducated soul from taking advantage of the "positive rights" designed and constantly expanded by elite Ivy League graduates like Ted Kennedy who reassure each new "victim" that they deserve to be cared for? It would appear to this observer that those taking and spending the checks are considerably wiser than the people handing them out.

Summary

The imposition of controlling and restrictive measures on commercial activity from above represents a mercantilist policy. All government programs and policies, no matter how cleverly designed, create restrictions that limit activity. Such measures usually not only enmesh the actual workers in a tangle of taxation and rules, but also impose limits on trade, grant preferential status to monopolists, create a class of law breakers, and require enforcement procedures to monitor a wide array of centrist governmental bureaucratic obstructions. They restrain trade, reduce competition, and exclude many entrepreneurs from participation in business. And yet the goal of current intellectuals in Western democracies is to enact ever more centrist regulations wherever they see any "problem" that they think needs fixing. Joseph Johnston has given the warning, writing—in 1984, appropriately—that a "new class" of "civil servants, sociologists, educators, administrative lawyers, welfare specialists, and professional reformers" has emerged that "thrives on state subsidies and government power." To justify this dole, "the legislators must appear to respond with vigorous action to every problem that seems to concern a sufficient number of voters, even though the problem is in fact insoluble."[283]

Such excessive management of affairs from the top undermines national success and represents a return to the failed policies under mercantilism that the common people worked so hard to overcome. In the twentieth century, communism and socialism were widely advanced as "new ideas" by the great ideologues seeking authority for themselves. But they were merely presenting in repackaged form an already failed and disastrous experiment. Sadly, for the millions who suffered and starved, it required the past 100 years to re-iterate what had been already proven.

Chapter 10
How Religions Affect the Growth of Freedom

 *Theistic faith, which includes both belief in the power of God and trust in His love and care, is a source of courage which is stronger than Stoic resignation or existentialist defiance of the absurdity of existence.*
—Professor George F. Thomas

RELIGIONS THROUGHOUT HISTORY have influenced the behavior of their adherents. While autocratic political leaders have exerted a primarily physical restraint on their subjects, religions have exerted a mental and moral restraint. Since the fundamental source of progress lies in the efforts of common men and women, an appraisal of religions must examine how they affected people's behavior and their ability to act. We are not in this book directly concerned with the spiritual aspects of religious faith nor in the comforts it may provide. But to the extent that specific religious principles and practices either empowered common people or suppressed them, they may be judged as either beneficial or harmful.

In fact, differences in religious beliefs may explain why the inventiveness of the common men of Europe under Christianity eventually exceeded that of individuals elsewhere. Dinesh D'Souza asserts that it was Christianity which "introduced the idea of a divine plan for man and the world. In this view, history was not just one meaningless event after another: it represented the fulfillment of a story line—a story line that began with the Fall but would end in triumph."[284] This recognition of man's importance may have fostered cultural innovations that gave Christians a big advantage: i.e., the common-sense ability to separate their secular world from their religious world and the recognition that religion was supposed to help not hinder or limit their existence. While intellectuals have great difficulty dealing with the distinction between science and faith, it is child's play for ordinary minds.

Separation of Church and State

Throughout the long centuries after the fall of the Roman empire, through the Dark and Middle Ages, the Catholic Church frequently worked in concert with the monarchs to keep each other at the top. It was an unholy alliance, but fortunately it still did not create civil order for any extended period. Indeed, the very fact that the Church was based in Rome and competing for supremacy of power and riches against the various Crowns of Europe rendered the combination less monolithic than in regions where the rulers and priests were one and the same. The people of Western Europe were, thank goodness, a particularly rebellious lot, and they eventually took advantage of this schism. But before they gained the advantages of separating the religious from the secular they were subjected to a double team effort by those holding back progress. Papal endorsement of the divine right of kings to rule was just such an ongoing—centuries-long—hindrance to those struggling to institute reforms in the feudal and pre-feudal systems.

In the Middle East, where church and state were one monolith dictating behavior for all, Islam acted as a similar depressant. In the Islamic world, though, efforts at reform have always failed. One explanation for the long steady decline in Arabic civilization is the rigorous orthodoxy of the religion's leaders, who prescribe every detail of life and thought. George Walsh writes in *The Role of Religion in History* that after conquering Mecca, Mohammed imposed his Islamic based tribal value system. Prior to this occupation of Mecca, the merchants there had developed a thriving economy in which an individual could rationally advance his interests. It was the typically irrepressible free enterprise that most traders just naturally gravitate to. Islam ended this, teaching that tribal values, blood brotherhood, feuding, and tribal honor must prevail—not just for one's immediate tribe, but for the entire communal tribe of Islam. Followers were to welcome fate, banish pride, and accept one's total dependence on Allah. "The religion is called Islam, which means 'surrender.' An adherent to Islam is called a Muslim, which means 'one who surrenders.'"[285] This set of beliefs, with the preservation of tribal customs inimical to business, was crippling to free enterprise, free inquiry, individual initiative, and technological innovation.

The Catholic Church, by contrast, only shared authority with secular leaders, and therefore was rarely as oppressive as Islam in suppressing free inquiry. At least after 1000 A.D., divisions within the Church actually helped revive Classical Greek and Roman knowledge and practices.

The Church hierarchy, like the European monarchies, was sharply stratified by class distinctions. The Vatican ruled from the top, with the clergy in the middle and most of the varied orders of monks at the bottom. The call for reforms started, as it so often does, at the bottom. Beginning in the twelfth and thirteenth centuries, Dominican and Franciscan monks challenged the legacy of traditional Augustinian and Platonic thinking that sought to use reason to support theology. The monks asserted that religion must rely on faith and revelation alone, and that reason has a separate role—to freely pursue knowledge about scientific truths of the physical world. This was 300 years before Galileo was forced to recant. But the seeds of reform were planted, and like most human advances, it took centuries to gain the next step.

Ironically, it was the great Muslim theologian Ibn Rushd, better known in the West as Averrhoes, who helped shape this separation of the secular world from the religious. His extensive commentaries on Aristotelian logic attempted to fuse Greek logic with Islam. Known as the "prince of science," Averrhoes was the most eminent twelfth century Islamic scholar in Moorish Spain, and his books were widely studied for centuries in European universities. But his teachings found no following in eastern Islamic cultures; there the theories of Al-Ghazali prevailed. The latter is one of the most celebrated scholars in the history of Islamic thought—for his belief that all causal events and interactions are not the product of material conjunctions, but simply represent the doings of God. His book, *The Incoherence of Philosophers*, rejected all Greek thought, opposed the Mutazilites who sought reforms within Islam, and led the return to fundamentalism in Islamic society. Al-Ghazali illustrates how, to qualify in history as a great scholar, one doesn't need to be right—you just have to write.

Fundamentalist beliefs prevailed within Islam, and the reformer-scientist Averrhoes ended up being stoned in the great Mosque of Cordoba and exiled from the seats of learning. He reportedly complained that there is "no tyranny on earth like the tyranny of priests." Averrhoes could have been the Martin Luther of Islam. But his ideas never found fertile ground. The unfortunate theories of the intellectual scholar Al-Ghazali won out and led to the decline of Islamic science.

When historians mention a religious impact on historical progress, it often has to do with how the Reformation in Europe and the consequent proliferation of Protestant sects diminished the power of the Catholic church and permitted a greater degree of free thought among the people of Europe than was allowed, say, under Islam. But this divergence had begun centuries earlier. Indeed, it was as early as the thirteenth and fourteenth centuries when Thomas Aquinas, Duns Scotus, and Occam "made a definite distinction between theological and philosophical truth; they placed theology on a pinnacle, but they placed it where it could no longer obstruct research. . . . Which manifestly released scientific inquiry from dogmatic control."[286] Scotus and Roger Bacon advocated the right of individuals to pursue scientific inquiry as a legitimate activity quite apart from religious observances. Such individuals, "by clearly separating the sphere of intellect from that of faith . . . intended to liberate theology proper from its dependence on classical philosophy."[287] Their arguments carried on those made over a hundred years earlier by Averrhoes that science and faith could stand shoulder to shoulder without mutual interference.

In an ironic twist of history, the monumental Greek science of logic from a remote past had been saved initially by Eastern Christians in the sixth century; then, in turn, translated into Arabic in the ninth century; then transmitted by Islamic librarians to the West around the end of the first millennium. Their arrival helped kick-start the widespread scientific investigations that were to make the West supreme. Islamic leaders rejected these writings and Greek thought. The fundamentalists won after their greatest scholar Al-Ghazali snuffed out the calls for Islamic reform. Any talk about scientific inquiry and human logic contradicted their theology that Allah was in charge and that any independent thinking was prideful and sinful.

The Reformation

Near the end of the Renaissance, around 1500 A.D., dissatisfaction with the Church that had been gathering for over a century erupted into open rebellion. Common sense and the exigencies of the marketplace caused many individuals "[to question] the morals and righteousness of the clergy, the good faith and propriety of their celibacy, and the justice of papal taxation. . . . In studies and lecture-rooms a wider-reaching criticism of the methods of ordinary Catholic teaching was in progress."[288] These questioners were inspired in part by the newly available Aristotelian works on logic and a host of Roman and Greek ideas that had arrived in long lost texts from the Middle East. But more importantly, the excesses of the Church were evident for all to see—the lavish lifestyles of the leaders, their vast landholdings, the corrupt sale of indulgences, and the constant flow from all over Europe of large sums of money to Rome. Like most monopolies, sixteenth century Christianity had reached a point of no return—its sheer size, costliness, and suffocating influence had become too burdensome on those it was supposed to serve.

Two men had much to do with ending all this: a lowly priest and

Martin Luther, a miner's son challenged the Pope and revolutionized Christianity

the printer who made possible the wide dissemination of his views. In 1517, "an obscure friar in a remote German university town posted ninety-five theses on the door of the castle church of Wittenberg in the best tradition of medieval academic controversy. . . . With explosive speed, preachers and printers promulgated the increasingly radical views of Martin Luther." By 1648, "a century of dubious battle had accomplished a lasting division of the continent between Catholic and Protestant states."[289]

The Protestant Reformation started in Northern Europe, and its appeal was heightened by Germany's other contribution, invented a half-century earlier, the Gutenberg press. Luther's translations of the Latin Scriptures gave believers direct access to the Bible and eliminated dependency on clergy to transmit the Gospel. In addition, the new Protestant faiths proved very compatible with the spirit of economic and political freedom that energized the cities of the Hanseatic League and the Italian city-states.

According to historian Kenneth Clark, "Whatever else he may have been, Luther was a hero; and after all the doubts and hesitations of the humanists, and the hovering flight of Erasmus, it is with a real sense of emotional relief that we hear Luther say, 'Here I stand.'"[290] The Reformation created a massive change in the structure of governments and religious belief starting in the sixteenth century, and these supported a burst of creative energy borne of increased freedom of thought. The new era was marked by expanding commerce in Holland and England. It was the time of Marlowe and Shakespeare, and the people who attended the plays in Stratford-on-Avon were independent and boisterous, with a diminished awe of their leaders and clergy. They were enjoying their heady victory over established authorities, a victory arising from the Renaissance of economic freedom and free thought of the fourteenth and fifteenth centuries.

Machiavelli pointed out how the corruption and secular ambitions of the Papal State in Italy invited much open criticism of the Church and paved the way for the decline of its reputation: "Nor can one can make a better conjecture about its decline than to note how those peoples who live closest to the Church of Rome, the head of our religion, are the least religious. And anyone who considers its foundations and sees how different its present practices are from what they were, would conclude, without a doubt, that its ruin or its scourging are close at hand."[291] Machiavelli wrote these discourses between 1513 and 1518, reflecting the critical attitude of many in Western Europe even as Luther in 1517 was posting his ninety-five theses on the door of the castle church in Wittenberg. Europeans were ready for reform and welcomed Luther's bold demand for change.

Machiavelli refers us to a similar protest and revolution of thought in the Greco-Roman era. It had to do with the Oracle of Delos, which long "filled the world with wonder and devotion." But once the oracle "began to say what was pleasing to the powerful, and this falsehood was discovered by the people, men became unbelievers and were ready to subvert all their good institutions."[292] Thus, the common man eventually became disillusioned with the oracles and then the Church as a result of the obviousness and blatancy of their excesses. And this led to the search for new beliefs. One could argue perhaps that the evolution of Christian theology has been shaped by the actions and needs of common people, and that the clergy and theologians, just like the economic and political philosophers, have for the most part struggled to keep pace.

The Reformation illustrates the complexity and subtlety required of any analysis of religion and progress. Common people have had the ability to benefit from their faith in spite of their clergy's frequent failings and shortcomings, and to separate their faith from their secular lives. Intellectuals lack this subtlety, and, simply because established religions aren't perfect, often seek their destruction. It's the same lack of understanding that makes them want to destroy free enterprise—because it isn't as perfect as their utopian dreams. Leave it to the best and brightest to invariably throw out the baby with the bath water.

After the Reformation, Protestantism fostered an atmosphere of openness to ideas and the sanctification of the ordinary laborer and his thrift and prudence—both contributing to the entrepreneur's role in advancing the West. In addition, both before and after Luther, the "kinder and gentler" nature of Christianity occasionally emerged to soften the rigors of life for mankind. Most notably, Christianity has been largely free of some of the horrific practices of other religions.

Granted, there had always been an ongoing struggle by the organized church powers to suppress scientific advances that contradicted scriptural writings and the preaching of the clergy. This was true in both the East and the West. Even in the West, many heretics were burned at the stake or beheaded. Such dangers were ever present for the man that exercised his independence. But the evident truth of scientific discoveries could not always be suppressed, at least not in the relatively free nations of Europe—in which literacy was more widespread, a prosperous and well-traveled middle class was gaining strength, and habits of free and critical inquiry were embedded in many of its people.

The result was that the European advancement of science was allowed to continue in one sphere of life, even as most people continued to be pious in their spiritual lives. By contrast, fundamental Islamic practice, by discouraging all inquiry, slowed and halted progress. And in the Orient, some philosophies, for example Buddhism, counseled renunciation of any action. As Von Mises writes, in their view the "only way toward bliss and satisfaction is to become perfectly passive, indifferent, and inert like plants. The sovereign good is the abandonment of thinking and acting."[293]

Unfortunately for the "untouchables," the Hindu priests and the upper castes have never thought to act on their behalf. Instead they are consigned by birth to live lives beneath human dignity. "This is a violation of every freedom and anti-discrimination law we hold most sacred. . . . It is a horrible condemnation of an entire body of people in society."[294] As Professor Ward writes, this long-term adherence to such a practice raises huge problems of acceptability of a belief system that condones such behavior. But the problem is not the horrid caste system itself, but the failure to rectify it. The approach to history's grand panorama used in this book emphasizes progress—the dynamic nature of history. All religions have had their downside, but the way Christians thought, armed with free will and elevated by a respect for the individual—that was different. That is why there was a series of "Reformations" in Western history. Even in matters of faith, progress bubbled up from the bottom.

A Kinder, Gentler Faith?

Some writers have attributed the original rapid spread of Christianity to its "liberating" nature—the comfort and freedom from anxiety it provided to the common people who adopted its tenets. When Jesus criticized the Pharisees in Jerusalem, he spoke for the common people. He referred to the leaders of the synagogue as power brokers, doctors of the law. He criticized how they claimed to speak for the Almighty, and how they had excluded the common people from the church and used it for their own ends. He condemned the leaders for hypocrisy: "Ye blind guides, you strain out a gnat, but swallow a camel. You keep the letter of the law, and leave out the heart of the law. How can any of you escape damnation?"[295] In short, He was the first "Luther," demanding reforms so that ordinary men and women could reclaim their faith. Christianity was to Judaism as Protestantism was to Catholicism. Each newly reformed and revitalized faith led the common people of the west to new heights of endeavor. And both Judaism and Catholicism benefitted too, adjusting and reforming their own practices in the face of competition.

Henri de Lubac recalled how according to the pagan beliefs of the classical world, "the gods, or Fate, played games with men and women, often with lethal consequences; remember the interference of the gods in human affairs in the Iliad and the Odyssey, or Israel's constant struggle against the practice of child sacrifice demanded by the gods of the Philistines. . . ."[296] By contrast, Christianity had considerable appeal: the God of the New Testament "was neither a willful tyrant (to be avoided) nor a carnivorous predator (to be appeased) nor a remote abstraction (to be safely ignored). Under Christian teaching, humans were no longer the playthings of the gods or passive victims of fate—they were "empowered to lead lives of dignity, through the intelligence and free will with which he had endowed them in creation."[297]

Many atheists disagree with such explanations that claim any positive historical role for religion. One such atheist, the Oxford Professor Richard Dawkins, appeared on CSPAN to discuss his latest book, *The God Delusion*, and damned both fundamentalist Christianity and Islam equally as the source of great evil and repression. *Publishers Weekly* noted that "For a scientist who criticizes religion for its intolerance, Dawkins has written a surprisingly intolerant book, full of scorn for religion and those who believe in it." Dawkin's most scornful criticism voiced on CSPAN concerned the harshness that can be found in the Old Testament. Dawkins called the biblical Yahweh a psychotic, and ridiculed the story of how Abraham was spared the need to sacrifice his son on the altar. Now, everyone knows that parts of the original Jewish theology was harsh—an eye for an eye, a tooth for a tooth; but that was thousands of years ago. One thing Christianity did was soften and broaden the appeal of its adaptation of Judaism, thereby allowing it to grow exponentially. Dawkins deliberately ignores any understanding or recognition of history by not noting that change. As a true member of the intelligentsia, he lets his emotions—and his hatred for Christianity—dictate his logic and color his reasoning. And he errs in judging Abraham by today's standards. It was 3,000 years ago, a millennium before Christ was born, and Abraham was surrounded by pagans who had employed human sacrifice for centuries. Their superstitious notion to appeal by such ill-advised bribery to an angry and frivolous God was not easily reversed. Most humans still thought that thunder and lightning was a mean God about to whack them. The new monotheistic religions developed within the embrace of Judaic-Christian belief are what emancipated mankind from such horrific acts of piety. Abraham's experience represented a mega-progress in religious beliefs, helping to end human sacrifice, and ease the minds of mankind. Indeed, the subsequent rapid growth of Christianity was a step forward in civilizing the Western people, moving them ahead of others. The fact that Dawkins had to go back three millenniums for most of his examples of the "evils" of religion is an indication of both the weakness of his logic and the irrelevancy of his argument.

Thomas Cahill has testified to the "liberating" aspect of Christianity, telling of how St. Patrick quickly converted the Irish heathens in the fifth century to this more protective and reassuring faith. Prior to his arrival, the Irish believers lived in constant dread, for the Irish gods "were not the friendliest of figures. Actually, there are few idols that we have retrieved from barrow and bog that would not give a child nightmares and an adult the willies."[298] St. Patrick taught a different outlook: "This magical world, though full of adventure and surprise, is no longer full of dread. . . . The key to Patrick's confidence—and it is the sort of ringing, rock solid confidence on which a civilization may be built, an un-muffled confidence not heard since the Golden Ages of Greece and Rome—is his reliance on the 'Creator of Creation.' . . . Our father in heaven, having created all things . . . will deliver us, his children from all evil."[299]

Indeed, the notion that God made man in his image, and more-over, "loves me," had to be a number one ego booster and undoubt-edly gave believers added self-confidence. Professor George F. Thomas has described Christian love and its principle of agape, as "not measured out according to the value of the person loved, as human love is; rather, God is the Creator and His love is creative of worth."[300] This boundless and "perfect love," extended to all, with loving forgive-ness, had great appeal among Western men and women and removed ancient fears and banished frightful idols.

St. Patrick also liberated the Irish from the need to sacrifice their children on their stone altars to appease vengeful gods: "Christ had died once for all. . . . Yes, the Irish would have said, here is a story that answers our deepest needs. . . . It is our lives, not our deaths, that this God wants."[301] And, in this way, Christianity offered a rock-solid foundation, freed from fear, dedicated to human action—a new found confidence and independence on which a revitalized Western civiliza-tion could be built.

Free Will

The Christian concept of free will asserts that man should be and is free, and possesses the will and rationality to make his own deci-sions. To be free, first one needs opportunity for constructive action. Then one needs the willpower to do the right things, and that too can be derived from the ethical precepts and commandments of most faiths. The constant contentiousness of Christian congregations may have flowed from this concept of free will, in consequence of which they often felt empowered to challenge their clergy. This decline in servility to religious leaders helped open Western minds. Aware of his free will, a person will not long put up with calls for blind obedience.

There is, then, reason to believe that the structure of Christianity has supported the individual-empowering concepts of freedom, human dignity, and personal rights—clearly a positive influence on their societies. In contrast, the religions and philosophies of the Middle East and Asia did not typically help the common man or woman gain respect or, what is more important, rights. One of Islam's most characteristic pronouncements is brutally fatalistic: "It is the will of Allah." It is sinful for a Muslim to question a single word of the Qur'an. Oriental philosophies have also discouraged free thought, instead usually stressing order and obedience, tradition and manners.

Gautama taught renunciation, the virtue of forsaking material pursuits. After naming his infant son Rahula, which means "obstacle,"

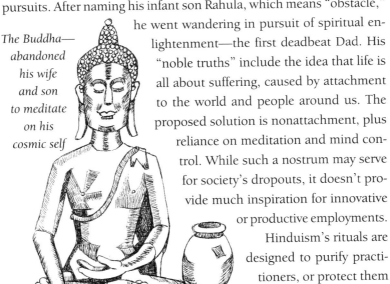

The Buddha—abandoned his wife and son to meditate on his cosmic self

he went wandering in pursuit of spiritual enlightenment—the first deadbeat Dad. His "noble truths" include the idea that life is all about suffering, caused by attachment to the world and people around us. The proposed solution is nonattachment, plus reliance on meditation and mind control. While such a nostrum may serve for society's dropouts, it doesn't provide much inspiration for innovative or productive employments. Hinduism's rituals are designed to purify practitioners, or protect them against the wrath of some god. Bathing in one of seven rivers in India can win karmic merit, so that in the next life one might return at a higher level of existence. But if practitioners fight to change life as it is now "rather than accept it, they upset dharma, the righteous order of society, and make [the] next incarnation even worse."[302] They might return as an animal, for example. And they can't eat meat, leftovers, or food that has been touched or smelled by another human being. Such passive acceptance of one's situation and deliberate privation are ways of being that restrict progress, not encourage it.

Christian and Judaic theology is based on the sacredness of individual human life, compassion, and free will. The last imposes moral responsibility on each individual. And where there is assigned responsibility, there has to be individual authority. Both the Christian and Jewish religions emphasize this elevated role of the individual, and this emphasis may have encouraged their followers to be more oriented toward individual action, constructive involvement, and creative effort. In Christian circles, there is no room for the shrug, or the excuse that "it is the will of Allah." That type of resignation may be heard among Christians when a loved one has been lost—an irremediable tragedy. But at least under circumstances where they can still have an impact, most Christians have a mindset aimed at purposeful intervention in matters of fortune. Some might even say that God helps those who help themselves.

Religion Versus Religion

Many theologians have noted the similarities among the Islamic, Christian, Buddhist, and Hindu faiths insofar as many of their original teachings urge ethical behavior—charity, compassion, honesty, frugality, etc. They all share a form of Christianity's Ten Commandments, in each case designed to provide guideposts for social interaction. These commandments ordering ethical moral behavior served as valuable guides and a useful legacy for mankind. A scholar versed in these religions could do a great service by compiling an ecumenical Ten Commandments combining the most valuable of these moral constraints. I believe it would not look very different from the Christian model. But would intellectuals understand the universal need and desire for at least a few absolute truths?

Although most religions share common ethical beliefs, the historical practices of each faith have varied greatly, and some splinter groups have wandered down undesirable paths of violence, racism, rigid orthodoxy, and persecution of both believers and non-believers. But each faith has also generally supplied a degree of positive support to the societies around them. Christianity likely stood out in this regard because it was richly laced with the Greek respect for the individual and its own principles of free will, forgiveness, and redemption. Christ's frequently quoted "fish" parable is inherently Calvinistic and capitalistic: "Give a man a fish and he will have food for one day; teach a man to fish and he will have food for a lifetime."

Those currently pushing an anti-Western agenda seem to relish pointing the finger at past failings of Western civilization. Thus they have tried to make Columbus a villain because some of his men killed Indians, or to castigate Western Europe for the Crusades, or condemn America for its past tolerance of slavery, or the Founding Fathers for writing the Constitution without giving women the vote. Flagrantly omitted from the indictment is the fact that the Western democracies have shown steady progress. Indeed, the Western democracies stand out for having slowly but surely broadened the principle of human rights and put all those past sins behind them.

Consider nine grossly abusive practices, many of which are still currently in effect in Oriental and Middle Eastern cultures. In India, English colonial administrators worked to end the practice of suttee— burying widows with their husbands. This reform is among the many beneficial influences that the British brought to India; benefits that lead Dinesh D'Souza to say, "Two Cheers For Colonialism."[303] In recent decades, Iran and Iraq have sent young children in human suicide waves to attack each other's forces. Islamic tradition allows and encourages the father or brothers of young girls to call them in and stab them to death for minor breaches of modesty, flirtation, or improper dress. It is an approved ritual, "Honor Killing," recognized by the authorities, honored by the culture.[304] For centuries, large numbers of young Chinese boys were castrated and enslaved to supply a cadre of eunuchs to wait on women of the Imperial Court. Too many Islamic priests encourage the most faithful in their flock to strap bombs to their bellies in order to blow up innocent civilians. In the 1930s and 1940s, the Japanese military regularly used Chinese prisoners for live bayonet practice, and Korean women prisoners as "comfort ladies" for the soldiers.[305] Female circumcision is still widely practiced in Muslim nations. In India, the huge class of "untouchables" are still forced to lead a subservient life of inferior status, and cattle are sacred as people starve. The large population of wandering sacred cows contributes to the disease and misery of the people by their scattered excrement. Under Islam, women are accorded few rights, restricted by onerous dress codes, and in many cases requisitioned to staff the harems of the elite rulers who keep them locked up like cattle, but powdered and perfumed, for their own sexual gratification and that of their guests.

These kinds of institutionalized practices are perhaps roughly comparable to some Christian abuses of yore. But the Christians ended most of their abuses long ago, while the Islamic and Eastern leaders still encourage them. Simple knowledge of chronology allows proper evaluation of which culture is improving morally and which is lagging behind.

Such practices can in no way help advance the interests of common people. It is self-evident that they are inimical to any minimal concern for human rights. The extraordinary thing is that all are still widespread, unchanged for centuries, even millennia. Only the first listed is now rare, thanks to the influence of English colonial administrators. Slavery has only been gradually outlawed in the Middle East during the past fifty years. It is hard to point at a similar listing of abominations (or even one) actively encouraged today by the institutions of Christianity.

Religion Versus Pure Reason

Philip Short has looked at the atrocities inflicted in Cambodia under Pol Pot and his Paris educated intellectual comrades who sought in the 1970s to "engineer" that society along Marxist lines.

"One and a half million people, out of a population of seven million, would be sacrificed to the working out of Saloth Sar's ideas"[306] He asks how can such a nightmare be visited on a people? "Why did so many Cambodian intellectuals throw in their lot with a movement that turned out to be so ghastly?"[307] "What is it about Cambodian society that has allowed, and continues to allow, people to turn their backs on all they know of gentleness and compassion, goodness and decency, and to commit appalling cruelties seemingly without conscience of the enormity of their acts and certainly without remorse."[308] Under the extreme communist system planned and implemented by Pol Pot, "An entire country was put in thrall to a dystopian ideal that negated anything and everything that was human."[309] And this nightmare was superimposed on a culture laboring under the tenets of Theravada Buddhism that suggests life is preordained and originality and initiative should be repressed, since all reward comes in the afterlife.[310]

Cambodian society lacked two concepts vital to Western society. First, the conception of righteousness and individual morality: "In Khmer legend, thieves go unpunished and live happily to the end of their days. Men are executed for deeds of which they are wholly blameless. Villainy is praised so long as it succeeds. Trickery is admired; honest conduct decried; and goodness regarded as stupidity. There is little place for compassion."[311] Second, women were suppressed as much as in Islam. It was customary for the numerous rulers to each keep hundreds of concubines. "Polygyny was a sign of virility, guaranteeing the fruitfulness of the realm."[312] Villainy, white slavery, and communism proved to be a poor mix. And, their new leaders' time spent in Parisian universities didn't help. There they were steeped in some of the more unfortunate elements of French intellectual thought—Rousseau's hatred for society, his romantic illusions about the simple rural life, and the Glory of the French Revolution. "The Terror was explained as 'an exceptional measure in exceptional times,' which took many innocent lives but saved the French Republic."[313]

Pol Pot and his intellectuals destroyed one and half million countrymen in an effort to create a new perfected society. Like the Jacobins, Japanese, Nazis, and Communists, they abandoned the moral tenets of virtually every religion to seek an abstraction based on pure reason. Those who rely on pure reason seem to frequently justify their amoral acts as essential responses to exceptional times when "the end justifies the means." Of such is the Kingdom of Hell.

In contrast, consider a tribute to the civilizing role of religion as given by the condemned communist functionary, Nicolos Rubashov: Arthur Koestler's 1941 classic that dramatically exposed the brutality of Soviet Communism tells Nicolas' story. After years of service to the Party, he is imprisoned, tortured, and awaits execution: "Looking back over his past, it seemed to him now that for forty years he had been running amuck—the running-amuck of pure reason. Perhaps it did not suit man to be completely freed from old bonds, from the steadying brakes of 'Thou shalt not' and 'Thou mayst not,' and to be allowed to tear along straight towards the goal. . . . And perhaps reason alone was a defective compass. . . . Perhaps now would come the time of great darkness."[314] For months he had been harried by his jailor who sought a false confession and sneered at Nicolos' moral soul-searching: "One may not regard the world as a sort of metaphysical brothel for emotions. That is the first commandment for us. Sympathy, conscience, disgust, despair, repentance, and atonement are for us repellent debauchery. . . . God is an anachronism. . . . When the accursed inner voice speaks to you, hold your hands over your ears."[315]

Arthur Koestler, like George Orwell, was among the few intellectuals who gradually recognized the horrors of communism and by the 1940s had become a fierce opponent. It took many of the New York intelligentsia another thirty to forty years to convert their beliefs from pro-communist to anti-anti-communist, and eventually, in a few cases, to anti-communist. But many still haven't admitted defeat and many of these are still trying to tear down the Commandments that have for so long provided the steadying brakes and moral compass that form the heart of Western civilization.

In summary, there are many differences in religious precepts and practices and the nature of those differences may well have contributed to the extraordinary success of the West. As a final example, the positive influence of women in some societies has to be considered in any analysis of economic history. They are half the population. And if the common people are a society's "ultimate resource," any system that forfeits the potential contribution of fifty percent of its assets has to suffer the consequences!

Critics of women's rights in the West show a marked ignorance not only of history but also of current practices around the world. There were no Florence Nightingales, no Helen Kellers, no Rosa Parks, or anyone like them in Oriental or Middle Eastern societies. These and millions of others who contributed in the West would still be stoned to death in much of the world for being so insolent as to leave their homes or expose their heads or ankles. To the extent that the imams of Islam have repudiated concepts of mercy, individual rights, respect for life, and rational debate, they may be blamed for the failure of the Islamic world to keep pace, and for the obvious misery and unhappiness of their peoples.

In any analysis of the impact of religion on societal progress, the historian needs a compass, a fundamental criterion for evaluating different religions. Armed with the Radzewicz Rule, this task is simplified: One needs only ask which religious practices freed and empowered the most common people: gave them the support, the faith, and the encouragement to act. Any such ennobling and empowering influences would certainly make that religion a positive force. Conversely, religious precepts may be deemed harmful when they held back the common people, discouraged active involvement, and stifled dissent and experiment. Such practices are easy to identify—and positive solutions are at hand. The record of Reform movements is everywhere in history.

Irshad Manji calls for such reform in *The Trouble With Islam: A Muslim's Call for Reform in her Faith*. "What's our excuse for reading the Koran literally when it's so contradictory and ambiguous? . . . We're in crisis and we're dragging the rest of the world with us. . . . Why are we squandering the talents of women, fully half of God's creation? How can we be so sure that homosexuals deserve ostracism—or death—when the Koran states that everything God made is 'excellent'?"[316] Clearly, there is much to reform, and Western intellectuals might be more usefully employed adding their voices for the end to such things as honor killing in the Middle East rather than bringing law suits in the United States to remove the "non-lethal" public display of religious Commandments.

Norma Khouri has also had the courage to speak out. She points to one of the great horrors of tribal Islamic custom, the ritual "honor killing" of women: "I must find a way to expose honor crimes for what they truly are: legalized murder; to break through the official Jordanian code of silence and find a way to make all Arab women's cries for justice and freedom heard around the world."[317] In 1998, the United Nations estimated that over 5,000 women are killed for reasons of honor every year, mostly in Pakistan, Jordan, Egypt, and Saudi Arabia. In November 2000, twenty countries abstained from signing a draft resolution condemning crimes of honor.

It is typical of the myopia and hypocrisy of Western intellectuals that they will oppose the public display of a Christmas crèche but remain silent about the very real human rights abuses chronically perpetrated under the aegis of other religions. That silence is what multiculturalism comes down to. It is an example of the kind of nonsensical ideology that academics will often champion even though it ignores the difference between good and evil, right and wrong, what helps the common people and what cripples the common people. History demonstrates the folly of any claims that all cultures are equally praiseworthy, that all religions have played equally positive or negative roles in mankind's advance, or that poverty and despotism are as beneficial as affluence and freedom.

Chapter 11
200 Years of Failed European Diplomacy

It was [Europeans], after all, who made the twentieth century the darkest in history . . . it was they who invented and put into place the two most criminal regimes ever inflicted on the human race.

—Jean-Francois Revel

A "BEST BOOKS" LISTING recently featured William Shirer's *Rise and Fall of the Third Reich*, but characterized it as the "one book that should be read about how one of the greatest cultures of all time fell under Hitler's spell, resulting in World War II and the deaths of 80 million people." Another listing noted that Shirer's book is a "unique analysis of that dictatorship and the evil genius of its architect." Such descriptions exemplify a common mistake among the West's literati. By blaming German nationalism, and one particularly insane political leader, they miss the real culprits. The Germany of the 1920s and 1930s, a fertile seedbed for Nazism, had been over one hundred years in the making. Hitler merely capitalized on the work of the country's intellectuals, who had so diligently laid the foundation for Nazism's worst features.

Although Germany had times of great artistic and industrial success, its governing structures had almost always been autocratic. There never had been any lengthy record of successful free elections, and the ordinary people had little or no experience with democracy. The separate principalities had only been united into one nation in the late nineteenth century under Bismarck and the military-industrial elite retained a tight grip on the nation. Even before unification, however, there were well established university communities, and as Shirer spells it out, it was the intellectuals and philosophers from that academic elite who destroyed the nation. Many of today's academics have sought to slide over that inconvenient fact and shift the blame onto Hitler.

Other academics, always ready to blame the West, will argue that the "harsh" surrender terms demanded at Versailles at the end of World War I, and other punitive measures, so degraded the surviving German state that it was forced to seek revenge. These apologists ignore the fact that Hitler was merely the last of several German autocrats that sought supreme power. Bismarck, the Prussian generals, and Kaiser Wilhelm had already established almost a hundred year record of aggrandizement based on the superman and racial purity themes of their "great" philosophers. For a hundred years before Hitler's arrival and the Second World War, the European leaders, diplomats, and their countless treaties and agreements had failed to avoid virtually constant warfare. This violent and aggressive disregard for laws and morality stemmed in part from the teachings of the Continental philosophers.

Shirer details Hegel's argument that one must not "be squeamish if the heroes, in fulfilling their destiny, trample or 'crush to pieces' many an innocent flower."[318] Nietzsche opined: "When a man is capable of commanding, when he is by nature a 'Master,' when he is violent in act and gesture, of what importance are treaties to him? . . . The strong man, the masters, retain the pure conscience of a beast of prey; monsters filled with joy, they can return from a fearful succession of murder, arson, rape and torture, with the same joy in their hearts, the same contentment in their souls as if they had indulged in some student's rag. . . . To judge morality properly, it must be replaced by two concepts borrowed from zoology: The taming of a beast and the breeding of a specific species."[319] These brilliant philosophers had clearly found a way to blot out the "accursed inner voice" of mankind's conscience. It is a case study strongly suggesting for all future societies that pure reason alone is not a sufficient guide for humanity.

By the time the opportunistic Hitler came on the scene, there had been over six generations of Germans exposed to these horrid concepts of amorality by their academics, their great thinkers, and much of the European elite. The German people were unfortunate in rarely having had a democratic government to complement and protect their many cultural and industrial accomplishments. Instead they were held subordinate to or indoctrinated by their flawed leaders and academics.

In *A Study In Tyranny*, Allan Bullock observes that Hitler was not the originator of Nazi principles but a product of the anti-religion and anti-Semitic ideas that had been common in Europe for the prior one hundred years. Leonard Peikoff makes a related case in *The Ominous Parallels*, that contending philosophical ideas dominating Germany, more than existential crises, are what made Hitler possible.[320] Daniel Jonah Goldhagen has also focused on the historical background extending over a hundred years before Hitler's birth to explain the fanatical anti-Semitism endemic among many Germans: "The unmatched volume and the vitriolic and murderous substance of German anti-Semitic literature of the nineteenth and twentieth centuries alone indicate that German anti-Semitism was sui generis."[321] The famous call for genocide "had been coined by Heinrich von Trietschke, the most prominent of the disaffected liberal intellectuals who embraced anti-Semitism. He was writing in 1879, yet he expressed the transcendent appeal of anti-Semitism in Germany."[322] This widespread madness had started almost a century earlier with Johann Fichte, another great intellectual and resident philosopher at the University of Berlin.

Europe, the origin of a few occasionally free societies and the mother of the industrial revolution, had matured during the eighteenth and nineteenth centuries. But with the widespread advent of the intellectuals, European civilization now commenced a decline. It was the complex, radical, insane ideas of its "great" thinkers that destroyed the cultures that had witnessed momentary occasions of greatness.

European Diplomacy on Trial

During the past two centuries, while the people of the new United States of America were crisscrossing their continent with railroads and building a free and vibrant society, Europe was repeatedly ravaged by war, starting with Napoleon's disastrous march on Russia in 1812 and eventually proceeding to the destruction of French armies by Bismarck's newly united German states in the Franco-Prussian War of 1870-71. From roughly 1890-1910, European leaders struggled to maintain their elaborate treaties and private pacts, taking time out for a couple "small" wars arising from disputes over imperial holdings. By the early 1900s, the major powers of Europe were locked into elaborate treaty arrangements designed to preserve a balance of power. This period witnessed a sophisticated diplomatic dance, orchestrated by the luminaries from all the European governments. But in the end, their tango failed miserably and led to the horrors of World War I.

Professor Walter Phelps Hall described WWI as the war no one wanted, the war everyone tried to prevent. However, the three major European authoritarian governments, Russia, Germany, and Austria, became so involved in their competition for territory that a war broke out that quickly became global in scale. Initially it was primarily "the old quarrel between Austria and Russia as to who should control the Balkan peninsula. . . . That quarrel came to a head with the diplomatic defeat of Russia at the Congress of Berlin in 1878, and smoldered and festered until it broke in 1914, the immediate cause of World War I." France had no interest in the Balkans but remembered the humiliation of losing Alsace-Lorraine when they were defeated by Prussia in 1870. "The pang of losing them slowly dimmed; but the desire for revenge did not die, and when France saw her chance to ally herself with Russia in the nineties she did so. From then on, the division of Europe into two armed camps became a sinister fact. . . . In theory European alliances and counter alliances were all defensive in character; but so complicated had they become by 1914 that escape from them in that fatal year proved impossible."[323] The European diplomats then stood by, helpless, as a world-wide conflagration threatened the very existence of every major European nation.

Germany's aggressive attacks quickly overran Belgium, then stalled after partly penetrating the defenses of France. They were living out their philosophers' dreams of the strong crushing the weak. With

German armored forces twenty miles from Paris, America contributed a million men to the battle of the Argonne Forest and, after years of trench warfare, the tide was turned. The Democratic president, Woodrow Wilson, the former professor and president of Princeton University, also had a dream: to make the world safe for democracy by waging a war to end all wars. Germany was eventually forced back, after a years-long conflict that cost millions of lives.

Allied troops drove the Germans back and most European nations regained their independence. But they could not keep it. The complex treaties and unwritten agreements that closed the First World War left many festering sores and vengeful nations that were not healed by the acclaimed diplomats of Europe. When Germany was driven into bankruptcy by onerous reparation agreements, her default on payments would give France the excuse they needed to march into and "take back" the Ruhr. With the treaties broken and the heartland of Germany's heavy industry taken away by force, German passions were inflamed, and its people became even more receptive to Hitler's vengeful message. In short, the leaders, the academics, the diplomats, and the philosophers of Europe had done everything wrong; the result was World War II. The ordinary people had done nothing—except keep their countries running, fund their massive governments, and tolerate too long their leaders' incompetence.

The United States and Great Britain had to save the world again in the Second World War; and then, throughout the Cold War, only American resolve and power kept Communist Russia from occupying not only Eastern Europe but all of Europe. Europe may again need saving by Americans. But will the Americans oblige, or will they rule, as in their favorite pastime, "three strikes and you're out"?

Europeans would be well served if their common people threw off the failed ideas of their elites. The recent resounding defeat of the proposed European Union hints at the vitality and patriotism that remains in the hearts of Europe's citizens. In popular referendums, they rejected their leaders' call for a super large governing structure run by bureaucrats in Brussels. Tony Blankley has interpreted these votes as a sign of a possible European turnaround, "in which the people would break with the elites and start demanding policies that protect their cultures."[324] Given the recurring diplomatic failures orchestrated by the European elitist leadership, the common people would certainly be justified in reasserting themselves and their more rational thinking.

After the First World War, in an effort to establish a world body "to end all wars," the allies created the League of Nations. It failed in almost everything it attempted during the 1920s and 1930s. During the same period, European diplomats repeated many of the same diplomatic and military follies as before and allowed a second World War to develop on the Continent. This time France hardly resisted the German onslaught, having been undermined by dissidents from within, and was quickly occupied, exposing England to direct attack. Russia allied itself with Germany to divvy up Poland, but was sucker-punched when Germany invaded and penetrated Russia's heartland. Once again, an American Democratic president, Franklin D. Roosevelt, sent millions of soldiers overseas to defeat the totalitarian regimes. Then, undeterred by a consistent record of failure, the world's finest diplomats again created an international body "to preserve peace for all time." The experts had somehow missed the lesson: Those who don't learn from history are doomed to repeat it. And they did just that.

The United Nations proved unable to prevent the wars and genocide that filled the remaining decades of the twentieth century with carnage throughout the world. The past sixty years during which UN diplomats have met regularly to discuss peace have been as bloody as any preceding sixty-year period in history. Many people defend the United Nations by reference to its good purpose or noble intentions. However, in matters of government, results are what count—not intentions. Indeed, throughout history, it is not clear which caused more misery—noble intentions or evil deeds. Stalin's communism was defended by many intellectuals for its purportedly noble goals. The League of Nations and now the United Nations were sustained at a huge cost only for their "good" intentions, in spite of their failure to deliver good results. What is there to show for the millions killed in pursuing the Communist dream? What is there to show for the billions spent by the United Nations, its "peacekeepers" stationed in seventeen nations watching ineffectually as anarchy continues?

Unfortunately, as "Buzzer" Hall foresaw, the United Nations failed just as had the League before it. What's worse, most of its members do not even share the noble objectives its creators hoped to accomplish. And by perpetuating a failed approach, the organization reduces the chances of any alternative approach doing better, all the while draining energy and tax dollars. In 1947, Professor Hall wrote: "Opening sessions [of the United Nations] were held in London in January, 1946. . . . It was painfully evident that the UN would speedily become as helpless as the League of Nations if Russia constantly exercised her veto power. . . . The future of the UN is, of course, problematical."[325] Within a year of its founding he had recognized the failure of the organization. Many of today's brightest minds still do not, or do not want to, recognize that failure.

> *The twentieth century's dangers and disasters were largely attributable . . . to the specific insane ideas or mind-sets that took control of certain parties and populations . . . this contagion was found especially among those who considered themselves to be an intellectual leadership or 'educated' class or caste. And these were often minds of high IQ presenting sophisticated fallacies to a wider spectrum.*
>
> —Robert Conquest

Although he correctly diagnosed the futility of the United Nations, "Buzzer" Hall ended his book on a positive note: "The intelligence which creates an atom bomb should be able to find some way whereby men can live together in peace." Unfortunately, the half century since he wrote has supplied continued proof of the UN's uselessness. Its basic ineptitude is often compounded by scandal, corruption, and the often controlling influence of totalitarian regimes. The author cannot resist pointing out that the "intelligence that created the atomic bomb" was that belonging to the "hard-scientists," those firmly placed in the higher levels of rational and intelligent beings. In contrast, all those involved with the United Nations have been practitioners of the "softer-sciences," the bottom rung on the ladder of common sense, and those who least rely on reason and objective observation.

Spawn of the Intellectuals

The horrors of the twentieth century were largely brought on by European intellectuals and philosophers who promoted ideological systems of government planned by those at the top and imposed on those at the bottom. Robert Conquest blames the modern era's destructive ideologies on the philosophers' whose writings distorted or ignored "traditional English understandings of liberty."[326] This criticism of philosophers is similar to what Voegelin referred to as the all-too-common distortion by intellectuals of reality; how the great philosophers and their ideas are too removed from "the engendering experience." That is, they are out of touch with the real world around them.

In correspondence from 1934 to1964, Eric Voegelin and Leo Strauss examined the dangers of modern intellectual movements in Europe: "Strauss and Voegelin agree, then, that the political deformations of the twentieth century were anticipated by intellectual constructs of reality that depart from reality and restrict the horizon of human existence. . . . The events of the twentieth century demonstrated how deadly this seemingly 'intellectual' error could be, how the dream world of intellectuals could translate into the horrors of political domination."[327] In simpler words, they are stating that common people deal directly by their action and deeds with the real world, while the intellectuals in their thinking and writing deal with an imagined world developed within their own big brains that often has little connection with reality. The result is, at best, faulty theories and proposals; at worst, extreme, destructive and malevolent ideologies.

Conquest deplores the confusion in ideology that fails to capture the subtlety of the common man's actual achievements. He writes that "the success of the physical and other sciences in England in the seventeenth century, gave the French intelligentsia the idea that everything could now be determined by Reason—in whose name the Revolution was made—with the 'Romantic' input from Rousseau as part of the mold. . . ." The French "miracle" resulted in two centuries of wars, defeats, and decline. But the abstractions of the great intellects held sway: "Marx himself said that he combined German philosophical, English economic and French political ideas. And it is indeed in France that we find Revolution in the sense of the complete destruction of the existing order, and its replacement by abstract concepts—these latter formulated by, and dictatorially enforced by, theorists with no experience of real politics. . . ."328

Conquest criticizes John Locke for promulgating "scholastic generalities" and for confusing the issues—a common failing among reporters. However, in defense of Locke it should be pointed out that at least he did not promulgate the horrid ideas of genocidal supermen, or the need for the supermen to obliterate the weaklings. That task was taken on by many of the scholars and philosophers on the Continent around 1800 and persisted in universities and among much of the elite throughout the nineteenth century and up to WW II. Hitler's worst ravings merely repeated the worship of power, the hatred for other races, and the lust for conquest that had been set forth over the previous hundred years by Nietzsche, Wagner, Hegel, and a host of the "famous" philosophers whose infamous work is still admired and taught in Western schools and colleges.

A particularly noxious derivative of these "superman" doctrines can be seen in the debate over euthanasia. Some of its advocates have favored pushing the Darwinian concept of survival of the fittest to its logical conclusion: eliminate the weak. And they are found in all Western nations. British philosophers such as Malthus, Darwin, Galton, and Spencer in effect endorse the idea that the weak should be pushed aside by the strong. Advocates use euphemisms such as mercy killing or voluntary euthanasia, but in practice, the intent is often to get rid of the unwanted, the mentally ill, the old, and infirm.

Dr. Richard Fenigsen has reported that under Dutch medical practices, of the 25,000 cases in which life-prolonging treatment was withdrawn or withheld without a request by the patient, 35 percent were done with the intent to terminate life; and, 22,500 patients died of overdoses of morphine. In the *Report of the Dutch Government Committee on Euthanasia*, it states that there were 5,941 cases a year of active involuntary euthanasia and that the doctors, with a single exception, never stated the truth in the death certificates. These figures do not include involuntary euthanasia on newborns with disabilities, children with life-threatening diseases, and psychiatry patients. Dr. Fenigsen concludes that active involuntary euthanasia practices are regularly practiced as a part of common medical practice; in many cases neither the patients nor their families are informed of the choice being made for them. Thus the ideologies of the great philosophers did not die with Hitler—they can look up and see Holland carrying on their ideas. And, in America, a new bioethics professor was hired at Princeton who has advocated that "abortion" should not stop at 3 months, 6 months, or even at birth, because a human infant is not "viable" until some time later. By emphasizing pain and viability, he can conclude that less evil is done killing a newborn human baby than killing a healthy pig or an adult cow.

Princeton students, selected for their love of abstract reasoning, are drawn to his ethical conundrums and many have become vegetarians in order to lessen the suffering of animals. Albert Schweitzer wrote more than 50 years ago about the need to extend a reverence for life to the animal kingdom, but it is self-evident that one cannot equate killing a human to killing an animal. For this type of education, Princeton parents are spending $50,000 per annum? This is the stuff of Huxley's *Brave New World* and a clear-cut warning that, with or without Hitler, the intelligentsias are leading the decline of Western civilization.

Racism and Supermen

The German glorification of ruthless power and a supreme state to be led by a "superman" can be traced to Johann Gottlieb Fichte, the University of Berlin philosopher who delivered his "Addresses to the German People" in 1807 after Prussia's defeat by Napoleon at Jena.

His dream was that Germany create a new all-powerful state, led by a small elite of pure German blood, free of any moral restraints. It would subjugate the inferior decadent races: the Latins, the French, the Jews. These ideas were all adopted in the universities and become part of German culture. In 1814, Fichte was succeeded at the university by Georg Hegel. Hegel possessed a "subtle and penetrating mind whose dialectics inspired Marx and Lenin and thus contributed to the founding of Communism and whose ringing glorification of the State as supreme in human life paved the way for the Second and Third Reichs of Bismarck and Hitler."[329]

Next we have Professor Heinrich von Trietschke, who from 1874 to his death in 1896 taught and preached history in Berlin. "Like Hegel he glorifies the State and conceives of it as supreme, but his attitude is more brutish: the people, the subjects, are to be little more than slaves in the nation. 'It does not matter what you think,' he exclaims, 'as long as you obey.'"[330] He outdid Hegel in his love of force and proclaimed war to be the highest expression of man. He supported "the need" for the mighty to destroy the weak.

Then came Nietzsche, who prophesied that a coming elite would rule the world, from among whom would emerge a superman; "this man and the elite around him will become the 'lords of the earth.'"[331] These intellectuals, philosophers and historians, with their rantings about a superman, the supreme state, and the need to destroy inferior races, spewed their horrid notions for a hundred years before Hitler— even as America during those decades flourished as a beacon of freedom. This was the period when Lincoln ended slavery, women got the vote, labor unions were formed to protect workers, and every four years a new president was peacefully elected. Such democratic alternatives were known to the German intellectuals, but rejected by them. Their continued assertion of authoritarian ideas is a testament to the molding power of an intellectual elite when it controls a nation's schools, colleges, and press. They saw to it that the German people did not gain from America's democratic example. Instead, the populace was conditioned to accept the elites' twisted and inhumane vision of how a society should be organized.

Even the "non-violent" thinkers of eighteenth and nineteenth century Europe did their part in undoing progress. Enlightenment philosophers believed in a "science" of politics. It became popular to apply mathematics to human affairs, as if by means of some scientific theory, society could be perfected: "Condorcet (himself a mathematician as, of course, was Diderot) put forward the idea that given adequate statistical data, all social problems could be solved. . . . It is precisely the mindset that accepted a 'science' of politics that fueled the utopias of totalitarian systems."[332] Thus, the European intellectuals and philosophers came on the scene and disseminated ideas that ended progress toward liberty and substituted the utopian dreams of big government, bureaucracy, regulations, control, and conquest—all designed to create a more perfect order. It was this bad idea of the elites to apply science to political affairs that lay the seeds of centrist political programs designed to control and alleviate all society's and mankind's problems and has steadily sprouted into the bureaucratic nightmare of the EU in Brussels. This development represents the dark side of the Enlightenment era and the transition from the rise of Continental powers to their decline. It is no coincidence that these were the years when major European nations began their slide into irrelevance, and when millions made the wise decision to abandon ship and head for America.

George Weigel has written that the principles of consent in governance and the limitation of the state's power over the people "find their deepest roots, not in Enlightenment political theorizing but in ideas, ideals, and moral commitments first nurtured in European Christian culture."[333] The Church's claim to authority over men's lives denied the emperor any exclusive role, and that empowering concept dates back to medieval times. This duality of allegiance meant that "because God was God, Caesar was not God and neither were Caesar's successors, be they kings, princes, prime ministers, presidents . . . or members of the Politburo." Thus "an anti-totalitarian vaccine was injected into Europe's civilizational bloodstream,"[334] fostering the great advances in freedom that occurred in the thirteenth through seventeenth centuries in Florence, Scotland, Holland, and England.

It is interesting to speculate that the Enlightenment, which spawned the great "soft-science" thinkers like Hegel and commenced the secularization of Europe, in the late eighteenth and early nineteenth centuries, may have undone that immunization, and by abandoning the constraints of religion and established moral custom, helped usher in the age of totalitarianism. As noted in the chapter on Scotland, the 1750s and 1760s represented the pinnacle of that nation's advance, which had started 200 years earlier with John Knox's arrival. In 1768, John Witherspoon left Scotland for America, unhappy with how moderates like David Hume were beginning to "liberalize" religious thought. This was the point in time where intellectuals began taking the place of both God and Caesar—a substitution that bode poorly for the European continent. Less than fifty years later, Fichte and Hegel at the University of Berlin were teaching that "racially pure" and aggressively militaristic leaders, free of all moral constraints, should subjugate the inferior and decadent races. Somewhere between these two events, European advances and cultural success fell victim to the ideas of the best and brightest now controlling the European academies.

Those who came to America were spared the slaughter and oppression of Stalin's communism, Hitler's holocaust, the fascism of Italy and Spain under Mussolini and Franco, the horrors in Eastern Europe under ruthless Communist puppet governments, and, on a much lesser scale, the stultifying effect of socialism and lack of upward mobility common throughout even the best of European societies. And immigrants were vindicated when they saw that America had to repeatedly defend, liberate, and restore freedom to those European nations because of their inability to even defend their borders.

Europe: A Discredited Role Model?

Some writers have attributed Europe's decline to the growth of secularism, the loss of faith in religious beliefs that had probably helped inspire past accomplishments. In his 1983 Templeton Prize

Lectures, Solzhenitsyn endorsed what Weigel calls the "Slavic view of history, " which suggests that "the deepest currents of history are spiritual and cultural." Referring to the atrocities of modern Europe, Solzhenitsyn argues that the "failings of human consciousness, deprived of its divine dimension, have been a determining factor in all the major crimes of this century. . . . Europe, bursting with health and abundance, fell into a rage of self-mutilation. . . . The only possible explanation for this is a mental eclipse among the leaders of Europe due to their lost awareness of a Supreme Power above them. . . . The West did not perceive that this was in fact the beginning of a lengthy process that spells disaster for the whole world."[335]

While atheism may have contributed to the modern European's aimlessness, its prevalence does not provide the whole answer. It is very likely that even if the elites in Europe were to stop trying to eradicate all Christian observances from public life, and assent to treat it equally with other faiths—indeed, even if they were to fervently embrace Christianity as born-again Christians—such tolerance or embrace of religious faith still would not immunize Europe from the destructiveness of all their other bad ideas. The social engineers would still pursue international answers, bureaucratic controls, a world court ruled by dictators, an expanded welfare system on the brink of bankruptcy, etc. Eliminating atheism would not significantly reduce the threat of such faulty visions. And they would still seek to extend the failed record of agreements and treaties that for hundreds of years have never accomplished their stated objectives. One of the longest periods without major conflict lasted for only a few decades after the 1815 Concord of Europe signed in Vienna; and that period of relative peace may have owed more to the exhaustion of the participants in the wake of the devastating Napoleonic Wars than to the soundness of the agreement. Given this record, European leaders are in no position to recommend sound policy concerning international relations, which doesn't prevent them from staggering from one crisis to the next as they deplore America's "legitimacy," ridicule Americans' moral convictions, and subvert the war on terrorism.

Jean-Francois Revel argues that the anti-Americanism of contemporary European leaders stems from weakness and envy and represents an attempt to cover their own loss of influence since World War II. "It is in France that this loss—real or imaginary—of great power status engenders the most bitterness."[336] He paints a gloomy picture of the future of Western European countries, an outlook confirmed by their continued decline in the annual rankings of economic freedom based on World Bank figures. The heavy hand of central regulation and planning is plunging them back into the mercantilist quagmire of 200 years ago. In sharp contrast, several Eastern European nations, recently freed from Russian communist suppression, have already displaced Germany and France among the leaders in economic freedom. If current trends continue, these "new" European nations may soon surpass Western Europe in prosperity and influence. In the 1990s, when the failure of Russia's communist experiment became too glaring to be ignored, many believed that the history of socialism had ended; i.e., that the benefits of liberal economic practices would now spread to all countries around the world. Unfortunately, most of the intellectual elites, true to form, will not admit that their abstract theories are fatally flawed. It is their leadership, and their denial of what economic mechanisms have worked, that continue to retard European prosperity.

According to Gerard Alexander, average U.S. per capita income "is now about 55% higher than the average of the European Union's core 15 countries. . . . [I]f the United Kingdom, France, or Italy suddenly were admitted to the American union, any one of them would rank as the 5th poorest of the 50 states. . . . Ireland, the richest EU country, would be the 13th poorest state; Sweden the 6th poorest. . . . 40% of all Swedish households would classify as low-income by American standards. . . . Europeans now match or surpass America in most crimes, including violent ones. . . . Its ideologically lopsided political and intellectual elite is so potent that it may shape Europe's political identity as much as secularism and economic dependence do. . . . The unemployment rate is stuck around 10% in Germany and

France, and if anything this underestimates the true figure—even more unemployment is concealed through extensive job-training and early-retirement schemes."[337] Meanwhile, the benefits of their traditionally homogeneous population are being disrupted by large numbers of Muslim immigrants who resist integration and look primarily to their own religious leaders and local mosques for direction.

Robert Kagan associates the decline of Europe with the same faulty vision of "a small segment of the American elite [that] still yearns for 'global governance' and eschews military force."[338] However, that elite is not yet as dominant in America as it is in Europe. That helps explain why the American economy suffers from a lower level of governmentally imposed constraints and is therefore growing faster than Europe. And America's population is growing faster and getting younger while the European population is declining and getting older. He quotes *The Economist*: "'The long-term logic of demography seems likely to entrench America's power and to widen existing transatlantic rifts,' providing a stark 'contrast between youthful, exuberant, multi-colored America and ageing, decrepit, inward-looking Europe. . . . If present trends continue, the American economy, now roughly the same size as the European economy, could grow to more than twice the size of Europe's by 2050.'"[339]

Kagan also disagrees with those who believe the United States should look to European nations for guidance or support. The great majority of European countries, mired in their present moribund state, do not constitute useful role models except as a lesson in what not to do: never allow the central planners, the intellectuals with their flawed visions, to take over the leadership of your country. And, Kagan asserts, America need not seek the approval of others to gain some form of international consensus or legitimacy. Her moral authority does not come from the approval of other nations or international organizations, but from its own founding principles: "Because the principles and ideals upon which it was founded were unquestionably superior—superior not only to those of the corrupt monarchies of eighteenth- and nineteenth-century Europe, but to the ideas that had shaped nations and governments throughout human history."[340] When the torch was passed to the United States, it was a giant step forward. The millions of good people who left Europe have little reason to return.

In that last quote, Robert Kagan uses the three words "principles," "ideals," and "ideas" to refer to the cultural basis that made American culture "superior" to all others. Quite differently, William Shirer referred to the horrific "ideas" of German philosophers as unthinkably inhuman in their glorification of the strong exterminating the weak. Neither writer appears concerned about the climate, natural resources, or geography of these two countries, but instead emphasizes the differences in cultural conditioning. Clearly, there are sharp differences in the values, ideas, and principles that underlie different societies, and these differences have important consequences. In the next chapter, we will examine the nature of ideas and principles and their role in history with the object of discovering why some "beliefs" have helped their people, while others promote oppression, violence, and destruction.

Chapter 12
The Difference Between Principles And Ideas

 *A number of human convictions have persisted ever since civilization began, little changed by the passage of time; these seem to be permanent truths, which any civilized nation must reckon with or decay.*
—Russell Kirk

Heather MacDonald published *The Burden of Bad Ideas* seven years ago and gave it the subtitle, "How Modern Intellectuals Misshape Our Society." In that book, she spells out the burdens that the intelligentsias have imposed on the nation and how their destructive vision has undermined traditional American strength.[341] This placement of blame for harmful ideas on the intellectual elites of successful nations has been argued by other writers but has never received wide dissemination because, after all, almost all those who write, are intellectuals, and they choose to ignore such assertions, no matter their validity. Because the destructive role of intellectuals has usually come from the dissemination of their faulty and untested ideas, it is useful to raise the question—what has been the role of ideas in history?

The Nature of Ideas and Their Role in History

Thomas Sowell has written that "The role of ideas and ideologies in history is much more difficult to establish than is often believed. Neither freedom nor slavery, for example, was the result of ideas or ideologies. Freedom began to emerge where governments were too fragmented, too poorly organized, or too much in need of voluntary cooperation, to prevent its emergence . . . slavery existed wherever there were sufficiently vulnerable people to make their capture and enslavement profitable."[342] Thus, one could say that freedom and slavery represent mechanical formats sometimes used in governing social groups; systems that evolved in antiquity and continued in use for many thousands of years. Slavery may have been an "idea" to the first cave man who realized the advantages of making someone else do his chores, but it gradually developed into an institutional practice. Then, as people developed the principles of freedom, some individuals viewed slavery as an evil and "abolition" became the new idea. That was 200 years ago, and today, even that is so time honored it may no longer be thought of as an idea but as a fundamental principle—that freedom is the birthright of all human beings regardless of race or origin.

The dictionary defines "Idea" in a number of ways: as "a picture of anything in the mind," an awareness or activity; "a thought, opinion or fancy," a notion or an impression, a "view or belief," an idea of "what is desirable or ought to be," a plan of action, an intention, a groundless supposition, a fantasy, or a corruption of what is desirable or ought to be.[343] Clearly, there is a wide range of meaning—from a concrete plan of action to a fantasy or a mere opinion or notion. In the scientific and artistic realm, fantastical notions have been known to help break through inertia and enable new insights and innovation. In the art of governance, on the other hand, it has been the negotiated adaptations of existing structures by groups of men and women that have formed most useful innovations in governing structures.

While the brilliant new "aha!" discovery in science has on occasion paid benefits, such brilliant "ideas" in man's affairs have a poor history. The problem is that in both the hard and soft sciences, the vast majority of new ideas are flawed; they don't work. They must be tested to determine real-world results. Once proven over time, these suggested hypotheses become laws or principles. The failing of many soft science experts is that they take each and every idea they like (either emotionally, viscerally, or ideologically) and pursue it with little regard for contrary findings. Many of the major disasters in mankind's history were caused by just such irrational pursuit of faulty ideas.

Ideas, Principles, and Cultural Values

Russell Kirk has recognized this distinction between principles and ideas and writes about how ideas lost in mankind's earliest history have become principles.[344] He asserts that the success or failure of a society depends on how sound and true its underlying principles are: Western civilization has been based on principles "built up over a great many centuries . . . the accumulated accomplishment of countless generations of human beings . . . the product of innumerable thinking and working men and women, who came to agree that a particular concept is true. By an age-long process of trial and error . . . some human beliefs are found to be sound and enduring, while others are found to be erroneous and obsolete. Yet a number of human convictions have persisted ever since civilization began, little changed by the passage of time; these seem to be permanent truths, which any civilized nation must reckon with or decay." [345]

In this book, we have outlined the "stepping stones" of history—those rare isolated enclaves where their people employed and adapted just such fundamental principles. The cumulative knowledge gained in these locales contributed to the inexorable rise of Western civilization. The concepts of personal rights and freedom, the sanctity of private property, the need for representative government, the importance of an informed and independent citizenry, and the minimization of all forms of physical and mental oppression—these are no longer mere ideas—they have been enduring principles of good government at least since they were enshrined in Pericles' Funeral Oration over two thousand years ago.

Barry Goldwater emphasized this same point—that the principles that govern free nations have been proven in practice for thousands of years. He believed that the two most important principles validated by the historical experience of free peoples were the limitation of central governmental power and the maintenance of the freedom and self-reliance of the people. He called these principles the bed-rock that defined his "conservative" faith. He had little time or interest in social or lifestyle questions—he was not interested in imposing his judgment on such matters onto the people of the various states. "Social and cultural change, however desirable, should not be effected by the engines of national power."[346] He believed that such micro-managing of individuals' lives only serves to violate the principle of limited government.

This distinction between ideas and principles is important—the meaning of "idea" is fuzzy, but in some minds that are enamored with such things, its use often overly inflates the importance of mere notions or fancies. However, the word principle indicates something more reliable. Kirk thus emphasizes that the ideas underlying Western freedom are "ancient principles," not the brilliant "ideas" of the philosophers of the past few centuries. And it is useful to remember that those "principles" are not great and mystical or complex things—they really are no more exotic than simple mechanics—the basic parts that ensure a working government that is limited and yet empowering for the citizens.

Goldwater's faith in his understanding of conservative principles was due to their unchanging nature—circumstances and problems may change over decades and centuries, he wrote, "But the principles that govern the solution of the problems do not. . . . The conservative approach is nothing more or less than an attempt to apply the wisdom and experience and the revealed truths of the past to the problems of today. The challenge is not to find new or different truths, but to learn how to apply established truths to the problems of the contemporary world."[347]

Thus, sound principles can only be based on successful experience—in both hard sciences and soft sciences. That is why the case method—examining actual experience—is the scientific and rational way to advance social science as compared to venturing off into the abstract theories of philosophers. The case method would also be the best way to teach history, because it would keep the subject grounded in fact rather than opinion.

Past Practice Versus Theory—Case Method Versus Ideology

Some of the first and most successful attempts to establish good government occurred in Greece over two thousand years ago. The early Greek systems were built on written laws and constitutional forms of government. Thucydides recorded these achievements in words he attributed to Pericles in his "funeral oration."

"Our constitution is called a democracy because it is in the hands not of the few but of the many. But our laws secure equal justice for all in their private disputes, not as a matter of privilege but as a reward of merit. . . . We deliberate in person all matters of policy. . . . In short I say that Athens is the school of Hellas, and that her citizens yield to none, man for man, in independence of spirit, many-sidedness of attainment, and self-reliance in body and mind."[348]

This democracy developed in Athens had been already foreshadowed during the preceding centuries by earlier Greek and Phoenician societies. The various forms of government that were employed in those pre-Christian days were referred to in some detail by Alexander Hamilton, James Madison, and John Jay thousands of years later when arguing the need for the American states to ratify the newly written Constitution of the United States: *The Federalist Papers* appeared as campaign pieces in colonial newspapers and journals in 1787 and 1788. They were designed to explain and justify the detailed mechanics of the Constitution. The primary issues at stake were the degree of national power versus states rights, the powers and separation of the two legislative branches, and the separation of executive and judicial branches. Religious freedom and an enabled electorate were givens— subject to minimal debate.

There were many past societies whose experience could be drawn upon. They were illustrative case studies revealing the relative merits of different approaches to self-government. In Number 45 of *The Federalist Papers*, both the Achaen Confederacy and the Lycian Confederacy are referred to as federations that reserved considerable power to the central government and yet did not "degenerate into one consolidated government."[349] In *Federalist* Number 18, reference is made to the division of authority in the Achaen system between the municipal government, the senate, and the chief magistrate. Contrasts are made with the Amphictyonic confederacy and the other Greek republics.[350] Comparative operating details are given in Number 63 for the various elective bodies that operated in Athens, Sparta, Carthage, the Tribunes of Rome, and the Cosmi of Crete.[351] In Number 48, weaknesses in the constitution of Virginia are compared with those of Venice where excessive power ended in the hands of the legislature; "one hundred and seventy three despots would surely be as oppressive as one."[352] In Number 9, the Lycian confederacy is criticized for its reliance on the elected common council to appoint local magistrates; and the writers lament Montesquieu's praise of it as "a model of an excellent Confederate Republic."[353] They refer to the detailed governmental systems of Solon, Lycurgus, Romulus, the Swiss Cantons, and the United Netherlands. In Number 20, the Belgic confederacy is criticized as "imbecility on government."[354] In Number 20, believed to be mostly written by Madison with some contribution from Hamilton, it is declared: "I make no apology for having dwelt so long on the contemplation of these federal precedents. Experience is the oracle of truth; and where its responses are unequivocal, they ought to be conclusive and sacred."[355]

These writers believed that the laboratory of history, where the results of divergent practices could be observed and evaluated, was a much better source of instruction than general ideas and theories. It represented a way of thinking based on actual case histories where actual results could be evaluated in order to appraise the usefulness of different approaches. These writers anticipated the celebrated use of the case method at Harvard Business School centuries later, where the instructors wisely chose to study actual practices rather than dwell in the uncertainty of theoretical generalities.

Professors Alpheus T. Mason and Gordon E. Baker have minimized Locke's role in the minds of the Americans who formed the new nation. They grant that Locke's *Two Treatises of Government* was full of ideas, but "on the institutional side, it was of limited usefulness."[356] They point out that Locke's "constitutionalism boils down to political limits on government—those imposed at election time plus the faith that rulers and ruled alike would be guided by considerations of justice and common sense. The idea of a constitution limiting and superintending the operations of government forms no serious part of Locke's system. It has been said that Locke was 'unreasonable only in his faith in reason.'"[357] And Mason and Baker quote Jefferson's comment about Locke ("Locke's little book on government is perfect so far as it goes."). Jefferson's criticism was that the book was just theory with no practice. Typically, the great philosopher dealt primarily with the grand concept that man should have freedom and the authority to have a say in who his leaders would be. This was a known generality from all the stepping stones to freedom that we have covered in this book—going back millennia. The problem, which the Founders saw, was *how* to limit the government's power—to design the mechanical parts that would keep men free.

There is little reference to philosophers or theorists in *The Federalist Papers*. In Number 47, where Montesquieu is cited for his argument that legislative and executive powers should be separated, Madison writes: "If he be not the author of this invaluable precept in the science of politics, he has the merit at least of displaying and recommending it most effectively to the attention of mankind."[358] Here we have Madison anticipating the theme of this book—that the great writers at best serve as good "reporters." The other reference to Montesquieu is to deny his argument that republics were only suited for small regional arrangements and could not work effectively over large expanses. The colonists already knew that had been proven wrong by the confederation of the thirteen colonial governments so they ignored the great philosopher's admonition. The index to *The Federalist Papers* shows no references to Plato, Locke, Aristotle, only one to David Hume, and no other philosophers or political theorists are cited other than the two to Montesquieu referred to above.

This glaring and almost total absence of references to the great writers and philosophers is also evident in the 659 pages of James Madison's *Notes*, where he recorded the daily details of debate that marked the Constitutional Convention. Montesquieu is again the exception, but only with a couple citations, and those are of a "reporting" nature, such as where he "recommends" that type of representation used in the Lycian confederacy "as the fittest model for that form of Government."[359] And, notably the index to Madison's *Notes* is replete with references to actual "cases" of governing systems in numerous historic societies. Benjamin Franklin corroborated this reliance on precedent, not theory, on June 28th speaking to the delegates that "We have gone back to ancient history for models of government, and examined the different forms of those Republics which having been formed with the seeds of their own dissolution now no longer exist. And we have viewed Modern States all around Europe, but find none of their Constitutions suitable to our circumstances."[360] Thus the delegates looked to past cases, borrowing here and there, adapting a variety of known mechanics of government as needed to fit the American experience.

Judicial Systems and Case Law

The judicial systems of Western democracies also arose over centuries, not based on theory but by the gradual introduction of sound practices, actual cases decided, and a growing fund of legal precepts. These were fashioned by practitioners whose careers were deeply involved with day-to-day legal cases. One such, John Cooke, brought the King of England before the court in 1649 and set the legal precedent that a King is not above the law. Cooke's legal brief was based on both biblical and common law principles, and on that basis, Charles I was found guilty and beheaded. After winning the verdict, Cooke declared that "The King's judges have pronounced sentence not only against one tyrant but against tyranny itself."[361] Cooke was the son of a poor Leicester tenant farmer who risked bankruptcy to send his son to Oxford and the Inns of Court. Isaac Cooke came from poor but healthy farming stock, all members of the Puritan community, "whose smallholdings sustained their families" that lived on the countryside for twenty miles around the town of Burbage.[362] This farmer raised the boy that changed history. Another example of how progress in freedom emerged from the very bottom, supported by a defiant faith and nourished by the aspirations of ordinary people for freedom and justice.

John Locke was a teenager at the time of Charles' execution and years later would write about the principles of freedom that John Cooke had firmly established and documented in the courtroom. A student would probably learn more about government, freedom, and the power of the monarch versus Parliament by reading Cooke's legal brief before the court and the counter arguments than by trying to digest the hundreds of pages of Locke's tortured attempt to philosophize and generalize on the notion of liberty and freedom.

This process of building legal precedents supportive of freedom and individual rights was buttressed by many legal scholars and practitioners who advocated specific applications and interpretations to the issues of their times. It is noteworthy that one of the greatest giants of American constitutional practices was a professor, who was never called a philosopher, a political scientist, or a great writer of abstract theory. Instead he was a "commentator" who "reported" on past and present legal developments, arguing for one interpretation or another. In the introduction to Edward S. Corwin's *American Constitutional History*, the editors celebrate Corwin's life work and compare it to "the giants of American constitutional commentators—with Kent, Story and Cooley."[363] These were the practical individuals who helped

John Cooke, a farmer's son, the ultimate commoner, provided the grist for John Locke's mill.

develop the law and precepts that underlay the American judicial system.

And like the good reporter he was, Corwin gave credit to the past practitioners. He referred in considerable detail to the earliest practices providing liberty regulated by a set of laws and a constitution as recorded in works by Sophocles, Demosthenes, and Aristotle. "The traceable American tradition, however . . . took its rise from a considerable time after Aristotle. Its source is Cicero's effort to render into juristic idiom the Stoic conception of a universal order, a cosmos, based on a divine reason which directs alike the movements of heavenly bodies and the conduct of good men."[364] Corwin traces these principles of freedom up through the Magna Carta and into the subsequent growth of common law: "As the range of classes and interests brought under its protection widened, its quality as higher law binding in some sense upon government in all its phases steadily strengthened until it became possible to look upon it in the fourteenth century as something very like a written constitution."[365] Such were the principles of freedom and personal rights for citizens that were established piecemeal over the centuries by the unsung heroes who carved out advances in freedom long before intellectuals came on the scene to write about it.

The Source of Bad Ideas

During the past few centuries, the learned and well educated elites in the West have regularly praised the importance of "ideas" in history. This is because they, unlike most common folk, have had the time and the abstract reasoning skills needed to construct and toss around complex ideas. It has set them apart and helped them gain control over the leading academies and institutions of the West. However, it is arguable that outside of the hard sciences, these practitioners of complex ideas have done more harm than good. As John W. Danford suggests, "In universities today, the 'hard sciences' still maintain a strong commitment to truth and objective standards, while it is the humanities that harbor the radical nihilists, the postmodernists who deny that there is such a thing as truth."[366] Bruce S. Thornton makes the same point: In referring to the prevailing vision of many educated elites, he observes that they are rarely confronted with demands for empirical evidence and that their ideas frequently "are the plagues of the mind, the intellectual diseases creating the new epidemic of false knowledge."[367]

Robert Conquest makes reference to Dostoevsky's description of a human type "whom any strong idea strikes all of a sudden and annihilates his will, sometimes forever." Conquest suggests that "The true idea addict is usually something roughly describable as an 'intellectual.' . . . Intelligence alone is far from being a defense against the plague."[368] Thus the problem is not with "ideas," per se, but with their use—especially their continued use even after their failings have been clearly established. Conquest starts his book, *Reflections on a Ravaged Century*, by referring to the extraordinary misery, repression, and killing by advanced nations during the latest century. He then asks, "How do we account for . . . the ideological frenzy of the twentieth century? How did these mental aberrations gain a purchase? Who were the Typhoid Marys who spread the infection?"[369]

We have seen in the wide panorama of history that it has been the intellectuals who eventually dominate successful democracies. Conquest points a finger at philosophers and Locke in particular: "The origin of the modern era's ideologies lay in John Locke's derivation of scholastic generalities from traditional English understandings of liberty, thus excessively rationalizing, and at the same time limiting, or in a sense desiccating, the more complex reality."[370] There are in fact much worse culprits among the philosophers than Locke, but Conquest here is echoing Voegelin's fundamental point that the so-called great philosophers, in addition to reporting past events, add on complex concepts of their own—concepts twice removed from reality, and frequently dangerous to any who follow them.

It has been this promotion of dangerous ideas that have quite rightly besmirched the reputation of intellectuals. In surveying the ideological carnage of the twentieth century, noted historian Clive

James has indicated that a lot of intellectuals often "get it wrong." Especially in the twentieth century, he points out, they got it wrong. But he also suggests that anti-intellectuals always get it wrong. Now any opinion in the humanities prefaced with an "always" is truly suspect, but more to the point, James' opinion reveals the common confusion over the term "intellectual." We have endeavored to point out throughout this book that there is nothing wrong with people of intellect, per se—they sometimes contribute great things to mankind's advances. Even those active in the soft-sciences, the commentators who produce no works of art or scientific discoveries, can still be highly useful when they remain objective and rational in their generalizations, and if they test their theories and summaries to evaluate their usefulness and accuracy. The intellectuals who almost always "get it wrong" are the ones who will never admit to error and pursue abstractions even after demonstrated failure. They rarely rely on or even refer to established principles because whatever has already happened is never good enough for them—they want to dream up new and better ways. It is their ideas that hurt, because, unfortunately, ideas don't have to be good to be influential.

Do Good Intentions Trump Results?

To ask the question is to give the answer—one would hope. And yet, there have been numerous intellectuals who supported the Russian communist experiment, and who have stated that they never regretted their involvement, in spite of admitted failure, because the intent was so pure—the goal so noble. This even though millions of innocents were tortured, starved, and killed in furtherance of that goal, and those who resisted were sent to the Gulags. Such an intellectual's continued belief and lack of remorse confirms that ideologies to them are just mental exercises, divorced from reality—mind games, enjoyed, as Bertrand Russell has claimed, merely for the intellectual exercise. They do not wish to comprehend the consequences! As Thomas Sowell has pointed out, for them, reality is optional.

It is useful to point out that the question of intent vs. results could never arise in the hard sciences. A researcher may have fine intentions when he attempts to create some new form of inexpensive energy, or the alchemist seeks to turn straw into gold—indeed that is the motivation for the investigation. But the researcher gets no credit unless his procedure works. Every goal, each experiment, every new hypothesis is tested. As the Nobel Laureate mathematician-physicist Richard Feynman wrote, "I have the advantage of having found out how hard it is to get to really know something, how careful you have to be about checking the experiments, how easy it is to make mistakes and fool yourself."[371]

Some attempts at discovery for the physical scientist may hold out greater promise to help mankind than other ongoing experiments, but they are all evaluated critically until the one that works is found. In the softer sciences, intellectuals seem to believe that their intentions are more important than the results. And many voters will quickly support a candidate who expresses noble and grand intentions with little regard to their plausibility. Incredibly, such people have come to judge political and social programs by their alleged intent. So the generalized question is: Should virtue be measured by the intent or the results. It is known that a corrupt man sometimes can do good things, and, in contrast, good people can do harm with the best intentions.

If we were to assume that people are honest, rational, and all-knowing, their stated intent would be good enough, because the good results would inevitably follow from the intention. And for those who assume that all human problems can be solved by some governmental action, the declared good intent might seem sufficient—they would believe that it simply required some new law or regulation to accomplish the stated purpose. Their optimism and benevolent outlook would lead them to be charitable and hope for the best. But, even when they go along with such hope, why don't more people see the error of policies that, over a period of years, even decades, fail to accomplish useful results commensurate with their cost? How do the intellectuals cover their tracks? We know that they can fool some of the people all the time, and all the people some of the time. Unfortunately, those twin "achievements" have been sufficient to maintain the failed policies that are dooming Western civilization. By blurring the distinction between established principles and untested ideas, the elites have made it easier to "sell" their pet ideologies to the public. The solution is to look first to principles and beware of ideas, ideologies, and abstract theories.

Chapter 13
Totalitarianism and Genocide

*Ideas that claimed to transcend all problems, but
were defective or delusive, devastated minds, and
movements, and whole countries, and looked like plausible
contenders for world supremacy. In fact, humanity has been
savaged and trampled by rogue ideologies.*
—Robert Conquest

IN THE PRECEDING CHAPTERS we looked at the reasons why European nations were unable to match America's rapid rise in prosperity during the past two centuries. Europe's leaders also failed at peace—they allowed recurring warfare to ravage the continent throughout the nineteenth and twentieth centuries. People have said, "Never again," but history has a way of repeating itself. There can be no lesson learned unless we understand why this carnage happened.

European warfare up to the eighteenth century had been primarily characterized as localized battles over national borders. However, in the more recent wars of the past two centuries, the conflicts escalated to continent-wide, even world-wide wars fueled by destructive ideologies that encouraged a ferocity and fanaticism rarely seen before. Genghis Khan, Alexander the Great, and Charlemagne had been ruthless conquerors of vast territories. But their subjugation of the conquered never reached the fearful level of terror witnessed under Nazism and Communism. A new element infected these viciously authoritarian movements: the "totalitarian temptation" common among intellectuals who pursue abstract blueprints of government, plans that always place themselves at the top, dictating their ideas on governance to a force-fed populace. Worse than the most extreme religious zealots they demanded total acceptance of their beliefs and believed themselves wholly justified in employing any ends to achieve their visions.

This was the horror of "pure reason" unalloyed by the soft voices of conscience. Albert Schweitzer, who devoted his life to saving lives, has spoken eloquently on this subject. He begins by condemning Descartes' philosophizing, which begins with the sentence loved by all intellectuals: "I think, therefore I am." Dr. Schweitzer's comment: "With this miserable, arbitrarily chosen beginning, it finds itself irrevocably committed on the road to the abstract. It never finds the door to ethics and it is caught like a prisoner in a dead world—and life—view. True philosophy must proceed from the most immediate and comprehensive fact of consciousness—'I am life that wills to live in the midst of life that wills to live.' This is not a subtly reasoned dogma. Day by day, hour by hour, I move in it. . . . Ethics, therefore consists in this: I feel a compulsion to extend to all the will-to-live around me the same reverence for life that I extend to my own. The fundamental principle of morality so necessary for thought is given here. It is good to maintain life and to promote life; it is evil to destroy life and to restrict life."[372]

Schweitzer was not afraid to say what was good and what was evil. And, he lived by his creed, often stopping to save earthworms stranded on a roadway, or to release insects trapped in a window. The elementary and universal conception of ethics that he elaborated was founded on his reverence for life. "Upon this principle his whole philosophy of civilization was based."[373] What a contrast to

Albert Sweitzer, a great intellect, practiced medicine, banished Descartes, revered life.

those European philosophers who praised the strong when they destroyed the weaklings—and they were talking about human beings!

The Age of Reason—
The Enlightenment Becomes Unenlightened

In the past few centuries, major European governments were able to feed off the momentum of the hard sciences and the flourishing commerce nurtured in earlier times. A number of small independent regions in Northern and Western Europe had replicated the successful structure of the Italian Renaissance city states. Those vibrant economies and the ones mushrooming in Holland and Great Britain were paralleled by the cities of the Hanseatic League, i.e., the free enterprise bastions that dotted the Baltic and North Sea coasts from Holland to Russia. The spirit of freedom and the wealth of these free trading populaces provided a permanent infusion of capitalist processes into the most remote regions of Northern Europe. Their enterprises generated an increased affluence, in turn leading to the expansion of the intellectual classes that came to dominate the universities and other leading institutions of these nations.

The resulting heady periods have been generally referred to as the Age of Reason in the seventeenth century and the Age of Enlightenment beginning in the eighteenth century. However, most of the reason applied and much of the enlightenment gained was associated with the physical sciences, technology, finance, and industrialization. In the soft sciences, the political leaders, philosophers, the diplomats, and academics played a less than exemplary or enlightened role.

Today's academics, by their concentration on the "great writers" of these past periods, have created the impression that where there were glorious achievements, they were produced by the writers. Nothing could be further from the truth. The writers produced only books, and while there was great and useful fiction, the political scientist and philosophers were merely reporting on events, or espousing radical and mostly destructive new ideas.

Eric Hobsbawm has written extensively on this period, noting that in the eighteenth century "commerce and manufacture flourished brilliantly. The most brilliantly successful of the eighteenth-century European states, Britain, plainly owed its power to its economic progress, and by the 1780s all continental governments with any pretence to a rational policy were consequently fostering economic growth, and especially industrial development, though with very varying success. . . . The conviction of the progress of human knowledge, rationality, wealth, civilization and control over nature" that we know as the Enlightenment "drew its strength primarily from the evident progress of production, trade, and the economic and scientific rationality believed to be associated inevitably with both. And its greatest champions . . . were those most directly involved in the tangible advances of the time: the mercantile circles and economically enlightened landlords, financiers, scientifically-minded economic and social administrators, the educated middle class, manufacturers and entrepreneurs. . . . Such men everywhere flocked into the lodges of Freemasonry, where class distinctions did not count and the ideology of the Enlightenment was propagated with a disinterested zeal."[374]

Thus, as we have seen in earlier chapters, the flowering of freedom and individual achievement was primarily the work of ordinary workers and scientists, not intellectuals, academics or great writers; and the aptitude and propensity for mechanical innovation had deep roots among the ordinary workers of Western Europe. Indeed, it was the well expressed demands for freedom of expression in Holland, Florence, and the German cities in the sixteenth century and the resulting achievement of business organizations—and a huge trading-marketing web across Europe, the Americas, and Asia—that enabled writers in the soft sciences to attempt summaries and commentaries concerning the ongoing progress.

The Legacy of the Philosophers

Advances during the sixteenth and seventeenth centuries that were made in the physical sciences had a remarkable effect on the soft-scientists. They reasoned that if they applied the same scientific processes to human and social affairs, they could remake the world. Their goal, however, was quite different from that of a Galileo or

Newton. Those men investigated the puzzles of the physical universe and sought to pass on their discoveries to fellow scientists and innovators to help control and harness the physical world for mankind's betterment. The soft-scientists sought to develop new laws and governing systems to control the general public, thereby fulfilling their fantasies of ideal systems and creating a role for themselves at the top where they would be free to experiment with their abstract theories.

Hitler was only ten-years-old when his intellectual countryman, Dr. A. Ploetz, writing for industrialist Krupp, suggested that at the birth of each child, a panel of doctors should judge whether it was fit to live, and if not, kill it. In 1905, Ploetz was involved in founding The Society for Racial Hygiene and argued that racial hygiene and eugenics were the same thing. In the 1920s in Germany, Karl Binding, a jurist, and Alfred Hoche, a psychiatrist, recommended euthanasia for the physically and mentally defective. In 1923, Dr. Lenz, professor of racial hygiene in Munich, stated that euthanasia should be part of any racial hygiene plan. In 1935, these "brilliant new ideas" of the elites were endorsed by Dr. Alexis Carrel, on the staff of the Rockefeller Institute, who proposed that criminals and the mentally ill should be put to death by suitable gases. His book, *Man, The Unknown*, was translated into nine languages. Then, in 1939, a deformed baby was born in Germany, and Hitler authorized a lethal injection. With that precedent, the categories of "unfit" people multiplied. The Holocaust had begun, carrying out the "ideas" spread by the elites from times before Hitler's birth.

The abstractions of German philosophers of the eighteenth and nineteenth centuries tended to promote atheism and urge an all-powerful state. These two amoral concepts have a natural affinity because Christianity, which elevates the sanctity of all human beings, constitutes a roadblock for tyranny. The idea that it is "good" for the strong to crush the weak doesn't normally sit well with practicing Christians. Unfortunately, when it came to crushing the Jewish population, even the German church leaders remained passive. Consequently, a large part of the population embraced their philosophers' other big idea: to "scientifically" examine racial differences and condemn all non-Aryan races. After a hundred years of promotion by the elites of the land, this idea became widely accepted, and filtered down to corrupt many otherwise decent folk. "Not only the churches and their leadership but also . . . virtually the entire German elite—intellectual, professional, religious, political, and military—embraced eliminationist anti-Semitism wholeheartedly as its own."[375]

Richard Wagner, the composer of majestic and triumphal music, excellent accompaniment to Hitler's blitzkrieg armored columns, spoke and wrote at length about Jews as being less than human: heinous criminals, terrestrial demons, the "plastic demon of the decay of humanity."[376] Wagner had learned from many teachers, all of them the product of a century of German academic "learning." Hitler's worst ravings of bile and hate merely repeated utterances by Germany's intellectuals and academics, who, like Hollywood scriptwriters, provided him with plenty of material.

Most students of history are familiar with British Prime Minister Neville Chamberlain's momentous meeting with Hitler in Munich in 1937, when Western leaders weakly remonstrated against Hitler's blitzkrieg invasions of neighboring nations. In accordance with their long-standing record of diplomatic failures, these leaders arranged a big conference and patiently explained that it was contrary to international law to invade, ravage, and enslave other countries. They had apparently not read Hitler's book, *Mein Kampf*, in which he had clearly adopted the teachings of German intellectuals and philosophers of the past 100 years: that there is no morality other than power. Armed with the radical nationalistic and racial ideas of Hegel and Nietzsche, Hitler was so fiercely belligerent that the other European leaders could only appease him, slink home, and watch numbly as he invaded one nation after another. What is less well known is that Neville Chamberlain's nephew, Houston Stewart Chamberlain, had lived in Germany for years, endorsing and ennobling the Nazi message of hate. He "was one of the first intellectuals in Germany to see a future for Hitler—and new opportunities for the Germans if they followed him."[377] This younger, "smarter" Chamberlain, a brilliant English intellectual, had adopted

Germany as his own country and was held in thrall by Hitlerian doctrines of power and might. He was fervently in sympathy with the totalitarian messages of Schopenhauer, Hegel, Fichte, and Nietzsche, the "great" German philosophers who favored the imposition of revered and all-powerful leaders over the common folk.

H. S. Chamberlain also worshipped the racial ideas of Wagner and the other leading intellectuals who spread this fanatical hatred aimed primarily at Jews. Many ordinary Germans, especially intellectuals and academics, adopted and supported the most inhuman ideas of cruelty and mass murder, which had now become "politically correct" in Germany. Hitler, a gifted politician, sensed this national predisposition to not only blame the Jews for the nation's weakness following World War I, but to regard them as sub-human. The German people were thus subjected to a triple blow made possible by the intellectuals: first, the long-standing socialist thinking behind Bismarck's welfare programs, which had since the prior century encouraged Germans to prefer safety to independence and freedom, and to venerate big government; second, the demagogic line preaching victimization, the notion that the Germans' economic problems were caused not by their leaders' foolhardy launching of the Great War, but wholly by the other countries their Emperor had attacked; third, the scapegoat of racism. Based on those three defective visions of reality, "an enormous number of ordinary, representative Germans became—and most of the rest of their fellow Germans were fit to be—Hitler's willing executioners."[378] In the seventy years since, too little has changed on the continent. The proposed EU constitution, 400 plus pages long, reflects not any desire to protect liberty or rights, but merely to enshrine the "right" to an income and the ever-greater encroachment of centrist bureaucracies.

The Growth of Totalitarianism, Concentration Camps, and Genocide

While Hitler was invading and occupying much of Europe during the 1930s, Japanese armies invaded and occupied much of China and Southeast Asia—the so-called Rape of China that resulted in an estimated thirty million deaths. The Chinese "died in military operations, for being guerrillas, for possessing some food, for being in the way, for being a girl, or just because a bored Japanese soldier wanted to have some fun. Entertainment included rape, dousing people with gasoline and lighting a match, forcing sons to rape mothers, shoving sticks of dynamite up girls' vaginas to blow them up, cutting fetuses out of pregnant wombs, and chopping off countless heads."[379] Western leaders protested; in 1937 the League of Nations held meetings to denounce the violence and aggression. But Japanese subjugation of much of Asia and Indochina continued for several more years. As the United Nations would in later years, the League stood by helplessly, unable to stop the carnage. Finally, the encircling Yanks, prepared to invade the Japanese homeland, and showing their determination and power with two nuclear bombs, succeeded in ending the carnage.

Germany committed similar aggressive acts, attacking one country after another. One of their first mass atrocities occurred in Spain, where they were allied with Fascist forces seeking to overthrow the new born republic. This antagonism reached its horrible conclusion in Guernika, the traditional meeting place for the assembly of citizens that led the Basque part of the nation. In spite of attempts at negotiation, "the only possible solution, according to Franco, was the complete annihilation of the Basque nationalists." But like all those who had tried to conquer the Basques, Franco's efforts failed. The German officers Hitler had dispatched to help Franco took over the campaign. "Colonel Wolfram von Richthofen, cousin of the World War I ace known as 'the Red Baron' . . . explained to the Spanish how aircraft could be used to destroy the morale of the enemy before a ground assault."[380] They agreed that no attempt would be made to spare civilians.

The assailants had all the latest planes, artillery, and armored units, while the Basques had only revolvers, rifles, and grenades. The Nazi forces advanced slowly, destroying town after town by aerial bombardment, after which advancing armored forces killed and leveled all before them. Still it went slowly, until finally, as they approached Guernika, the attackers chose a market day—Monday, April 26, 1937, at 4:40 P.M., when the center of town was full of peasants selling their crops—to unleash "a sort of deadly air show, displaying all that was new in German and Italian attack aircraft. . . . The bombers dropped an unusual payload, splinter and incendiary bombs, a cocktail of shrapnel and flame personally selected by Richthofen for maximum destruction to buildings. As people fled, the fighters came in low and chased them down with heavy caliber machine guns."[381]

At the 1937 Paris World's Fair in the Spanish Pavilion, Pablo Picasso's famous mural displayed the Guernica bombing. This painting has ever since stood as a symbol of the horror of war. But it should also be viewed as a symbol of lost opportunity and the dangers that come from intellectuals, for in 1937, Hitler was just getting started. Though his deeds and words had made clear his intentions, no nation stepped forward to stop him. And so the horrors of Guernica were repeated across Europe hundreds of times over, inspired by the European intellectuals who had originated Hitler's every hateful utterance. The mural tells us: "Never underestimate the power of the academics who control the minds of your children." It also tells us: "War is horrible, but there will always be conflict, and clear distinctions and judgments must be made, and blame correctly assigned." It serves as an example of what happens when the weak-hearted fail to promptly subdue vicious aggressors. Such weak hearts were in the streets in force the very month the Basques were being strafed by machine guns; "one million American college students had shut down campuses across the country in the fourth annual 'peace strike' as they recited the American version of the Oxford antiwar oath: 'I refuse to support the Government of the United States in any war it may conduct.'"[382] As the saying goes, students must be liberals if they have

> *Totalitarian ideologies are adopted because they rationalize resentment. . . . It is not the truth of Marxism that explains the willingness of intellectuals to believe it, but the power that it confers on intellectuals, in their attempts to control the world.*
>
> —Roger Scruton

any heart; but in another ten years must be conservatives if they have any brains. A braver spirit was displayed by the Basques themselves, who withdrew into their country villages and spent the next eight years of wartime ferrying refugees across their mountain strongholds and through their ports to safety.

Despite the anti-war movements, the continued aggression of the Axis powers, culminating in the attack on Pearl Harbor, swayed public opinion sufficiently to support President Roosevelt's decision to enter the war. The resulting American military actions freed the European nations from foreign domination, as well as Singapore, Malaysia, Taiwan, Thailand and a host of other occupied lands. The victory also created free democratic systems and more open economies in Germany and Japan, successfully imposed by occupying American forces intent on "nation building" in two societies where democratic rule was virtually unknown.

Secular Utopias and Other Dreams

The institutionalized inhumanity in Germany, Russia, and Japan in the 1930s and 1940s illustrates the depravity that can spread throughout a society and erase centuries of civilizing advances. The governance of these three nations was no better than Idi Amin's gruesome rule of Uganda thirty years later. None had had any significant experience with democratic or individualistic traditions. They lacked the institutionalized habits and values that buttress faith in self-reliance and personal responsibility and that respect the sanctity of every human life—habits and values that informed the dominant ethical norms of the few successful Western nations.

Each of these temporarily degenerated countries also shared a common animosity toward Christianity, and, for that matter, denied the existence of any moral or religious codes that called for the dignity and humane treatment of individuals. And in each case, the indoctrination of hate and viciousness flowed from the top—from the leaders, the elites of the land—never from the common people at the bottom. The horrors came solely from the faulty vision of their intellectual leaders and great philosophers, a vision that was quickly adopted by the academics and political leaders. Their dreams of building secular societies devoid of moral truths could only end in a nightmare for the whole world.

A common defense by those who cooperated with their leaders' demonic policies is that they were ordered to do it. This defense may suffice for minor evils, but one might expect revulsion from any human ordered to support and execute the heinous mass crimes on the scale practiced by Hitler, Mao, Hirohito, and Stalin. There are always a few bad apples in any population, but it required many thousands of active participants to operate the gulags and extermination camps of World War II. In comparison, the American military has a regular load of about three hundred courts-martial in process at all times to punish those who go beyond accepted rules of engagement— out of a couple million total personnel in the armed forces—a more law abiding ratio than found in the general population. There were no such courts-martial for the Germans and Russians who beat the inmates, drove them like beasts into cattle cars, and who ultimately dropped the poison gas crystals though the air vents and stripped the gold fillings from a million dead bodies.

How can one explain the extent that ordinary Europeans accepted and carried out atrocities on such a widespread scale? What forces within their societies led them to such deeds? Leonard Peikoff has argued that it is the intellectuals who lead societies, modify customs, and choose a country's direction. In established successful societies, they usurp control over the leading institutions and gradually influence all those in their societies with their ideas, theories, and concepts that Peikoff describes as exercises in "unreason." When generations of students have been exposed to their abstract visions, the new generation loses the ability to apply practical common sense. "In a population taught to think rationally, [Hitler] would have had no chance."383

By contrast, the common men and women who built the stepping stones to progress in certain laboratory societies were largely free from aristocracies and intellectuals and were united by certain enabling beliefs, customs, and cultural mores that reinforced their initiative and effort. Their teachers and clergy emphasized hard work, fair play, consideration for others, and useful effort aimed at bettering society and their children's well-being. The nurturing process for Japanese and German youth under the dictators of the 1930s taught hate, violence, and unspeakable cruelty. Similarly, hatred is emphasized in many of today's Islamic schools, where children are led in anti-Western chants about the Great Satan and the need to destroy the infidels. Such "students" become suicide bombers that want to kill innocent civilians. Similar conditioning made the children in Japan, Germany, and Russia willing agents who would carry out the twisted dreams of their leaders.

In describing the ominous parallels between Nazi Germany and modern America, Peikoff writes that the main source of unreason "is not the churches, but the universities. Virtually every department in the humanities and social sciences today openly attacks reason and glorifies irrationality. In philosophy, for example, they teach that reasoning is an arbitrary game divorced from reality. In psychology, one school (the behaviorist) says that man has no mind, while another (the Freudian) says that the mind is really run by irrational drives. Our universities are the real source of irrationalism in this country and of the idea of self-sacrifice for the community and of the push for ever bigger government; in other words, the sources of all the central ideas of Nazism."[384] And these ideas, whether we speak of the German philosophers' glorification of power or the Marx-Lenin-Mao-Pol Pot style of belief in a secular utopia under communism, were all simply attempts at fulfilling abstractions of intellectuals.

Eric Blair has written that the notions of these modern thinkers were not new. They endorsed the ancient attempt by a few with centralized power to control the many. Like all such attempts at coercion, "their consistent effect was to limit the arena of ideas. . . . If this was enlightenment, it was an Orwellian one, a true nirvana of extincted individual consciousness and oblivion to external reality. But then, that's just where Winston ends up at the end of 1984, when he has won the victory over himself so that he may love Big Brother. That is how he now censors himself to think (or rather, not) what Big Brother wants, automatically."[385]

The Age of Enlightenment

It is worth comparing what was happening during the Enlightenment in the American colonies with what was happening in Europe. Some of the main figures of the European enlightenment were Descartes, Pascal, Bayle, Montesquieu, Voltaire, Diderot, Hume, Vico, and Rousseau. These soft-science philosophers tried to emulate the great physical scientists like Galileo and Newton, by applying reason to their social theories. They tended to argue for rights for citizens, but not "for a radical transformation of society. All of them, like Voltaire, defended enlightened absolutism."[386] They wrote vast tracts on their ideas concerning social and political matters, but rarely spelled out the full needs of freedom that were to be carved out by the Founders of the American Republic.

Meanwhile each American colony was operating under a state constitution and elected assembly, overseen by an appointed governor/administrator. The colonists drafted simple pamphlets protesting the oppressive regulation imposed by the British Parliament and monarchy. They revolted and established a new free republic. Its leading exponents spent years as the American ambassadors in London and Paris during the last decades of the eighteenth century. They translated and explained the Constitution, to the declared admiration of the European intellectuals. And yet none of those successful governing practices were adopted in a single European nation. Instead, The French Revolution became an orgy of excess, where reason was lost, and the Reign of Terror negated the very objectives of the revolution. Then Napoleon inaugurated 150 years of warfare that dehumanized civilization in Europe during the nineteenth and twentieth centuries. It is typical of academics that they have maintained the reputation of the European leaders, philosophers, and diplomats who in fact accomplished so little to maintain the well-being of their people.

Kenneth L. Grasso has written an excellent article about "the intellectual framework" that Enlightenment thinkers constructed to summarize the institutions of freedom and individual rights that had already been instrumental in making their birthplaces part of the modern world. He suggests that this intellectualized framework actually unraveled the foundations of European progress in three ways. One group of great thinkers argued for increased power for central governments to engineer progress; a second group diverged radically to support totalitarian extremes as seen in many of the German writers and academics; the third group pursued theories fostering an extreme search for unlimited personal freedom.

This third approach results in the "rejection of the possibility of an objective order of truth and goodness, towards the view that 'truth' is simply what the individual happens to believe, and the 'good' is merely what one happens to prefer."[387] This exaggerated form of "freedom" goes beyond the individual's desire to live and work in an established benign society governed by certain rules of conduct. Instead, it provides a Platonic carte blanche to "do as one will." On the other hand, the first two groups with their penchant for central management destroy freedom. The wiser, more practical Americans, on the other hand, in drafting their Constitution chose to create a careful balance between centralized governmental power versus individual freedom—and also wisely chose to not even consider that middle idea about following supermen and totalitarian extremes.

The superiority of the American achievement lies in it having emerged, fine-tuned by argument and compromise, out of intense negotiations among practical men who looked to ancient principles and historical examples of actual governments for guidance. Quite differently, the three "unraveled" theoretical conclusions that Grasso deplores, emerged from the armchair musings of abstract Enlightenment thinkers.

That three-way divergence among the intellectual theorists is telling for another reason: Most people would like to think that for most problems there is one best solution—possibly, a couple reasonable ones. But intellectuals rarely agree with each other. Most of their writings are aimed at disputing each other's writings. Now, it may not follow that therefore only one intellectual at any point in time can be "right," and all the others must be wrong, but their frequently wide disparity of opinions should warn the person of average intellect that a large percentage of those widely varying opinions have to be of dubious value.

Historian Christopher Dawson laments how Enlightenment thinkers furthered the secularization of Europe: "History has shown that no true solution is to be found in the direction which the eighteenth-century Enlightenment took, i.e., by constructing a purely rational philosophy of religion based on the abstract generalities that are common to all forms of religion. For deism is nothing but the ghost of religion which haunts the grave of dead faith and lost hope."[388] We have argued that Christianity, as an independent source of authority, had inoculated Europeans against any monolithic control by their monarchs. One could also argue that Christianity similarly protects modern man from his own egoism, effectively for most common people, but not sufficiently for those who actually believe that their pure reason can fashion a perfect world.

Grasso refers to "The ascendancy of what Sandel has termed the liberalism of the unencumbered self."[389] Thus, intellectuals, who customarily take good ideas and push them to ridiculous limits, were soon espousing the notion that individuals should be so independent as to be unbound by any moral and ethical rules at all. "By producing an intellectual universe in which everything is permitted, it leaves liberalism's commitment to the rights and dignity of the person suspended precariously over a moral and metaphysical abyss."[390] Under the exaggerated liberalism of Enlightenment thinking freedom has mutated into "What Murray terms 'the ancient idolatrous error of the self-sufficient man, who regards himself as the sole architect of his own freedom, single author of the values that govern his life, ultimate judge of right and wrong, true and false.'"[391]

The moral relativity that emerges from this exaggerated ideal of unlimited personal freedom is an unavoidable companion to atheism, which seeks to remove the limits and restrictions imposed by Christianity. Those limits did not prevent the giants of the Renaissance from great discovery and innovation. In fact, the ethical rules inherent in Judeo-Christian heritage had directed and sustained most of the institutions and individual conduct that led to the great advances in mankind's well-being long before the Enlightenment philosophers came in and distorted both the foundation and means that enabled freedom to spread throughout much of the western world.

The conceit of Enlightenment philosophers was that they sought solutions not from reality, not from historical case studies—but from their own intellectual abstractions. They had the arrogance to seek, not modest improvements, but wholly new directions: "When Cordorcet sets himself to write a complete history of the progress of humanity, he condemns almost every institution which the societies of the past had evolved, and attaches supreme importance to the progress of intellectual enlightenment in the mind of the individual. As pure taste could create the perfect work of art, so pure reason would construct a perfect society. . . . This absolutism of method was as characteristic of the nature worship of Rousseau, as it was of the rationalism of the champions of progress, and both these currents united in the French Revolution in an attempt to make a clean sweep of the past and to construct a perfect society on the foundations of pure doctrine.[392]

Grasso concludes that "the modern quest for freedom is in crisis; that much of the responsibility for this crisis rests with the ideology through which the modern West has tended to conceptualize this quest; and that Dawson is correct that Enlightenment liberalism has proven itself 'incapable of maintaining' its noblest ideals and aspirations 'by its own inherent resources'—that just as it 'did not create these moral ideals, so, too, it cannot preserve them.'"[393]

In summary, it can be suggested that the Enlightenment, at least in the areas of philosophy and the soft sciences, did more harm than good. Piggy-backing on the continuing progress of the hard scientists and businesses, the philosophers claimed credit for what they had not produced—the rapidly increasing freedom and prosperity that dated from the work of the Dutch, Scots, and English in the 1600s, and to the many stepping stones even before that. And, to the extent their theories led to the advancement of totalitarianism, centrism, social engineering, and the disintegration of constraining moral codes, they did great harm.

The intellectuals, in other words, may have meant well—but their reporting was inaccurate, their digressions proved destructive, and they were oblivious that as they wrote, American farmers and merchants were creating a more perfect union, based more on the scribblings of mere pamphleteers than on their weighty tomes. One of the failings of almost all academics and scholars during the past 200 years is their preoccupation with those continental European philosophers, mostly French and German, who generally did such a poor job of reporting the progress of freedom, sound governmental structures, and the sources of prosperity. They rarely looked to the demonstrated American success during the eighteenth and nineteenth centuries in fashioning the freest and most prosperous society in the world. And they rarely even acknowledge the American and British pamphleteers, preachers, and newspaper contributors who were more clearly enunciating long-established principles of political and economic freedom.

In previous chapters we have cited the works of Bernard Bailyn, who details the major impact of these lesser mortals, whose writings did not rise to the academic standards of the deepest thinkers. There is no need for an academic to interpret the works of Thomas Paine, Cato, John Trenchard, Sam Adams, Thomas Gordon, John Dickinson, or Algernon Sidney. These individuals laid out the case for liberty and freedom in simple language, producing succinct essays that were widely read by ordinary people. These numerous popularizers of freedom were the talk radio of their day. They appealed directly to the common people and championed the Rights of Man in stirring words that directly influenced events. "The People, when they are not misled or corrupted, generally make a sound Judgment of Things. They have natural Qualifications equal to those of their Superiors; and there is oftener found a great Genius carrying a Pitchfork, than carrying a White Staff."[394]

In that last sentence, Cato attests to this book's thesis that common people are often wiser than their so-called superiors. However, he also made our point about why the origin of freedom occurred in locales unburdened by intellectuals: "Besides, there are not such mighty Talents requisite for Government, as some, who pretend to them without possessing them, would make us believe: Honest Affections, and common Qualifications are sufficient; and the Administration has been always best executed, and the Publick Liberty best preserved, near the Origin and Rise of States, when plain Honesty and common Sense alone governed the public Affairs, and the Morals of Men."[395]

Unfortunately, in nineteenth-century Europe, plain honesty and common sense were pushed aside by the academicians and philosophers that came to dominate the schools and institutions of the continent. The English and American libertarians were ignored in favor of more elaborate and passionate ideologies of extremist intellectual thought.

In Communist Russia, Nazi Germany, and Imperial Japan, on all sides of the world, the ideas of the leaders, intellectuals, academics, and philosophers enabled the ruthless, expansionist, and destructive forces that so set back the forces of liberty. They were not working for a known reality, but seeking to fulfill a fantasy constructed from theory. Relying on the ideas of Marx and Lenin, communist tyranny held sway in Russia, where Stalin's regime was responsible for the murder of millions of its own citizens and those of the neighboring nations it seized and occupied.

The same century saw the end of the European hegemony as the torch of individualism and liberty passed to the United States. Given this historical record, how can anyone still look to Europe for guidance on international affairs, politics, economics, or judicial and legal wisdom?

Chapter 14
The Problems of Mature Societies

> *Beware intellectuals . . . (they) follow certain regular patterns of behavior. . . . That is what makes them, en masse, so dangerous, for it enables them to create climates of opinion and prevailing orthodoxies, which themselves often generate irrational and destructive courses of action.*
>
> —Paul Johnson

SOME OF THE FREEST NATIONS in history have gradually become victims of their own liberality, with license overtaking liberty, and then, over-burdened by excessive populist policies, they end in mob rule and chaos. It is common place to think of all this as a recurring pattern—the rise and fall of nations. When final collapse comes, the failing societies usually fade into oblivion; but not always. "Such intellectual constructs are too neat," Tony Blankley reminds us. "They are often also historically contradicted. China has repeatedly emerged from decadence back to youthful vigor, as she is doing currently."[396] China's current economic revival coincides with its adoption on the mainland of some of the business freedoms allowed under Hong Kong's capitalist system. Currently, the government is giving its peasants formal deeds to their property. Nothing in human affairs is predetermined. Declines can be reversed—provided enough people make the right decisions and act on them.

America's success has persisted for almost four hundred years, a span comparable to that of Greek and Roman society at their height. The question may well be asked whether America's ascension to an all-time peak of prosperity and comfort will now be reversed, with the nation relegated to a peripheral role in the world—or are new peaks yet to come? And is Europe on the edge of an even more dire precipice?

The answers reside in the citizens of each nation—whether they still exercise an active, common-sense approach to problem-solving, still have the independence, self-reliance, and grit required to maintain freedom. After a society reaches maturity, its sheer size and affluence may create added burdens and less commitment. Unless the people remain vigilant, new ideas and faulty visions can take-over and lead to decline. Survival will not be decided by natural resources or the environment. Barring a meteor strike, it will not be decided by climate or luck. Just as all past progress was achieved by individuals at the bottom, so the future vigor of society can flow only from the actions and beliefs of those ordinary citizens who make the system work. Are they self-reliant, or do they believe that the world—i.e., their government—owes them a living? As Joseph Johnston put it, "society's attitude toward the relation between man and state is more important than any set of constitutional or political principles. . . . [T]he task is hopeless if the preferred relation is one of gratification and dependence."[397]

America's extraordinary success was built on the fierce self-confidence of each individual that confronted the wilderness and built homes, businesses, and lives for themselves and their families. They were beholden to no one. That will not be true of an America in which the ideologies of excess compassion, moral relativity, and victimology finally overcome the independent American spirit. Whether the problems of maturing societies can be resolved without precipitating the decline of those societies depends on whether the attempted solutions come from the wisdom of the crowd, or from an elite trying to force-feed ideological cures from above.

In *The Wisdom of Crowds*, James Surowiecki prolifically illustrates the seemingly paradoxical thesis that masses of half-informed people usually not only make wise choices, but wiser choices than those of the experts. He cites how a rural incident alerted statisticians to the principle. At a country fair passers-by were offered the chance to guess the weight of a large ox. The estimates of cattle dealers and farmers were separated from those of the general public. In spite of their unfamiliarity with farm animals, the average of the laymen's guesses was considerably closer to the actual weight of the ox than the average of the guesses made by those with expertise. This wisdom goes beyond mere weights and measures: Many writers allude to Jefferson's comment two hundred years ago: "State a moral case to a plowman and a professor," the founding father wrote. "The former will decide it as well and often better than the latter, because he has not been led astray by artificial rules."

But crowds behave intelligently only if the individuals composing them act independently. In cases where a few "leaders" take control and the public apathetically follows, the opportunity for the wisdom of the crowd to be expressed is wasted. When the public has been brainwashed or numbed into conformity, or their thinking channeled by political correctness, then they, too, like the experts and intellectuals, will be "led astray by artificial rules." Such a decline in the nature of its citizenry is the curse of mature societies.

Charles E. Tomlinson has developed the unique argument that this decline in rational thinking is primarily caused by people being subjected to too many "fuzzies," the obscure pronouncements of intellectuals. He explains that these "large balls of fluff" can be multi-layered, but "never say anything outright." The most obscure fuzzies, which are by design subject to a great number of interpretations, frequently grow to immense size, and to be understood by the general public, these require repeated explanations from so-called experts.[398] If too many people waste time trying to unravel them, they won't have time to work, and their society will collapse.

Don't laugh—there is a larger kernel of truth in Tomlinson's book than in much of what passes as today's intellectual thought. The following sections examine the ways citizens can be led astray by the faulty and fuzzy thinking of their elites.

The Temptations of Big Government

A successful democracy requires involved and independent citizens. It is more important that these citizens possess common sense and simple logic than an extensive college education. The laboratories of history—from Phoenicia to Greece, Florence, Holland, England, Scotland, and America—show how the common man, grappling with the realities of everyday life, built the mechanisms that enabled freedom to prevail. Philosophers and economists came later and sought to explain what the ordinary man had accomplished. They often failed. Because they were not involved in the building, they could not understand the mechanics—and many of their interpretations, laced with suggestions on how the government must do something to "make things better," have done more harm than good. Such prescriptions are the stock in trade of intellectuals, experts, consultants, and others who haven't actually participated in building a society but only swoop in after the fact to criticize and foster decline.

Thomas Sowell writes about the growing gap between firsthand knowledge and decision-making, a deficiency that arises with the expanding influence of intellectuals who rely on an abstract vision of what ought to be rather than on the practical experience of those who created the modern world. Ancient Rome was afflicted with the same syndrome: "Behind the self-weakening of Rome lay forces similar to those at work today in the United States and in the Western world at large: internal divisiveness and demoralization, rising welfare expenditures, a growing and stifling bureaucracy—and a rising political influence of intellectuals."[399] He affirms that "The characteristics of the intellectual vision are strikingly similar to the characteristics of totalitarian ideology. . . . It is consistent with this that intellectuals have supported and indeed spearheaded the movement toward a centralization of power in democratic nations. . . ."[400]

Sowell deplores the waste and inefficiency that results from this ascendancy of costly and ineffective ideas but goes on to expose a much larger and more destructive effect—the demoralization of a society. "No one supplies this demoralization more constantly or effectively than intellectuals. Again, this is not, historically, a new role for intellectuals. The intellectuals' vision has long taken precedence over any tangible reality. . . . If the social visions behind the French Revolution required the execution of tens of thousands of human beings . . . so be it. If the vision of proletarian communism or German racial purity required that millions be slain, so be it. Against this background, there is hardly any reason for surprise if current visions of 'social justice' do not moderate to accommodate military necessity, or if campaigns to discredit rival elites like businessmen or the military are so all-out that the consequences are the demoralization of a whole civilization and a weakening of the will to defend it."[401] This usurpation of power by an elite lies at the heart of the West's current weakness. Although only the common man has the firsthand knowledge of how things actually work, the intellectuals, experts, and pundits—all those who rely on ideology over reality—have increasingly interfered with his conduct of affairs.

Fareed Zakaria notes that democracy is a term with many meanings, can serve both good and bad ends, and cannot by itself ensure good government. What is necessary is "constitutional liberalism," i.e., "the tradition, deep in Western history, that seeks to protect an individual's autonomy and dignity against coercion, whatever the source—state, church or society."[402] He stresses the fact that democracy, which has to do with the mechanics for selecting government, free elections, and a wide enfranchised base, can give everyone a say in who governs them. But constitutional liberalism establishes the proper goals for the resulting government. Those who established the American constitution sought to limit those goals, to confine the role of government to two enabling functions: the protective and the adjudicative.

What happens when a society and government go aggressively beyond these two enabling functions to expand so-called "positive rights"? First, the justice of rewarding effort and performance is violated, and motivation reduced. Second, the administrative functions of assistance and regulatory programs add so many constraints on freedom that they reverse or partially negate the enabling characteristics of a healthy society. Zakaria calls for "self-control, for a restoration of balance between democracy and liberty."[403] But restraint will not come from state and national legislatures as they are currently operating. The elected and appointed officials have come under the virtual control of special interest groups and lobbyists, who can contribute significantly more than the individual voter to re-election efforts.

Joe Scarborough served in Congress and sheds light on this problem. His insights reveal that any new central planning project of the intelligentsia is, by its very nature, welcomed by every member of the governmental bureaucracy—they are all in league to maximize their self interest by expanding the national government. He points out that presidents, senators, and congressmen do not run the country. Instead there is a permanent establishment of "Fat White Pink Boys" whose one goal is to build their own empire. These career bureaucrats "populate the ranks of all congressional staff, D.C. lobbying firms, bureaucratic agencies, congressional committees, political consulting firms, White House cubicles, and just about every other desk at national party headquarters."[404] Scarborough testifies that these professional hangers-on are motivated primarily by their desire to keep their cushy jobs by expanding the scope of governmental operations. They undermine any reformer's efforts to reduce the waste and inefficiency in government. Allied with most members of Congress, these supporting staffs create an impassable log jam for any newly elected maverick seeking to end the trillion dollar back-scratching schemes that bloat congressional appropriations budgets.

Scarborough's book, based on his experience in Congress, details the existing process that allows unjustified subsidies to farmers, corporations, unions, and a host of other special interest groups. He suggests that all reform movements are doomed to fail from the start because of the way that lobbyists and bureaucrats have tied themselves in with elected representatives.[405] He reveals a world of unbelievable selfishness and vindictiveness at the center of modern American government. The hungry denizens of official Washington leap at every new do-good program advanced by big-government liberals because it increases their pay rate and job security. Thus, there is a huge and growing alliance of people with one end in mind—growing the federal bureaucracy. It isn't just the intellectuals but also all those who benefit from their utopian agendas.

Fareed Zakaria was cited above for his warning that such governmental growth, and its increasing control by elite organizations, carries the danger of creeping fascism. The dilemma for mature success-ful nations is that their new elites succumb to a totalitarian temptation and seek to augment their control over the country's destiny by expanding the scope of governmental activities. However, there is a more prosaic reason for this cancerous growth in government, this unusual alignment of interests that work against good government: The very structure of how it all works dictates the undesirable results we observe. Changing the structure and incentives of those involved might reduce the evils that the current system encourages. When Maurice McTigue described his successful reforms in New Zealand, he suggested that such major changes were easier to adopt under their Parliamentary system of government than they would be under the rules that govern our congressional operations. That is an indication of how formidable is the essential task ahead.

Rights Inflation

> *History makes it plain that unless restrained, government proliferates to a point where its cost bankrupts the people at the same time it robs them of their freedom."*
>
> —Ronald Reagan

Alan Dershowitz notes that the Bill of Rights evolved in response to actual experiences with injustice. They were aimed toward "acknowledged wrongs rather than on idealized perfection. . . . Rights come from human experience, particularly experience with injustice." Such rights were built "from the bottom up, not the top down," and were not based on the teachings of abstract philosophy.[406]

Many educated people have been misled to actually believe that the American patriots operated from a blueprint of ideas that philosophers had bequeathed them, so it is refreshing to read Dershowitz's explanation that their creation arose from actual experience, not abstract philosophy. Sowell makes the same point in *Knowledge and Decisions* when he contrasts the French revolution with the American thinking of late eighteenth century—the carnage and ultimate failure of the former arose from the very fact that it "was based on abstract speculation on the nature of man by intellectuals, and on the potentiality of government as a means of human improvement. The American

Revolution was based on historical experience of man as he is and has been, and on the shortcomings and dangers of government as actually observed. . . . Their constantly reiterated references were to 'experience, the least fallible guide of human opinions,' to 'the accumulated experience of the ages,' . . . to 'the popular governments of antiquity,' and the history, economics and geography of contemporary European nations."[407] By such references to *The Federalist Papers*, Sowell underscores the point made repeatedly in this book that the American system of government was based, not on theories or "ideas," but on over two thousand years of historical case studies, taking the best features and avoiding the worst features of hundreds of representative governments.

Specific rights were added to the Constitution to prohibit the government from performing certain actions that history had shown to be oppressive and unjust. Thus these Bills of Right were "negative" rights—the government could not seize a person's private property, invade his home, hold him in jail for an extended time without trial, nor try him without letting him face his accuser. These shalt-nots—negative because they designated what the government could not do—served to limit governmental power.

The citizens of those days wanted government to provide an army, courts, roads, and basic infrastructure, but otherwise to leave them alone. Indeed, the three-thousand-year struggle for freedom had been to achieve safety without oppression—freedom from governmental injustice and restrictions while still gaining the enabling functions of an honest, moral, and lean central government. With the American Constitution and Bill of Rights guaranteeing this freedom, the citizens could work freely and achieve prosperity. Americans were soon renowned for their self-reliance and independence of spirit.

There have been many adjustments made in American government over the past 100 years. As affluence grew, the size of the government grew, and it now resembles a populist democracy more than a federal republic. The growth of so-called positive rights has eroded freedom from big government. Restrictions and regulations as well as higher taxes are the price of all government programs. By their very nature, expanded government and increased handouts can only create shriller demands, more waste, and increased corruption. When half the electorate depends on a government dole or subsidy or for their very employment, can they truly make a rational choice between a fiscally prudent candidate and a tax-and-spend politician? When the current expansion of positive rights reaches the point at which 51 percent of the electorate is "taking" from government and only 49 percent are producing the wealth that supports government programs, a slippery slope will have become an avalanche. In a culture dominated by the quest for special favors, eventually a majority of voters will simply elect those politicians who promise the most goodies. This process has been accelerating, fueled by the activists and academics who favor centralized controls and who see no end to the opportunity for government solutions. The belief that every condition of life can be improved by an activist central government is the result of a vision of man and society that contradicts everything understood by the framers. It reflects the utopian dreams that lay at the heart of the failed communist experiment, but which are still cherished by Western intellectuals.

"Positive rights" give politicians, and the "Fat, White Pink Boys" that Scarborough castigates, something to do—divvy up the pie—and allow them to claim that they are helping the sick, the infirm, the aged. In fact, they are parceling out special favors to selected beneficiaries, with special consideration given to large donors and vote-getters. Of course, they claim credit for these expensive programs with grandiose talk of wonderful intentions. But when their legal staffs are through drafting them, they turn out to be mostly pork and handouts for selected groups. Promoted as a means to help those most in need, the programs actually serve those most influential, such as corporations, teachers' lobbies, blocs of minorities, environmentalists, select farming interests, social workers, government employees, and retired people to name a few of dozens of powerful lobbies each seeking to get ahead of the other.

Relatively little goes to the working poor. Yet this group, even when paying no federal income taxes, lose up to a quarter of their pay in payroll taxes, state income taxes, sales taxes, and taxes on their homes and personal property. Thus no one can escape subsidizing the largesse of the affluent experts and intellectuals who work incessantly to expand the scope and cost of governmental programs.

David Shipler, author of *The Working Poor*, admits that it's tough to find someone in this country whose poverty "is not somehow related to his or her unwise behavior—to drop out of school, to have a baby out of wedlock, to do drugs, to be chronically late to work."[408] He thus affirms Dr. Theodore Dalrymple's argument that it is the notions of intellectuals that perniciously encourage the dysfunctional habits of those at the bottom. By subsidizing illegitimacy with welfare payments, the liberal Left's policies helped create the surge in fatherless children. In many urban areas, more than half the children are illegitimate. As Larry Elder writes, "In 1960, out-of-wedlock births accounted for 2 percent of white births and 22 percent of black births. By 1994 the rates had soared to 25 and 70 percent, respectively. . . . Women learned they could 'marry the government,' making a fifth wheel out of the biological fathers of their children. . . . Lyndon Johnson's well-intentioned War on Poverty created the greatest uptick of illegitimacy in America's history. This huge number of children without involved fathers underlies nearly every major problem in America—bad schools, crime, unemployment."[409]

A perverse effect of these trends is that a larger and larger proportion of American children are raised in "families" with the least ability to nurture and discipline them. So welfare advocates invent still more positive "rights" as the solution: public day care and head start programs to undo the harm done by previously endowed "rights." Few of these programs were ever requested by the common men and women. Instead, they were designed by the self-appointed "champions of the poor" and reflect their unrealistic vision of welfare programs that have so many unintended but dire consequences.

Bypassing the Voters

It is a hallmark of American politics to criticize special interests, the groups that lobby for special favors. The concern is healthy but has been largely unsuccessful. Today the elected representatives and appointed bureaucrats in America are more beholden to special interest groups than ever before. Every politician has become dependent on contributions from these groups. Both the politicians and lobbyists now employ large staffs of lawyers to make sure they successfully evade the ever-changing rules, rules deliberately designed with loopholes to keep the cash and favors flowing. The influence of these shadowy groups exerts great influence on the government, bypassing the voters, and therefore represents a perversion of democracy.

We have examined some of the societies where freedom developed; they were able to flourish because their governments tended to provide only protective and adjudicative functions. There were few organized groups or lobbyists seeking subsidies or attempting to wreak major cultural changes. However, representative governments have always tended to expand the scope of their activity, and it has generally been to the elected official's advantage to offer more and more benefits to his supporters. The average citizen goes about his business, caring for his family, as more importunate types traipse to Washington in search of special favors. This would not be so bad if those seeking favors had no more clout than the typical voter; but when the elected officials enact rules that allow large political donations from those seeking special treatment, the relative importance of the common people is severely diluted.

As the Federal Register swells with thousands of bills and regulations the power of the government over everybody expands greatly. This in turn makes it essential for those interested to attempt to direct the details of government programs. Two types of lobbyist emerge: those concerned with preserving or advancing their economic well-being and those concerned about legislating their pet social, religious, and ideological projects. The lobbyists seeking economic advantage can in turn be divided into two categories. Initially they seek favors, subsidies, or laws to limit their competitors or encourage their businesses. Then, as such discriminatory practices are enacted, many other groups are forced into defensive lobbying. For example, manufacturers of cloth might seek tariff protection from foreign suppliers to reduce competition and allow them to charge higher prices. But then garment manufacturers might be forced to oppose that in order to maintain the better prices and varieties of cloth gotten from overseas suppliers. As a result, many lobbyists are merely protecting themselves from threatened legislation that would hurt them. Their contributions operate much like the "protection" money paid by shop owners to neighborhood gangs.

The other class of lobbyists, the social-agenda-driven organizations, are usually established by individuals seeking major changes in America's winning playbook. Rather than pursue their agenda at the ballot box, they resort to covert pressure on legislators and bureaucrats. They set up corporate organizations with attractive sounding names like Concerned Citizens For Justice, and using modern PR and fundraising techniques attain considerable power. Unfortunately, this power is often directed by a small cadre of individuals whose actions are not very transparent to their membership or supporters. They can even be controlled by a foreign government, a single millionaire with a personal mission, or a radical group devoted to the demoralization of the nation. In any case, the power that derives from their gifts to political campaigns undermines the concept of democratic voting. The actual voters are relegated to an inferior position in the minds of the politicians.

Attempts to eliminate the evils of lobbyists and campaign financing abuses have generally failed because those involved don't want to end the gravy train for all concerned.

Several approaches to accomplish reform have been suggested. First, enact spending limits to limit a candidate for office to a government established maximum. This has been held to be a violation of Free Speech rights under the First Amendment to the Constitution, because the candidate has the right to get his message across without limitation. Second, just use "clean" money supplied by the government to candidates. This of course opens a Pandora's box of potential abuses as candidates vie for part of the handout. If the government pays people to run for office, many enterprising individuals will enter races just to spend the funds with no intent of actually winning. This has been of limited use because the enacted rules require the candidate to agree to "voluntary" limits on how much he will spend. Third, ban or limit contributions deemed to be "soft money," which is somehow supposed to be more insidious than "hard" money. This approach is transparently a sham because the distinction is first, not important, and secondly, never clear. Fourth, limit contributions by most groups, unions and corporations, but allow them to give through PACs, "astro-turf" groups, various tax exempt corporations, etc. These "reforms" are, of course, just a new form of money laundering, calling gifts okay if funneled through the right entity. Fifth, ban all political donations from every type of corporal entity and allow only individual gifts from registered voters, subject to a maximum from any one person. This last would eliminate the financial power of the lobbyists and restore power to the individual citizens.

Many states have tried to do what the feds haven't done. Iowa, North Dakota, Pennsylvania and Texas prohibit labor unions, regulated industries, and associations from contributing to candidates' campaigns. Arkansas, California, Connecticut, and Kansas limit the amount contributed to election committees and political parties. As in the case of welfare reforms made during the past few decades, the real campaign finance reform movement has sprung from the grassroots as America's communities in a few states seek to correct current abuses to our political process.

While public funding remains popular, and is supported by many of the would-be office-seekers, it would create new injustices as to who would qualify for the government hand-outs. The best solution, that recognizes the most important asset in the country, is to find the solution that maximizes the influence of individual voters on their elected representatives. It is the only simple and effective way to eliminate the power lobbyists gain from gifts that are in effect bribes. It may also help to take a new look at the concept of "free speech." The right to support and promote a candidate of one's choice may be an exercise of free speech, but that advocacy right should logically only extend to the words uttered or financed by individuals. Democratic voting rights are meant to be extended only to individuals—we don't let General Motors vote—so all corporate organizations could be well removed from the process.

Barry Goldwater argued for this point in his 1959 best seller, *The Conscience of a Conservative*: "In order to achieve the widest possible distribution of political power, financial contributions to political campaigns should be made by individuals and individuals alone. I see no reason for labor unions—or corporations—to participate in politics."[410]

Under representative government, the citizens delegate authority to their elected representatives, reasonable in view of the huge population and the complexity of lawmaking. However, there is no need to delegate campaign financing to a wide variety of independent groups and organizations. Goldwater looked on these organizations when they sought to influence legislation and elections as "the enemy of freedom . . . and the champions of freedom will fight against the concentration of power wherever they find it."[411] He believed that "The Federal Corrupt Practices Act does forbid such activity. That legislation has been circumvented by the 'education' approach and other devices; and Congress and the courts, in effect, have looked the other way. The only remedy, it appears, is new legislation."[412]

Goldwater's book was written in the late 1950s before the advent of large special interest organizations and the conversion of the huge non-profit foundations to political activism. Otherwise he well may have also wanted their "educational" purposes to be barred from political activity. All the special interest groups that claim to have lofty purposes have only one objective in mind—to allow a small controlling clique to magnify their financial power so that they, as individuals, can exert more influence than other individuals. This process corrupts democratic principles, because most individuals are too busy earning a living and living their life to start their own lobby—so their influence is overshadowed by the elites running the lobbies. In fact, it is a violation of the spirit of democracy to allow such organizations to gain influence over the people's elected representatives. The wisdom of crowds comes from each person acting independently. Once they allow a group with a special interest to exercise their free speech for them, their balanced wisdom and common sense will be lost.

Government as Mother

We have seen that in history's newly emerging societies, the people were quite content and successful when their governing system was devoted to only the essential roles of protection and adjudication. These conditions were conducive to freedom—enough safety to empower individual activity, without so much intrusion as to hamper it. Such rights-protecting systems of limited government are more important to a society than democracy per se; a democracy or "liberal" government does not necessarily promote freedom. Indeed, governments that grow too "liberal" reduce freedom. Education, the rule of law, the protection of private property, and the curbing of excessive regulation and taxation are what enable freedom of action for individuals.

The legal structures that provide an environment allowing free economic expression, the product of centuries of slow development, are well-known and can be readily nurtured and maintained. If the purview of government expands much beyond that basic purpose, it undermines that purpose. "The rules of the protective state do not specify a 'public interest' because there is none," according to Joseph Johnston. "Instead, public officials concern themselves with preserving the conditions under which private ends may be pursued. The affirmative state, on the other hand, chooses a goal to be pursued on behalf of everyone. . . . As Michael Oakeshott has shown, the vocabulary of the affirmative or goal-oriented state tends to be military (the 'war on poverty'), and it relies on the organizational structures of administration, command and bureaucracy rather than adjudication and arbitration of disputes. It spawns overseers, bureaucrats and inquisitors, whose function is to supervise adherence to the path of virtue and conformity. Civil law gives way to administrative command.

People are treated not as free individuals but as subjects to be treated, hospitalized and nurtured—and, of course, taxed to pay for all these privileges."[413]

Although there are some affirmative roles that the central government can and should play (such as national defense, maintaining the judiciary, police forces, and some highway and bridge infrastructure), Johnston calls for carefully measuring these and delegating as many as possible to the private sector or to the lowest level of government possible. Above all, it is a question of restraint. Rousseau, like the radical mob leaders of the French Revolution, was no fan of moral restraint; he advocated individual choice no matter how irresponsible or licentious and blamed all social evils on the government. His writings encouraged the idea of citizens as "victims" needing help, and he condoned resistance to all restrictive societal norms. Like most intellectuals, he lacked the subtlety of moderation and pushed his ideas to the limit. However, he apparently believed sufficiently in the beneficence of the state to deposit each of his illegitimate newborn babies on the front steps of the state orphanage, where their life expectancy, with luck, might extend to a year or two. He defended such abandonment by claiming Plato had proven that the state best rears children. With the hypocrisy that only an intellectual can rationalize, he condemned the government as the source of man's problems, but relied on it to ameliorate the consequences of his own bad behavior.

Rousseau is thus the perfect role model for all later drop-outs and malcontents adept at rationalizing personal moral failures. He not only rationalized it but blamed others, fostering both a culture-wide victim mentality, and a knee-jerk resort to the government for direction and support. This view represents a 180-degree turn from the cultural-religious notions of self-reliance and personal responsibility that built the Western nations to pre-eminence. The increasingly "soft" America that Michael Barone warns of has forgotten the virtue of responsibility and attending to consequences. As Alan Dershowitz warns, the excuse-making and evasion of responsibility that now "abound in every sphere" of public and private life "breach the social contract and rend the very fabric of democracy. We must stop making excuses and start taking responsibility. What is at stake is far more than the punishment of criminals and the deterrence of crime. It is the very nature of our experiment with democracy."[414]

Trust-Fund Babies

For nations as for individuals, the downside of wealth is that it makes everything too easy. Too much of what the West's citizenry enjoys has been inherited, not earned, and many are ignorant of the effort needed to create and sustain this prosperity. Worse, the intellectuals keep telling them they are "victims"—yes, that's right, the freest and most affluent people in the history of the world, victims. And that it's the giant corporations, big oil, the drug companies, religious nuts, and Anglo-Saxons white men who are ruining society. The motives are transparent. Since intellectuals have not contributed to the building or maintenance of modern prosperity, and are often driven by resentment and self-importance, they feel obliged to attack the actual source of their country's success and to damn those who are actually making the products, supplying the goods, creating the jobs, raising functional children, practicing the work ethic, and otherwise manifesting the moral and responsible attitudes that made the country free and prosperous.

Charles Tomlinson puts it this way: "The rational choices of our ancestors provide most of our needs in the areas of food, shelter and clothing today, even though the first man who discovered how to cultivate corn is shrouded in the mists of our history, the first spear maker is an ancient memory, the first fire keeper even more removed. Because we can pass the products of our minds down from generation to generation, we have built a tremendous storehouse of knowledge which, coupled with our benevolent nature, allows us to support those who cannot, or will not, contribute without even noticing their burden."[415] However, the forward momentum of a nation can last only so long. It is the nature of man to build societies by the application of his reason and his work ethic. "No other means are open to him; nothing else will work! No shell, no fur, no fangs—it's think or die for man. It has been that way for eons and will be that way as long as we survive in this universe."[416]

Those individuals that consider current prosperity as a given are not only ignorant of history but are living in a fool's paradise. Their major concern is how to divvy up the pie handed down to them from prior generations. They do not care about the right to live in freedom, nor the right to work in peace, but rather seek a new right—to live without thinking or working.

The demagogues of today's populist democracy encourage this dependency because it secures a large group of voters more interested in stated intentions and hand-outs than in end results. They have seen to it that "It is possible to survive in the twentieth century as a hitchhiker on the minds of others. . . . [W]e have evolved a survival system which, acting over long spans of time, is so benevolent as to allow most men to go through life repeating the motions discovered by men generations before, following the codes of conduct imposed on them by governments and religions, and managing to make it from cradle to grave without focusing their consciousness on anything more important than their whims of the moment."[417] This is the kind of greedy and narcissistic citizens that autocrats seek to cultivate. Such citizens will give up freedom before comfort and security. This is the kind of people that will rarely know the satisfaction of personal accomplishment. It represents a type of life which Tomlinson describes as "contrary to the requirements of man for happiness," a subject that he describes as "a topic for another stump session."[418]

The danger is that like many trust-fund babies, Americans will squander their inheritance. Successful dynastic families employ restrictive trusts with principal held sacred and only income paid out to reduce the chances that their children will squander their financial inheritance. Unfortunately, there is no equivalent mechanism to preserve the cultural legacy of nations. In the past, Western nations relied on their schools, churches, families, and social institutions to impart enough wisdom and common sense to each new generation to enable them to carry on the work of civilization. If such training and education are not effectively provided, the citizenry will lack the knowledge, resolve, and discipline to maintain that inheritance. Children today are at greater risk than ever, and the steady increase in illegitimacy and dependency presents a bleak picture for their future. And there is at least one self evident truth left—the schools have been failing the children and the nation for decades.

America has the financial and military momentum inherited from past generations that makes current generations live easily—too easily—especially if they do not appreciate how it happened and how it must be preserved. This legacy is a wonderful gift to all today, but it may be a curse tomorrow if it serves to hide the enfeebling signs of maturity that face us. The challenge before us is to reverse the progressive decline of self reliance and moral character that lies at the heart of the decline of nations.

A New Elite Emerges

Journalists have often been called the Fourth Estate because of how their provision of the news influences national affairs. They have served a useful watchdog function, exposing the sins of the three original branches of government—the executive, legislative, and judicial. But these days the major media are allied with a larger and more dangerous offshoot of modern government—the shadowy special interest groups that furtively operate to re-direct national affairs to fulfill their agendas. These groups cloak themselves with noble-sounding titles like Coalition for World Peace or Americans for Justice, and claim to be pursuing worthy goals like the protection of freedom and rights. They get good press because they share the same anti-American agenda as the news media.

A turning point in this effort to change how America works occurred in 1966 when McGeorge Bundy, who had been National Security Advisor to the Kennedy and Johnson administrations and former Harvard dean, was appointed president of the Ford Foundation. In the previous job, he had spent five years helping mastermind the escalation of the Vietnam War, but he was to do the nation even more harm in his new job at Ford. In that role, he pioneered something new. Instead of using these huge tax exempt funds to aid the poor and the hungry, or fund research to eradicate disease, he pioneered a program of "advocacy philanthropy."

The common men and women of America don't appear on the boards that control these huge piles of tax-sheltered funds. They are run by those over-educated, soft-scientist, idea-driven individuals who never created wealth or jobs, but who in affluent mature societies are able to administer from on high. Private foundations provide a haven for such people, where they can earn huge salaries, contribute zero to the economy, and spend billions on their anti-American campaigns, with unfortunate results. "They promoted ideas that led to legislation, and then sought to influence the regulatory bodies and federal courts that implemented and interpreted the laws. Thus, Ford and Bundy helped develop an institutional structure that, by means of litigation and the leverage it exercised over administrative agencies, could push its favored programs beyond any limits contemplated by the politicians who enacted them."[419] Other major foundations like the Carnegie and Rockefeller, led by like-minded intellectuals, hurried to follow the same path, "Over the long run, the Bundy approach was instrumental in inventing what is now a familiar phenomenon on the American political scene: the well-placed advocacy group nursing a grievance against American society and seeking compensation on behalf of its members."[420] These huge tax-sheltered corporations, controlled by individuals with a narrow activist agenda, have been able to use their vast resources to fund like-minded individuals and groups, influence academics through financial grants, and undermine the interests of ordinary citizens who are generally ignorant of the pernicious behind-the-scenes influence of these shadowy organizations.

The new elites have also taken over at most major media outlets where "polls document the lopsided, Left-leaning nature of newspapers all across the country."[421] Larry Elder reports that among journalism students at Columbia University, a whopping 40 percent believe in government ownership of corporations; that only two percent of Washington, D. C. journalists call themselves conservative and about 90 percent voted for Bill Clinton in 1992, as versus 43 percent of all American voters. This bias has a significant effect on public opinion in general, and a negative effect on the silent majority who are too busy to get involved.

"Although cultural fraud has any number of variations," according to Jack Cashill, "one can discern a general pattern: The hard Left attracts the intellectual Left with its almost Rousseauvian purity and rawness. The intellectual Left in turn intimidates the soft center Left that so dominates America's news production into silence and/or compliance. The news producers educate the open-minded center and the less informed liberals in their audience."[422] In that way, the bad ideas of the intellectuals get passed down to the society at large.

Academics—Teachers or Ideologues?

Over the past few decades, the intellectuals' notion of remaking the world into a communist/socialist Garden of Eden has spread throughout academia. The collapse of Communist Russia raised no question in their minds. The biggest harm done by the faulty vision of today's academics is the twisted notions imparted to the youth. Although American schools and colleges excel in many of the hard-sciences, the soft science subjects concentrate on the abstractions and anti-American thinking of the professors. It has always been the case that these teachers, enamored with the great philosophers, have given their students an overly elevated respect for such theorists. The case method of instruction in history or political science would have grounded their charges in more practical ways of thinking. However, it has gotten worse with the message now being given that the biggest problems are pollution, gender rights, gay rights, and the lack of a world government. The result is that today's students in the humanities are actually being hurt by their education, their thinking process dulled, and their attitudes corrupted.

The controversial new theory embodied in the Radzewicz Curves indicates a direct relationship between years of schooling and a decline in wisdom and common sense, also known as "EQ." Note that the impact of today's soft-science schooling can vary for different

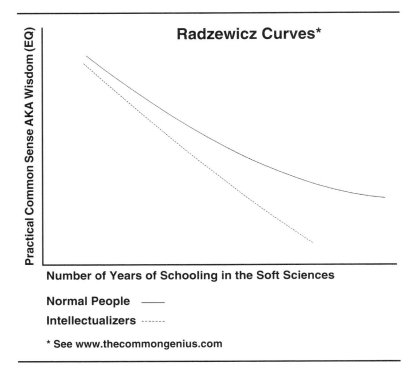

types of students. For simplicity, we have divided students into two broad categories, although refinements might provide further insights.

For "normal students," the decline in wisdom continues with each additional year of schooling in the soft-sciences but at a declining rate, because such individuals have a significant degree of resistance to abstract concepts that defy reality. However, for students with a predilection for abstract thinking, the decline is linear and more precipitous. Thus, there is a concave line for normal students and a straight line for the more intellectual types. Although the concave line can never reach zero on the vertical scale, there have been cases where some of those in the other group have done so. In either case, children concentrating in the soft-sciences are left scarred from ever being able to think clearly on governmental issues—which is exactly the object of most of their teachers!

The Loss of Moral Certainty

Intellectuals often espouse contradictory policies because they do not accept the need for a logical framework underlying their ideas. Clever as trial lawyers, they can talk their way around the most controlling facts to any conclusion they like. Instead of relying on a few simple beliefs, the intelligentsia rely on raw brain power—the kind of mental agility that gets good grades regurgitating data on tests. In love with their own big brains, they have recently taken to criticizing the IQ and schoolboy grades of presidents. But Ronald Reagan proved how wrong they are. In spite of an inability to conceptualize grand theories, and in spite of his possibly average academic grades, and even though he often forgot the names of French premiers, he understood the honesty and worth of the American people.

The common people, in their naïve simplicity, are attracted to ideas that are honest and logical—ideas founded on basic principles. Most do not understand why there are twenty thousand employees in the State Department, or why the government gives billions of dollars in foreign aid to dictators. They are not crippled by moral uncertainty over capital punishment, especially when it is limited to the most heinous murderers. But most intellectuals oppose any capital punishment. Their opposition "is not," as George Will writes, "because the intellectuals, having finer sensibilities, abhor killing more than other people do." Rather, they are victims of their own relativistic theories and have become shorn of any moral certainty; "doubt is the black-lung disease of the intelligentsia—an occupational hazard now inflicted on the culture as a whole."[423]

However, the intellectuals have no uncertainty about their favorite ideologies. Their support for Russian Communism bordered on fanaticism. Actually their doubt and certainty fluctuates with their objectives.

They will denounce Christianity but defend Islam, denounce capital punishment but defend euthanasia and abortion, attack police brutality but ignore Stalin's mass exterminations. And to advance their agenda, they will rewrite history. Radical intellectuals may not be sure what values or morals are, but they display great certainty and arrogance in asserting their fanatical ideologies.

In *Unholy Alliance*, David Horowitz provides the names and backgrounds of hundreds of individuals and organizations that have worked, mostly in university settings, against the interest of America. They are still at work: "The disappearance of the Soviet Bloc has had only one consequence of note. It has lifted the burden of having to defend . . . an indefensible regime. Because the utopian vision is no longer anchored in the reality of an actually existing socialist state, the Left can now indulge its nihilistic agendas without restraint."[424] Such stubborn persistence in a failed cause is hard to believe, but consider the case of one of thousands of die-hards: Gerda Lerner, history professor at University of Wisconsin. Lerner began her career in Central Europe as a Communist but emigrated to America in the late 1930s to escape Nazism. She abandoned the Communist Party in 1956 after Khrushchev went public with the already well-known Stalin massacres. But she never rethought her devotion to the revolutionary cause. She joined the radical Left as an anti-anti-Communist. "She went on condemning the democracies of the West, opposing the Cold War against the Soviet Union . . . and became a pioneer of radical feminism . . . writing one of its canonic texts, 'The Creation of Patriarchy' and in 2003, during the conflict in Iraq, one of the founding members of Historians Against the War."[425] Her radical career spanned three generations, and easily transitioned to each new revision of "the progressive cause."

There are thousands of such people teaching in western schools, winning awards in the academic bastions that fund them and protect them. Knowing their intentions, it is folly to believe that they teach an accurate or beneficial history course. Although Lerner later admitted being duped, she did not give up her fanatical dreams: In *Fireweed*, she writes "Like all true believers, I believed as I did because I needed to believe: in a utopian vision of the future, in the possibility of human perfectibility. . . . And I still need that belief, even if the particular vision I had embraced has turned to ashes."[426] Such is the irrationality and fanaticism of the radical Left. Unfortunately, that vision can be attractive to many whose charitable hearts are bigger than their rational heads. But, only a lazy mind will tolerate ideas that are supported merely by noble intentions and allegedly beneficial results.

The problem is that, taken as a whole, the message being taught is nihilistic. In order to replace the existing culture with their new vision, those advocating change must first tear down the values, traditions, and institutions that made America what it is today. Students subjected to years of such propaganda are designed for an amoral and mechanistic universe devoid of inspiring loyalties and emotions. Without a moral compass and taught to let personal feelings trump duty and responsibility, these graduating classes may prove unfit to preserve the legacy handed down to them by their forebears.

Rot Always Comes from Within

In the eight sections above, we have sketched out the ills of maturity that are catching up with America. Grave as they may seem, each of the problems could be readily dealt with except for the growing moral uncertainty, the blurring of right and wrong, and a loss of confidence in the principles that made America the most free and prosperous nation in the world. Those that seek to remake the American culture rely on this blurring to accomplish their goals. The tradition of compromise that marked American politics is anathema to their hardened objectives. The country is stuck in stalemate. Both political parties battle to hold onto their position of power, while the problems facing the nation go on hold. As Bernard Goldberg suggests, on the one hand, we have crazies; on the other wimps.

Most writers, when describing today's problems, focus on the *symptoms* of decline, because they fail to recognize the cause. It is typical for "experts" in the field of education to point to the deterioration in our nation's schools and recommend that if we spend more we can cure the problem. However, we have been spending more and more for years with no positive result. The problem with our schools lies elsewhere and until the fundamental problems are addressed, no amount of money will help. Similarly, the problem with foreign aid is not the amount of aid given but the way it is provided and to whom it is directed. Unfortunately, the constant failing of the new intelligentsia-elites that have come to dominate most policymaking is to not understand the causes but instead rely on their centrist top-down planning agendas—and that usually means throwing more money at all problems. Their approach not only doesn't work, but it will bankrupt the nation's taxpayers.

Solutions to today's problems must come from the practical people that have been pushed aside by the so-called experts. America's success has grown steadily for generations. Current stagnation stems from the moral and political confusion and ideological antagonisms created by those who only critique the real players, the nation, and its history. It bears repeating that today's security, affluence, leisure, and freedom did not arise from anything done in the recent past. Today's blessings are the result of the constant forward momentum of the past two centuries. Each generation of Americans contributed to this rise. The challenge before us is to recognize the lessons provided by the collapse of prior civilizations. If that challenge is met, it will be possible to overcome the destructive influence of the uninformed but strident critics whose sole objective is to rule the common people from above. Only if common wisdom prevails can we hope to pass on to our children a nation still on the rise. The alternative is to go down in history as the first generation to squander our parents' legacy.

Chapter 15
Are We Destined to Decline?

The main responsibility for the century's disasters lies not so much in the problems as in the solutions, not in impersonal forces but in human beings, thinking certain thoughts and as a result performing certain actions.
—Robert Conquest

THOMAS SOWELL HAS CALLED the century just past "the century of the Intellectual, and nowhere more so than in politics."[427]

Predictably, this development did not bring forth any wondrous achievements other than in the hard sciences. Intellects of the softer persuasion tried unsuccessfully to apply reason and science to socio-political affairs. Their attempts were doomed to fail because they treated reality as optional and human nature as something that could be safely ignored. The growth of their influence resulted, however, in what Robert Conquest calls "the ravaged century." Their ascendancy may represent the biggest threat yet to the survival of Western civilization. Recall that the Rule is: Intellectuals are absent during the rise of societies, proliferate during their maturity, and become dominant during their fall. By their very nature intellectuals create managed societies, centrist and even totalitarian in nature, in order to administer their top-down directives on how to make things better. And that approach always fails because managed societies forfeit the genius and common sense of their citizens.

During the past half-century, intellectuals have often fueled, sustained, and apologized for totalitarian governments and programs. The most harmful dictators of the century—Hitler, Lenin, Pol Pot, Stalin, and Mao—offered world visions that appealed "not just to the gullible masses, but to the intellectuals, including scholars, literary giants, and others with impeccable credentials in the world of ideas."[428]

Each of those five dictators were allied with the vast majority of their nation's intellectuals—all collaborating in pursuit of an ideal society perfected by reason and stripped of religious dogmas. They were fully prepared to use even the most ruthless experiments in social engineering to accomplish their unrealistic dreams.

What totalitarian movements have in common "is a sense of a revelation grasped only by the anointed, a revelation that needs to be imposed on the benighted masses for their own good. Could anything be more of an ego trip, or more in keeping with the intellectuals' exalted view of themselves, or their resentment at seeing wealth and power in the hands of lesser beings?"[429] The intellectuals supporting the five dictators mentioned bear primary responsibility for the death of tens of millions of Europeans, Chinese, and Southeast Asians during the past seventy years. Although some of the major Western nations avoided a similar bloodbath, it was not thanks to their intellectuals. In fact, those resident intellectuals were more often than not cheering on and apologizing for the ruthless dictators. They even cheered for the convicted spies that worked for the Russian communist leaders during the Cold War. Many of those spies were the intellectual darlings of the liberal Left in America. Some still defend Alger Hiss whose guilt has been fully corroborated by documents emerging after the collapse of the Soviet Empire.[430] The vision that inspires such treason and refuses to confront reality is an intellectual vision. The minds that are able to deny conclusive evidence and persist in anointing false arguments are intellectual minds. Such minds are alive and well in America and play leading roles in our institutions. America's future depends on whether those minds triumph in destroying the nation or whether the common people can unite to throw the rascals out.

Of Mice and Men

In *A Conflict of Visions*,[431] Thomas Sowell argues that our policy debates are ultimately animated by the clash of conflicting views of the way the world works and the way human nature works: The liberal

Left believes that society is more to blame than criminals for criminal conduct; the conservative right believes that individuals are responsible for their own behavior, even bad behavior, and that criminal conduct is justly punished. The Left believes in equality of results, and so advocates affirmative action and welfarism; the right opposes social engineering and believes in equality under the law. The Left seeks equal results; the right seeks equal opportunity. The Left believes negotiation is a more potent instrument of foreign policy than armed might; the right that negotiations can only be conducted from a position of military strength. The Left believes in central economic planning, with themselves as the intellectual elite doing the planning; the right believes that individuals should make their own choices, and that government should be more hands-off.

The position you take on each of those questions is determined by whether you deal with man as he is—or as you hope he might become. The positions taken by those on the Left can only be supported if human nature can be modified—through social engineering—in such a way as to render all men saints. Those on the right base their position on the unchanging and basically selfish nature of humans.

Now, few people, even the most optimistic idealists, dispute the egocentric behavior of almost all men. To dodge this obvious but awkward fact (because it rules out all their utopian fantasies) intellectuals have generally endorsed William Godwin's 1793 assertion that "Men are capable, no doubt, of preferring an inferior interest of their own to a superior interest of others; but this preference arises from a combination of circumstances and is not the necessary and invariable law of our nature."[432] Godwin's logic is typical intellectual doubletalk— the common man knows that while the lion does not "invariably" kill the gazelle, and that although the snake's bite is "not necessarily" poisonous, it would be stupid to bet against either eventuality.

People are selfish. That is why they will normally prefer a personal interest, no matter how trivial, over a public interest. Allan Bloom explains how *Gulliver's Travels* makes this very sobering point: "Swift is surely one of the funniest men who ever lived. His misanthropy is a joke; it is the greatest folly in the world to attempt to improve humanity. This is what it means to understand man."[433] Jonathan Swift's satire explores different cultures and forms of government and support's the well-known truism that life among human beings can never be ideal. Any governing culture that has a chance to provide a satisfactory environment for its people must be designed to accommodate the extraordinary variations in human nature.

The two conflicting visions of man's nature are manifested in what Michael Barone calls hard America and soft America.[434] The twentieth century witnessed a major tilt to the softer side with massive increases in government programs designed to help everyone who might need assistance. America's softening was the product "not of mass politics . . . but of intellectual elites. Such elites were purveyors of what historian Robert Wiebe calls 'bureaucratic' ideas, 'peculiarly suited to the fluidity and impersonality of an urban-industrialized world.' . . . These Progressive-era reformers, the products of the new universities' faculties and professional middle classes, were eager to reform society in line with what they deemed to be scientific principles."[435]

Barone sees the efforts in the 1960s and 1970s to expand welfare, grant racial quotas and preferences, legislate affirmative action, and be more lenient on crime as profoundly misguided. "While the civil rights movement had sought to allow blacks into Hard America, the new public policies actually confined more Americans, black and non-black, into a Soft America where poverty and crime were chronic." Led by the elites' exaggerated demands for hand-outs, "the great mass of well-meaning Americans who wanted a Softer response to crime and welfare dependency had in fact increased and perpetuated misery."[436]

A similar critique of the activist leaders of a soft vision was made by Milton Friedman. In his *Capitalism and Freedom*, he writes: "In the name of welfare and equality, the twentieth-century liberal has come to favor a revival of the very policies of state intervention and paternalism against which classical liberalism fought. The nineteenth-century liberal regarded an extension of freedom as the most effective way to promote welfare and equality." Friedman emphasizes this point by arguing that there is no middle ground with socialism—those liberals who have finally recognized the horrors of Communism, or "totalitarian socialism," now seek to defend "democratic socialism." Under that more palatable name, they seek "to adopt the essential features of Russian economic arrangements and yet to ensure individual freedom through political arrangements. The thesis of this chapter is that such a view is a delusion, that there is an intimate connection between economics and politics, that only certain combinations of political and economic arrangements are possible, and that in particular, a society which is socialist cannot also be democratic, in the sense of guaranteeing individual freedom."[437]

Friedman and Barone have outlined by these observations an essential element of how the new soft-science elites bring on the destruction of their societies. They give new names to their same old failed programs and develop new arguments for their adoption. They just don't give up. They undermine the culture that made the society great in the first place. They seek to turn men into mice. Like Trust Fund babies and those they "help," they are happy to squander an inheritance they neither appreciate nor understand. Barone observes, "The advocates of Softening hated the idea of imposing middle-class mores on black Americans, but middle-class mores are necessary for achievement in Hard America, and underclass behavior makes such achievement impossible."[438]

The concepts of individual responsibility and self-reliance were the essential foundation of those ordinary people who built the stepping stones to modern freedom and prosperity. When the people of a nation are gradually shorn of such enabling character, their incentive to act atrophies. Given a continuing dose of anti-American propaganda by their teachers, and brainwashed with the need for centrist governmental "solutions," a once-great people now face the inner rot that Michael Savage so effectively ridicules: "Wake up, sheeple! America has been infected by a mental disorder that is virtually destroying everything your ancestors handed to you on a silver platter."[439]

In his own book about this conflict of visions, *The Great Disruption*, Francis Fukuyama argues that restoring the traditional values and good habits of mind that made America great is a Herculean task, because there are so many with an opposing vision more interested in eliminating all values than fostering them. Robert M. Pirsig says that what's "coming out of the urban slums, where old Victorian social moral codes are almost completely destroyed, isn't any new paradise the revolutionaries hoped for, but a reversion to rule by terror, violence and gang death—the old biological might-makes-right morality of prehistoric brigandage that primitive societies were set up to overcome."[440] He distinguishes between the need to constantly liberalize intellectual thought on scientific and governmental operations, and the need for restraints on personal and social behavior. It will always be necessary to limit the ever-present potential for undesirable behavior of individuals, but that doesn't mean a society must shackle free scientific thought. Intellectuals, as usual, confuse the issue by demanding tolerance and open-mindedness in all areas of human behavior.

This excessive tolerance and permissiveness that permeates both the public schools and entitlement programs has relegated large segments of the population to regress into poorly educated and welfare dependent underclasses. Pirsig believes that the "paralysis of America is a paralysis of moral patterns. Morals can't function normally because morals have been declared intellectually illegal by the . . . metaphysics that dominates present social thought."[441] The Great Society policies that have spawned social and economic ghettos both urban and rural not only create misery for the underclass, but deny the nation the essential and beneficial contribution of all its people.

A Vision of Despair

The moral doubts of the intelligentsia largely spring from their belief that man is not responsible for his actions. Now, everyone knows that all men are on occasion irresponsible, and that some men are very irresponsible, but that, by and large, most men are responsible most of the time, and that letting them off the hook of personal responsibility and accountability would only encourage more bad behavior. In essence, societies must deal with man as he is. The intellectuals, on the other hand, who like their theories pure and unsullied by the normal variations in human nature, have chosen to deny personal responsibility for behavior. That way, their understanding of reality has no exceptions—everyone is irresponsible and needs their help. Neat and tidy, but obviously absurd—the intellectual's mind is a thing of wonder! The next step, when they realize they can't mold or control everyone the way they want to, will be to go to Huxley's genetic tampering solution—designer babies—so that, after a generation or two, the common people will finally become pliable and orderly.

In the meantime, having denied free will and virtually eliminated the idea of personal responsibility, they are left with a moral relativism that renders them unable to react against the evils found in all societies. One consequence is the breakdown in families and the rapid growth in illegitimacy, especially for inner city black families, where such births approach 75 percent of the total.[442] This has served to remove the hope and opportunity of any upward mobility for many American children. It is unrealistic to expect a child from a dysfunctional home to progress in the world as easily as a well-parented child. Bill Cosby has criticized those in the black community who ignore the need to reverse this destructive breakdown in essential societal norms. While the ideas of intellectuals and the welfare policies rewarding victimhood are a large part of the cause, Cosby is calling for individual responsibility and action. Addressing the growing tendency of youth to wear baggy long shorts low enough to show their crack, he asks parents: "Are you not paying attention? People with their hat on backwards, pants down around the crack. Isn't that a sign of something? Or are you waiting for Jesus to pull his pants up?"[443] Excellent questions that few of today's politically correct thinkers dare to ask.

There are basic inequalities among people, but these can be at least ameliorated by good training and parenting. In the past, a child was expected to grow up fast, be responsible, and pay the consequences for misdeeds. Today, the reigning notion is that you are almost automatically a victim and that the government is obliged to help you. Fathers can't be located. The schools get saddled with children unprepared to behave or learn even the rudiments of reading and writing. To compound the problem, the schools teach them that all societies have been equally meritorious, that there is no right or wrong, and that everything is relative . . . except the "inhumanity" of Hiroshima, the bigotry of internment of Japanese in World War II, the apartheid of South Africa, the plight of American Indians, and the horrors of colonialism and the military, all designed to make them hate Western civilization. As Johnny Cash lamented, "Can you blame the voice of youth, for asking: What is truth?"

In Britain of late, a few have sought to reverse this decline in moral certainty. *Times* columnists Oliver Kamm and Douglas Murray see the need to restore classical liberalism and a leadership world role for their country. Murray "paints an optimistic portrait of a nation no longer in love with its own decline and ready to respond to an agenda of tax cuts, a smaller state, an assault on welfare dependency, immigration controls, and tough law enforcement. Inspired by practical commentators like Leo Strauss and Allan Bloom, Murray proposes a restoration of authentically liberal education, with an end to the cultural relativism that he holds responsible for the fact that 'a large proportion of the people our educational systems are producing are not very nice.'"[444] However, such ideas have been opposed for decades by the British diplomatic, academic, and political establishments, from both sides of the political spectrum. The paucity of bold calls for reform shows how extensively the faulty visions of Left and Right alike have infected society and the education of our children.

Julian Simon has tried to explain why the harmful ideas of the new elites in the West have spread and infected so many of the people within these free and prosperous nations. His book, *Hoodwinking The Nation*, explains why so many believe "false bad news." He explores the nature of the false news; its production by researchers, politicians, and organizations; its dissemination by the press and television; and why we tend to accept "that body of false statements."[445] His explanation reinforces Sowell's concept of a faulty vision: that "a set of unsound ideas undergird the newspaper and television stories and provide the intellectual infrastructure that gives these stories credibility. These ideas fall into two categories: misunderstandings of the nature of resource creation and population economics, and misunderstandings of the nature of a modern complex social-economic system."[446]

It's not just the soft scientists who promulgate this "overabundance of false bad news." At least in the areas of environmental and population doomsday scenarios, many hard scientists have created unwarranted public fears that have little basis in fact. Simon counters these doomsayers and gives the facts that refute hysteria over alleged evils like DDT and Agent Orange. And he documents how Albert Gore's book, *Earth in the Balance*, is "as ignorant a collection of clichés as anything ever published on the subject. . . . Gore seems unaware that the solid scientific consensus is that there was no observable damage to humans from living near Love Canal. . . . The entire book is filled with this sort of environmental gossip, backed by no sources, and contradicted by solid data."[447] Simon points out that contrary to popular understanding, "There is broad scientific consensus that the air and water in the United States are getting cleaner rather than dirtier, that natural resources are becoming less scarce rather than more scarce, and that there is no quantitative evidence that population growth is detrimental to economic growth in poor countries or rich ones."[448] And yet a large number of Americans believe many of the environmental myths that not only divert attention from real problems, but result in legislation and regulations that do only harm.

> *Why don't democracies work? Because they are only temporary states. . . . They can only function until a majority of voters discover that they can vote themselves money and other goodies from the public treasury.*
>
> —Joseph Farah

Simon's analysis of polling data on people's beliefs and understandings on these subjects indicate that there is a major discrepancy between what people know personally about their own situation and neighborhood, and "what they think is happening 'out there.'"[449] They get their local knowledge from their own faculties and senses, and their knowledge about everyplace else from the media. When polled, the citizens respond accordingly about what they have been led to believe, and the media then touts these beliefs as proof of a national consensus, further compounding the credibility of their false news. Of course, the polls are often contrived to confirm whatever results are desired. (Truism: Accept no poll or statistic as fact) Simon argues that after this process of misinformation, "the abstract aggregate judgments" of the people are not consistent with what would be the sum of their individual judgments.[450] Just as when buying soap, the common man and woman can be led astray by a constant barrage of misleading information.

To the extent that they accept the Left's destructive indoctrination, children will be hobbled; they'll lack the habits and perspective needed to participate in and benefit from the American dream. These children are, in Julian Simon's words, a part of America's "ultimate resource"; and the leaders of the liberal communities are demonstrating great cruelty by failing to heed the warnings of critics like Kamm, Cosby, and Murray. The future of America and Europe's democracies may be influenced by such pressures as terrorism, pollution, the deficit, and immigration. But far more important in determining survival will be the habits and beliefs of the next generation, the very ones being conditioned to oppose any strong effort to control, punish, interrogate, or incarcerate criminals, perverts, and terrorists. This is soft America gone nuts.

Since the Greeks first put man on a pedestal as an almost sacred hero, such belief has been an integral part of mankind's ascent. Heroes, by nature, are responsible—they not only attempt to lead exemplary personal lives themselves, but go the extra step and help others. There are few heroes living on welfare. Intellectuals have done much in the past few hundred years to undermine the concept of personal responsibility. Sigmund Freud and B. F. Skinner are among those who have cast doubt about the independent man. Their harmful concepts suggest that man is a helpless puppet whose actions are predetermined by biological and environmental conditions. That vision of despair helps create a large victim class that the elites can minister to. They dispense monetary rewards to those who accept the bait. Thus, intellectuals, constitutionally unable to participate in the real world, are compelled to create well-paid, superior roles for themselves as academics, social engineers, pundits, education experts, psychotherapists, critics, foundation heads, etc. And some of them have even baser motives. They know that undermining personal responsibility undermines the foundations of freedom and will help topple democracy and capitalism. They have been very effective, imposing a large burden on those beneath who must bear the costs and consequences of their schemes.

Crime, Punishment, and the Fate of the West

In *Suicide of the West*, James Burnham calls for a reassertion of "the pre-liberal conviction that Western civilization, thus Western man, is both different from and superior in quality to other civilizations and non-civilizations. . . . Unless Western civilization is superior to other civilizations and societies, it is not worth defending; unless Westerners are willing to use their power, the West cannot be defended. But by its own principles, liberalism is not allowed to entertain that conviction or to make frank, unashamed and therefore effective use of that power."[451] Writing in the mid-60s, Burnham recognized the difference in vision that splits America: that since what America is differs from the liberals' utopian vision of what ought to be, they oppose America and its underlying values.

No external enemy can "murder the West": no external enemy can even begin to match the overwhelming reach and power of the major Western democracies, at least not as long as those nations have the will to survive. But exercising that will means applying the hard lessons of history, not the soft fantasies of the intellectuals. Reversing the decline means upending mountains of bureaucracy, hordes of establishment "leaders" in schools and colleges, and vast special-interest advocacy groups. It is a Herculean task, for the downward momentum is strong and the time is late.

Mature societies need not implode. Nothing in human affairs is preordained; everything depends on what individuals at any point in time decide to do. Just as most individuals can turn their lives around by practicing self-discipline and following a few simple rules, so can a declining nation be freed from the sclerosis of established bureaucracies, special interest groups, and academic pundits. New Zealand benefitted two decades ago by just such reforms. They were exposed to a lot of "tough love" and some "cold turkey" adjustments. Just one of their reforms eliminated all farm subsidies over an eight month period and yet within two years the farmers were more prosperous than before.[452] They cut the federal colossus by almost 50 percent over a decade! But although it can happen, it rarely does, for the entrenched centers of power that seize control at the top, the intellectuals and bureaucrats, don't want to give up control. It would be too painful for their egos and pocketbooks.

The problem is not just one of efficiency, or wasted government budgets, or the unintended consequences of laws and programs that subvert the culture. The radical members of the intellectual Left pursue an even more extreme agenda, what Eric Blair has referred to as "the weapon of Marxist Critical Theory. Critical Theory is based on the observation that Westerners, intoxicated with capitalism and inculcated with a love of freedom, would never throw their lives away for a Leninist style socialist revolution in the West." The path to revolution "begins with an attack and undermining of the dominant culture of the society."[453] Thus they seek to destroy and discredit Christianity, capitalism, the family, morality, sexual restraint, patriotism, nationalism, and conservatism. Easy-going Americans are bemused, unaware of the cumulative damage being done. It has been said that we are tolerating ourselves to death, for as long-suffering and overly tolerant parents look on apathetically, their children's minds are being deformed.

The defeatist attitude of the liberal Left reached a high point under President Carter in the late 1970s. He told the American people that they better get used to being number two, or three, or worse. He was so morally uncertain that he could not even bring himself to support Solidarity's call for support when the Polish workers union dared challenge their communist oppressors in Moscow. It took the AFL-CIO Longshoremen, defying both President Carter and the State Department, to announce a supportive boycott of all Polish shipping. The strikes vaulted Lech Walesa into prominence in Gdansk and his "illegal" Polish trade union caused the first major crack in Soviet hegemony. Carter had been afraid of "provoking"

The union electrician from Gdansk that helped topple the Communist Empire

the Soviets and remained so unsure of who was in the right that he deplored Ronald Reagan's later description of the Soviet Union as "evil." National confidence was eventually restored by the Reagan administration and its optimistic vision of America as the brilliant "city on a hill," but the vision of despair and uncertainty, rampant among Carter's "team," was there for everyone to witness.

The intelligentsia have often created the doubts and confusion that precipitated a nation's decline. The only option for freedom-seeking people has always been to go somewhere else, to get a fresh start free of such encumbrances. It can only be hoped that with the improved communication derived from the Internet and the activity of bloggers, the common people will finally be able to negate these destructive forces and reverse the decline of their homelands. Or perhaps the new technologies will enable them to discover the next enclave, so enterprising individuals can get there first. Unfortunately, that may not be an option. When Rome fell, there was no place to go, and the Dark Ages ensued. Today, even the most alienated American intellectual can't find a better nation on earth than America herself to abscond to.

If the West does collapse in our lifetimes, it will not be for lack of power, money, or resources; it will not be from pollution, bad luck, the failure to sign a treaty, or a refusal to negotiate with dictators. Internally, the nation can be defeated only by intellectual and moral weakness, the twin failings of intellectual elites: a lack of common sense, of rationality, of moral certainty. The liberal ideological vision encourages and rationalizes the decline of Western society. It tries to teach our children to accept a status comparable to that of the least developed nations. It ridicules the middle class mores that strengthen the nation, denies the superiority of Western values, and undermines the prosperity and success bequeathed by those who created the modern world.

If the worst-case scenario should come to pass, the only satisfaction for the common people unable to leave for a freer land will come from watching their intellectual betters kowtow to some autocrat, "reciting specified verses, and prostrating at a nonnegotiable angle, all at assigned times of the day"[454] to worship a new God. But that would hardly compensate for the loss of our freedom. To prevent this outcome, Americans must wage total war against the new layer on top: the intellectuals, the fourth and most dangerous branch of government.

On the Relative Significance of Things

Accountants must sort through and substantiate huge amounts of detail before they can certify that a corporation's financial statements fairly present the results of its operations. That certified veracity of corporate profitability provides the foundation for investment activity. However, many approximations go into the final statements because it is impossible to prepare a precisely accurate bottom line number, such as the earnings per share. To ensure that their result is "substantially" correct, the accountants rely on a finely tuned sense of "materiality." That means they concentrate on what is "significant," not getting bogged down in relatively unimportant details. The final number, though never theoretically precise, is highly useful in measuring the performance of the company. This same reliance on the "relative significance" of things should be applied to most aspects of life, because it is eminently practical and logical, and most everything in life is even more uncertain than accounting numbers. The principle applies especially to deciding which issues of public policy are most in need of repair or tinkering because otherwise we waste time on relatively unimportant issues. For example, in the first 100 days of the newly elected 2006 Congress, very little meaningful legislation was enacted—a large portion of the bills passed had to do with renaming federal buildings!

It is hoped that the historical review in these pages of how societies grow, mature, then stagnate and decline gives the reader an idea of the fragile nature of things as well as the importance of zeroing in on what is crucial versus what is superficial. If an individual has been induced into a Trust Fund mentality that assumes all the freedom and abundance of the West is a given—they may actually believe the most pressing problem now is simply how to divvy up the pie. They may be quite prepared to squander their inheritance, to invade and live off the principal bequeathed to them by the work of those who built the West. Such is the attitude of those who push for more and more government programs, increased subsidies to every clamorous group, more and more taxes to pay for their latest ideas, and more and more regulations to fine tune the way people live their lives. That road is the road to decline. The grandchildren of such people will have little left to inherit except for the debts and failed dreams of their ill-advised parents.

There is another road, and it is not turning back the clock to the good old days, attractive though that might appear. Instead, a way must be found to adapt the extraordinary system of government we have to the needs of the future. There are important changes needed, significant matters, and they can only be addressed if we the people put our emphasis on what is relatively the most important issues facing the nation. When those key problems are isolated, the next step is to demand action, not phony band-aids and mirages like the recent campaign finance reform acts, or the illegal alien legislation.

Congressmen no longer solve problems; they paper over them, attempting to accommodate every special interest group that approaches them. Nero allegedly fiddled while Rome burned, but Congress goes a step further. While the nation's future is at stake, they spend the majority of their time investigating each other, over trivialities, over who leaked what to whom, over what the meaning of "is" is, over their opponents childhood indiscretions, and holding hearing after hearing where each senator vies for a media moment. They have no grasp on what is "significant" or on the relative importance of things. Indeed they avoid any issue of substance. And the media do not set any course, concentrating instead on garish stories of gossip, "leaks," gloom and doom, and innuendo to fit their political agenda.

The result of this dismal myopia is that what needs doing rarely even gets looked at. And the seemingly big questions, such as the war on terror and the adventure in the Middle East, which preoccupy so many in counterproductive second-guessing, may turn out to have not been the biggest problems facing the nation. Any rational and balanced approach would address the other larger challenges facing the nation. It is just possible that if the media, special interest groups, and lobbyists left the legislators alone for a while, our elected representatives might just find the time and seclusion to debate and solve the real problems facing the nation. Under current PC rules they have to mince their words carefully lest they become the next public firestorm of controversy—the thought police and speech enforcers are everywhere.

Catching the Next Wave

Alvin and Heidi Tofler have written about the major changes needed if America is to keep up with the modern world—and, to prepare for a new "Third Wave" of civilization. The first major advance by mankind was the Agricultural Revolution, a few millenniums ago when hunter gatherers began to grow their own food and domesticate animals. The second major "wave" was the Industrial Revolution of several centuries ago that witnessed, for those few nations that were open to such innovation, huge advances in the production of food and merchandise with a resulting growth in affluence. Today, history is advancing rapidly toward a new age based on "Information" and computer/Internet capabilities.

According to the Toflers, "The Third Wave brings with it a genuinely new way of life based on diversified, renewable energy sources; on methods of production that make factory assembly lines obsolete; on new, non-nuclear families; on a novel institution that might be called the 'electronic cottage;' and on radically changed schools and corporations of the future. The emergent civilization . . . carries us beyond standardization, synchronization, and centralization, beyond the concentration of energy, money and power."[455] These predictions lay out some of the significant types of policy questions that the country's leaders should be focused on. Instead, all we get is screaming and hollering about the latest leaking of gossip, finger pointing over alleged wrongdoing, or a battle over a personality clash among the star-struck denizens of Washington's inner beltway.

Other commentators have predicted, like the Toflers, that massive changes will come from the instant availability and communication of information on the Internet. A heartening example is how an individual blogger brought down Dan Rather and the CBS network after they aired forged documents about President George W. Bush's military service record. As Daniel Flynn writes, "Thinking with your ideology rather than your brain makes you susceptible to be duped. Dan Rather and CBS are finding this out the hard way. The CBS eye is blinded by ideology."[456] The bloggers who repudiated CBS's documents are a testament to the "little guy" that this book celebrates, and further proof that progress comes up from the bottom. An alert "freeper," trawling the boards at FreeRepublic.com, under the anonymous name of "Buckhead," questioned the typography of Rather's memos and called them forgeries. He did this at 11:59 P.M., less than four hours after the 8

P.M. airing of *60 Minutes.* Buckhead's claim flew around the Internet and by the next morning had elicited more supporting evidence that CBS had actually tried to pass off faked documents.

CBS News executive, Jonathan Klein, attempting to stonewall the story, ridiculed the blogger as "some guy sitting in his living room in pajamas" (how low and common can you get!). In contrast, he praised the professional news team housed in a Manhattan skyscraper with its "multiple layers of checks and balances" (how high and mighty can you get!).[457] Intellectuals, academics, and spokesmen for several Leftist organizations went way out on a limb for a week, defending CBS until the bloggers overwhelmed them with the facts. The common man, because of a window of opportunity and freedom, occasioned in this case by the Internet, was able to topple the arrogant media elite who were caught spreading false bad news from on high.

Such media sins, however gross they may be, are still, unfortunately, a small problem compared to the gridlock and scandals that have frozen the centers of our state and federal governments into irrelevance. In *The Sovereign Individual,* the authors address this collapse of American governance, but, on a hopeful note, speak of the coming death of politics as we know it. In short, government has gotten so bad, they say, it will self-destruct. They explain that politics began with the early stages of industrialization and ever since has preoccupied itself "with controlling and rationalizing the power of the state. . . . Now it is dying. A widespread revulsion against politics and politicians is sweeping the world. You see it in news and speculation on the hidden details of Whitewater, and the poorly disguised murder of Vincent Foster. You see it innumerous other scandals touching President Bill Clinton. You see it in reports of embezzlement by leading congressmen from the House Post Office."[458] And the same corruption and incompetence has been displayed in all major Western capitals as well as the United Nations. "Almost everywhere you turn in countries with mature welfare states once thought of as well governed, people hate their political leaders."[459]

Davidson and Rees-Mogg compare the current bloated and inefficient national governments to the situation in 1500, when the people of the West rose up against the egregious sins of the Church that in those days dominated their societies. After that, the secular power of government increasingly exerted power to balance religious institutions. Unfortunately, after 500 years, the state has assumed the abusive role the Church once played. "Mass democracy and the concept of citizenship flourished as the nation-state grew. They will falter as the nation state falters, causing every bit as much dismay in Washington as the erosion of chivalry caused in the court of the duke of Burgundy five hundred years ago."[460] Such a massive displacement of centralized authority could save America from its incipient decline. That may be the only way to free the "elected' officials from the distractions and corruptions of office. A means must be found to change the manner in which they operate; to discourage practices where they pander to the public but respond only to lobbyists and special interest groups, and demean our people by encouraging a victim mentality and expanding the modern populist welfare state. The liberating empowerment of the world wide web may allow ordinary people to throw off the socialist and centrist policies that burden today's world. But it will require structural changes in how legislative bodies operate, and a massive reduction in the bureaucracies that administer the current smothering web of laws and regulations.

The Toflers point out that it has been difficult to reverse the ever-expanding twentieth century state socialism that "led not to affluence, equality and freedom, but to a one-party political system, a massive bureaucracy, heavy-handed secret police, . . . and repression of intellectual and artistic freedom. Setting aside the oceans of spurting blood needed to prop it up, . . . every one of these elements is not just a way of organizing people but also—and more profoundly—a particular way of organizing, channeling and controlling knowledge."[461]

Today's politically correct restrictions on speech and the kowtowing to multiculturalism and diversity have already corrupted our schools, colleges, and governmental agencies. The policies of controlled speech and thought are Orwellian in nature and the natural outgrowth of the elites that seek to dominate America's institutions. "In fact, behind each of these elements we find a single obsolete assumption about knowledge: the arrogant belief that those in command—whether of the party or state—should decide what others should know."[462]

The parallel between the massive governmental leviathans of today and the oppressive medieval church are clear, and the former needs a reformation as much as did the latter. "The Medieval Church five hundred years ago, like the nation-state today, consumed more of society's resources than it ever had before, or ever would again. The Church then, like the state today, seemed incapable of functioning and sustaining itself on even record amounts of revenue. Just as the state has come to dominate late-industrial economies, spending more than half of all revenue in some Western European countries, so the Church dominated the late-feudal economy, draining resources and retarding growth."[463] The current fevered attempts in most municipalities to over-ride Proposition $2\frac{1}{2}$ show just how incapable these governments are of functioning even with record amounts of revenue.

It is important to distinguish between nation states as they are currently mismanaged and such entities as they might be reformed. Intellectuals have recently deplored nationalism and nation-states, blaming the Nazi and Communist atrocities on their organizing structure, or "nationalism," rather than on the distorted ideas of their academic and intellectual elites. It was Stalin and his utopian ideology, not the Russian state that killed millions of Ukrainian peasants. There is nothing wrong with nation-states and flag-waving patriotism, per se; indeed, loyalty to one's homeland will usually increase unity and teamwork.

Today's elite have taken to criticizing "nationalism" because they want to create a bigger worldwide bureaucracy to rule over everyone. The better path is to mend the nation we have by decentralizing power to the lowest levels of government possible. Simplifying and downsizing would achieve some economy and efficiency and return more power and freedom to the people. Giving up sovereignty to international agencies, as many of the academic elites recommend, is the exact opposite of what is needed.

Davidson and Rees-Mogg suggest that "the nation- state will be replaced by new forms of sovereignty, some of them unique in history, some reminiscent of the city-states and medieval merchant republics of the pre-modern world . . . governments will find that they must compete like corporations for income, charging no more for their service than they are worth to the people who pay for them. The full implications of this change are all but unimaginable."[464]

But they have one thing in common—they must be smaller and more responsive to the individual citizens. These changes cannot be based on abstractions. They do not require changes in the nation's basic beliefs and values. They should not be based on any ideology. They must, like all past governmental advances, be simply mechanical. They can be made gradually, adapting the existing successful structure of Western economies to new simpler systems that are more responsive and less costly. The downsizing of central governments and a massive reduction in laws and regulations would help remove impediments to individual creativity.

The possibilities of downsizing have been advanced by a call for a new concept of what makes up a useful "community." Spencer MacCallum has challenged the common assumption "that an expanding population necessitates increases in the size of formal organizations in society and, correspondingly, increases in the use of force to restrict liberty among persons. With these assumptions, men have accepted more and more enslavement as the necessary cost of fecundity."[465] He foresees a new form of society, one where all individuals can interact without the stultifying shadow of governments overseeing their activities. The recent spread of Internet communications makes his vision both plausible and imminent. MacCallum suggests that "A new social capability, an authentic art of community, already has emerged in tens of thousands of small beginnings. . . . Might not these beginnings contain the empirical seed of a new social integration which will ultimately permit men to be truly creative in their community affairs as they have begun to be in their material world, therein producing new environments appropriate to the infinite process of differentiation—and, with this, the ever increasing potential for fulfilling association—of the individual human spirit?"[466]

Instead of calling for a return to the warm and natural pleasures of rural life, which is not practicable for many, MacCallum has offered an insight into a broader potential for each individual to reach out to many others but still remain in a supportive community of fellow human beings.

Desirable change will never come from the established elites who will only seek to hold onto their power. And the radicals that want big changes are driven by a faulty vision that will only create havoc: "We have in every society a fringe of pseudo-revolutionaries, steeped in obsolete Second Wave assumptions, for whom no proposed change is radical enough. . . . Yet what lies ahead . . . is not a replay of any previous revolutionary drama. . . . The creation of new political structures for a Third Wave civilization will not come in a single climactic upheaval but as a consequence of a thousand innovations and collisions at many levels in many places over a period of decades."[467]

Here, the Tofler's endorse the principle that historical advances always came from small changes, as practical individuals constantly tinkered with the mechanics of governance. In the meantime, as these changes are achieved piece by piece, it is essential to undo the restrictions currently depressing free thought in our schools, colleges, and public institutions. Shuffling congressmen and presidents will not end the political paralysis. "There is no possibility of restoring sense, order and management 'efficiency' to many governments without a substantial devolution of central power. We need to divide the decision load and shift a significant part of it downward."[468]

Another observer of today's political stalemate is James Ronald Kennedy, who has called for a reformed society, true to its original format when it was founded, sheared of the centrist and managed abstractions put in place by the uninformed elites. His recent book,

Reclaiming Liberty, suggests that all Americans can enjoy life and prosper in a bold new atmosphere that encourages personal account-ability, self-determinism, and the satisfaction of personal accomplish-ment.[469] These cultural values that Kennedy wants restored are the very ones that empowered early Americans, and are also the same attitudes that we described as being sabotaged by the elites of mature nations who have a different vision—one where they administer from above to a flock of helpless victims way below.

This approach mirrors that of Barry Goldwater who agreed that change in the mechanical operation of government is constant and necessary, but all such changes should be based on the enduring underlying principles that provide the foundation of freedom: "Cir-cumstances do change. So do the problems that are shaped by the circumstances. But the principles that govern the solution of the problems do not."[470]

Kennedy proposes a reaffirmation of "States Rights," which would restore the federalist system of limited central government that was envisioned by the Founders. Some such amendment may be needed to make the existing Ninth and Tenth amendments effective because "under our current liberal/socialist political system, the federal courts are the final arbiters of the limitations imposed upon the federal government by these amendments."[471] Kennedy's argument con-demning "judicial overreach" was reinforced recently when a court ruled that a woman growing marijuana in her California back yard strictly for personal use and only within the bounds of her property was in violation of the Interstate Commerce clause. That is how far-stretched federal authority has become under the current politicized judiciary.

Alvin and Heidi Tofler call for all Americans to participate in shaping changes for the better in our governance. They call for "tremendous pressure from below" because our leaders are so en-meshed in their positions of power that they will look only to solutions that embellish their status. That is why today's leaders favor activist judges, to increase the centralized power of government. It is why they oppose school vouchers and private social security trust accounts—

such innovations return power to the people. That is why they extend amnesty and more and more free benefits to illegal aliens—to boost the percentage of Americans beholden to government. The entire U.S. governmental bureaucracy is bloated and unresponsive to the interests of the working man and woman. Those entrenched seek only to hold onto their seats of power and avoid any reform movements that would make the government leaner, more efficient, and less costly.

The Toflers point out that, "What is needed, we believe, is a clear distinction between rear-guard politicians who wish to preserve or restore an unworkable past, and those who are ready to make the transition to what we call a 'Third Wave' information-age society."[472] The Toflers have addressed some of the significant issues that face the country. Instead of wasting time on trivialities, we must concentrate on the major issues that will determine our future. Other newly re-organized nations have adopted many of the mechanics that led to Western supremacy and are making huge strides forward that could leave America behind if the current decline is not reversed. It is up to the people to force another Reformation—not a religious one this time, but rather, a major modification in the way our government functions to meet the challenges of the next five hundred years.

Chapter 16
What's So Great About the Common Man?

*These [common] people . . . ask no questions; they
live, seemingly, for the day; they waste no energy or
substance on the effort to understand life; they enjoy the physical
experience of living; . . . If they are wise, surely the rest of us are fools.*
—George F. Kennan

THE COMMON MAN is no paragon. He can be cantankerous,
shallow, aggressive, opinionated, bigoted, envious—in no way the
polished gentleman we might hope for. Anyone who has served on a
jury of his peers and tried to reach consensus can harbor no illusions
about the perfection of the common man. Indeed, it is the innumerable failings of ordinary people that make the science of governance so
difficult and the realization of utopias impossible. Nevertheless, from
the common men and women of any society springs the genius that
moves the world.

It is really just a matter of numbers. In recorded history there have
been millions, eventually billions, of common men and women. The
old European monarchies, or chauvinist Islam, or stratified India,
extinguished the potential of their citizens. But open and upwardly
mobile societies have welcomed and encouraged individual potential.
Most of the great presidents and prime ministers have come from the
lower or middle classes. Most millionaires in Britain and America are
self-made, having emerged from modest economic origins with little
help from their families or governments. These freer societies draw on
the best individuals from every stratum of their populace. No one need
be excluded. All individuals are granted an equal opportunity to
contribute, and it is up to them all to show what they are capable of
accomplishing with their lives. Out of this chaos emerge the uncommon men and women who move mountains and advance the well-
being of all the others.

The United States, to its credit, was among the first to get it right. In the past century it gave women the vote, and then began to draw on the rich capabilities of its minorities when men like Thurgood Marshall and Jackie Robinson made clear to nearly everyone that there was nothing inferior about being black. Jesse Owens, representing Uncle Sam, did more to repudiate Hitler's "master race" when he ran away with the 1936 Olympics in Berlin than all the intellectuals put end to end. In a caste system, many do not get this chance, and many extraordinary talents are consigned to the margins of society. The success of every country depends on enabling such talent to emerge. Yet in the vast majority of those nations sitting and posturing in the United Nations, most citizens are denied this opportunity. They deserve better.

Benjamin Franklin—of humble birth, a printer's apprentice, an American rags to riches story

The opportunity to achieve rights and safety for all mankind should not be lost because of petty and narrow self-interest. Karl Popper urges an activist approach, asserting that although history by itself may have no meaning, we can give it meaning; although history has no predetermined purposes, we can seek ends of our own. Each individual has substantial power to shape his course, if free to do so. This stirring challenge reflects the proactive attitude that enables the people of some nations to succeed, and the absence of which dooms others to failure regardless of climate or physical or monetary assets.

Where freedom reigns, when upward mobility is possible, people will strive and compete to succeed—and their societies will prosper. Conversely, when the doors of opportunity are closed, or when welfare programs provide a sufficient alternative, the energy and talents of many will lie dormant—and their societies will suffer the loss.

Karl Popper deplores the devotion of scholars to the history of power politics, heroes, and great events, since these elements have often proved to be the least noble or helpful. He suggests most history is taught as merely a series of facts, a recital of wars fought, and a listing of the major civilizations, without any connecting thread to provide meaning. Indeed, he says no meaning can be discerned nor is there any universal history of mankind. However, he does observe that any such synthesis "would have to be a history of all human hopes, struggles, and sufferings. . . . The history of freedom is that we are ourselves responsible for it, in the same sense in which we are responsible for what we make of our lives. . . . The life of the forgotten, of the unknown individual man; his sorrows and his joys, his suffering and his death, this is the real content of human experience down the ages. If that could be told by history, then I should certainly not say that it is blasphemy to see the finger of God in it. But such a history does not and cannot exist; and all the history which exists, our history of the Great and Powerful, is at best a shallow comedy."[473]

As I have also argued, great events and great men have indeed more often than not been comedic and harmful. But the historical progress that has occurred (despite the fumbling and butchery) rests precisely on those "human hopes, struggles and sufferings down the ages" that Popper celebrates. Through the ages, many unknown individuals assumed responsibility and helped to achieve freedom, human rights, and an open society. Those common people "gave history meaning" by bequeathing to us the legacy of free institutions that they so persistently pursued. It is their history of determined effort that is presented in *Common Genius*.

It has been the struggle of those occasionally free people that created modern freedom and prosperity; they demonstrated that with some degree of order and security, and unburdened by oppressive forces, they could and would carve out giant steps forward for all mankind. "The great advances of civilization, whether in architecture or painting, in science or literature, in industry or agriculture, have never come from centralized government," observes Milton Friedman. "Their achievements were the product of individual genius, of strongly held minority views, of a social climate permitting variety and diversity. Government can never duplicate the variety and diversity of individual action."[474]

Sidney Hook observed that the continued flourishing of the American experiment requires "a commitment as deep and sustained as that which inspired those who left us our heritage of freedom."[475] Each new generation must recognize the danger of lapsing into the trust-fund mentality that allows complacency and an ignorance of history to soften their resolve, and heed anew Whittaker Chambers' admonition that the support of freedom must be nourished "by a deep and sustained commitment that can match the power of the totalitarians' vision of control." The new totalitarians, hiding under the compassionate banner of paternalistic government, are fundamentally the same as the fascists and communists of yesteryear: they, too, seek control over the common people of America. It has always been thus.

Armed with historical knowledge, with appreciation for this heritage and how it came to be, a man would have to be very obtuse to cast such a society aside, or revile it for shortcomings real or imagined, or stomp on its flag. While there are many anti-American critics who do these things, one thing they don't do is leave; least of all those intellectuals and Hollywood celebrities who perpetually threaten to do so. By not leaving, they confirm that America is the best place in the world to live. They also thereby confirm that no other country has created its equal. That is why their criticisms of America mean no more than the nonsense that comes from a Monday morning quarterback, nit-picking his team's performance, un-bruised from the fray, suggesting untested alternatives, and bad-mouthing the team and its coaches.

And, in this simile, remember that the team—America—just won the Super Bowl—as it has every year for the past 200 years. Because that is what the United States has done in comparison to the rest of the world. And yet that very bitter and obtuse Monday morning quarterback wants to totally recast the team! Worse, if he is a true member of the intelligentsia, he will want to impose gentler "rules of engagement" to end all that pushing and shoving violence in the line of scrimmage! He might then even go on to suggest we not keep score—to avoid hurting the feelings of the losers! With friends like that, who needs enemies?

In the past fifty years, the political scene has changed. The extreme liberals and intellectuals have become what Bill O'Reilly calls the "secular-progressives," and no reform is radical enough to suit them. They are the unenlightened descendants of the European Enlightenment philosophers—the geniuses who claimed that pure reason—their big brains—could figure out how to make the world better, and ushered in a century of war and genocide to impose their visions. In *Culture Warrior*, secular-progressives (S-Ps) are described as the radical Left that supports public control of corporations, guaranteed income for everyone through greatly expanded welfare and redistribution programs, the end of any reference to religion, and a passive-pacifist foreign policy. The S-P movement "wants the United States to decline in power. It wants a new world order where global consensus would rule and the superpower model of our time would recede into obsolescence."[476] Those would be wonderful things if we could rely on the United Nations to govern all nations lightly and honestly. But they can't even govern themselves—their own organization—which is more corrupt than the American Congress! The idea of "one-world" government is a utopian fantasy. Progress will only come from going in the opposite direction—returning as much authority as possible to the lowest level of government, where ordinary people can keep an eye on it.

The secular progressives, as O'Reilly calls them, would make the world a much more dangerous place—especially for America. "Can you picture Russia and communist China dominating the world? How about the combined Arab states?"[477] We have mentioned the need to put things in perspective, recognize the relative significance of the issues facing us, and such a balanced judgment should ally many from both the Left and Right, the liberals and conservatives, to stand up to those who would destroy the country. The questions of animal rights, women's rights, minority rights, free prescriptions for the elderly, and in-state tuition for illegal aliens are just distractions—they are very far from being the biggest problems facing the nation. The radicals bent on destroying the nation have used those issues to divide the electorate. They continue to fool a lot of the people a lot of the time with these smokescreens. After all, they are intellectuals and very smart at playing with ideas and concepts. They have just never made anything work.

Unfortunately, those voters wanting to turn back the radical centrist policies of the Left must turn to the Right and thereby nourish corporate subsidies, farm supports, an adventurist foreign policy, and related restrictions on personal freedom. In some cases, the "lesser evil" is difficult to pin point. Both major parties lean to an imperial presidency, foreign entanglements, a love for the inept World Bank and IMF, an inability to resist government handouts, and support for clandestine CIA operations. The two political parties, each in their own way, pander to the vocal well-established interest groups to stay in power.

Sheldon Richman has referred to this Republican/Democratic similarity as a welfare-warfare scheme whereby either side can enable its ruling class to expand its power and wealth. Each elite claims to be pursuing welfare or war "to serve and 'protect' its people," but the primary objective "is a grand scheme to enable a ruling class, through its complex bureaucracy and ideological smokescreens, to transfer wealth from the industrious classes to itself."[478] And those "industrious classes" are the common people who are given only this limited and inadequate choice in leaders. This situation forces the tax-paying producers to support not only what Richman calls the "tax-consuming aristocracy" but the heavy burden of all the government programs these elites create.

Hernado de Soto was quoted earlier on how the fox and the wolf may be very different creatures, but to a rabbit, it is the similarity that matters. So it is in American politics. Restoring all financial power over campaign financing to the people, acting individually and independently, is one way to rein in the existing perverse situation. Such power would make legislators more responsive, reduce the re-election of ineffective incumbents, and make third party candidates more viable. All three results meet the Radzewicz test: they enable each individual citizen to decide political outcomes and add to his authority over elected representatives.

The vast majority of Americans are proud of their country but believe government is too big; they respect all faiths, but believe it is good for children to pray and behave in school; they desire to help the poor in other nations, but see no use in the United Nations or wasted dollar aid; they believe in free speech, but resent the arrogance of large special interest groups who claim to speak for them; they are for education, but can't understand why it costs $40,000 a year to attend college; they support forgiveness, but think criminals should be punished.[479] They have observed the United Nations in action for half a century and fear any "New World Order" that gives such a distant, corrupt, and incompetent group the power to rule over us from the top.

If America's decline is to be averted, it will be averted by the common genius of her ordinary citizens. By relying on fundamental values, facing difficult truths, making hard choices, and seeking practical solutions, they can find the way to balance the security and safety of each person so they can work in freedom, but not live free of work. They can reverse the trend toward vast bureaucracies in government that oppress the people, and develop enlightened and lean public agencies that foster free enterprise. By resisting all acts that reduce the free constructive activity of individuals, they can steer clear of the pitfalls of mature societies. They can cast aside the failed vision of the intellectual elite that has sought to impose their destructive, valueless ideas to destroy a successful way of life—a way of life the elite did not build, does not contribute to, and cannot understand.

However, it will take a supreme effort by the voters to turn back the failed vision of their new elites. In Newt Gingrich's words, "These elites want a dramatically different world from the values and aspirations of most Americans. . . . Self-government implies that on these issues, the people should rule, but the liberal elite minority is winning and the popular majority is losing. . . . The entrenched lobbyists and entrenched bureaucracies will do all they can to minimize the changes no matter how vital those changes are to America's future. . . . Only a grassroots citizens' movement can insist on the level of change that is needed for our children and grandchildren to have a successful future."[480]

Alexander Deane has called for the middle class to re-assert itself, charging that they have "abdicated" their role as sustainers of the traditions and culture that made their country strong.[481] However, this charge may be unfair because it was the middle class' preoccupation with work, civic activities, and their familial responsibilities that had made the nation strong. They elected representatives to abide by the Constitution and to look after essential governing matters. This allowed the people to devote their energies to their personal lives and work. That arrangement is what made in Conquest's words a successful "consensual society." The problem arose when the intelligentsia arrived and made selected ideological issues into all-consuming programs and pursued them to the ultimate degree. Thus the problem may not be one of "abdication" but one of "usurpation," where single purpose advocacy groups pursue divisive agendas that only they desire.

The advent of special interest lobbying groups, headed by a small coterie of zealous single issue advocates, has made this divisive pattern a major unsettling feature in Western democracies. It might help if everyone got back to their work and if the legislatures did as little as possible. In fact, the latter should concentrate on reducing the size of government from some 40 percent of GDP to 25 percent, as the people of New Zealand have done over the past two decades.[482] It is a self evident truth that if congressmen worked toward more efficiency and less investigations, more forward thinking and less finger pointing, everyone would be much happier.

This need to recast government represents an unfair burden for the working people of the nation. Their job has always been to create economic plenty, more and more efficiently, undisturbed by the administrative functions of their elected representatives. There is nothing creative or positive about reversing the impact of the intellectuals. It should be unnecessary. Unfortunately, the new elites, allied with the academics, pressed by lobbyists and special-interest groups, gorging on false bad news, and encouraged by those who favor centrist controls and grand solutions to every minor human problem, have usurped power and altered the nation's course for the worse. It is a course of weakness and pandering to irresponsibility, ungrounded in any moral certainty and devoid of patriotism and sentiment. It is a road to decline, and it must be altered.

It has been forty years since John F. Kennedy enjoined us to ask "not what your country can do for you; ask what can you do for your country." That was a good speech, delivered with the irresistible Kennedy panache, but it changed the behavior of very few people. It is now time to heed the advice. Domestic policies in many democracies are spinning out of control and creating large constituencies of victims and financially-dependent individuals. The poor in lesser developed nations are making little or no progress in living standards. The struggling peoples of a hundred nations would welcome the opportunity to rely on their own initiative.

It is up to each person, each uncommon individual, to demand the sweeping away of impediments to freedom. And while each person's own country should always come first, the demand for reform should encompass all the nations and peoples of the world.

In his 2004 Inaugural Address, President George W. Bush praised the spread of democracy and freedom and urged the free world to assist that spread. This well-meaning desire to help the peoples of other lands echoed similar calls from presidents over the past hundred years, from Wilson and Roosevelt, to Kennedy and Reagan. These leaders recognized that what the Western nations had developed was special and valuable, and that people from all around the world now aspire to live in lands of opportunity. With the fading of the Cold War, and the demise of the communist experiment, with free enterprise and free economies on the rise, now may be the time that such dreams can be fulfilled.

A first step is to accept the primacy of de facto economic freedom over democratic symbols, and to concentrate on empowering the economic activity of every individual citizen by increasing the security of his person and property and eliminating oppressive controls. We should put an immediate end to all foreign aid to countries whose systems fail to give all their citizens equal access to advance up the ladder of economic opportunity, as measured by such analyses as the two annual reports published by the Heritage Society and the Fraser Institute.

Free nations can collaborate to end poverty and oppression throughout the world. This process should not be sought by force-feeding dogma or nation-building. It should be fostered by withholding all aid and comfort from those nations that have not demonstrated real progress in empowering their people, all their people, equally.

And, by defending the principles that built freedom and prosperity, the West may yet ward off its own decline, and reach ever greater heights of prosperity and achievement.

Acknowledgements

T HIS BOOK HAS REPRESENTED an adventure of sorts, a search for meaning. There are many people who have shared this effort—they will recognize their own ideas within the pages of this book. It could never have been completed without their help; nor without the perspective of many years experience.

At seventeen, my mind was opened to a wider world when I worked with the American Friends Service Committee and Bayard Rustin in their political endeavors. Their goals of world peace and civil rights for all people have a nobility we must never ignore. Responding to a natural youthful idealism, I volunteered to be a spokesman for unilateral disarmament. Seated in the Senator's office, I put forth the case and the Chairman of the House Armed Services Committee graciously thanked us for our ideas. A year or two later, I discovered George Orwell and Arthur Koestler, and like them, jettisoned my sympathy for Communist Russia and pacifist solutions. I owe a debt to all those who helped me pass quickly through this turbulent full circle in political ideology.

I have often admitted that as a quasi-intellectual, I am caught somewhere in limbo between those who love grand abstractions and the Joe Six-Packs who prefer simple answers. My parents influence— to keep both feet firmly planted on the ground—eventually ruled my thinking. Thanks must also be awarded to the examining professor who, after a dismal Doctoral Oral Exam, told me I just didn't have sufficient conceptualizing skills to deal effectively with abstractions. Taking that as a compliment, I abandoned postgraduate teaching and entered the realm of business and politics. There are countless individuals that have subsequently contributed to my education while I worked with middling success as an elected politician, an appointed office-holder, a faculty member, a businessman, an investor, carpenter, an accountant, auditor and business consultant, board member, landlord, professional trustee, farmer, sailor, and aspiring joke teller. Such active involvements, dealing constantly with the vicissitudes of reality, have protected me from the lure of abstractions and ideologies.

I also acknowledge a debt to my teachers, many of whom are referred to in these pages, and to the great Class of '54, many of whose authors are also referenced herein. It is unfortunate that today's academics have fallen so far beneath the titans of yesterday who instructed and inspired their students with an impartial and scholarly erudition, unmindful of restrictions imposed by political correctness. Professor Turkevitch never had to insert gender or diversity into his dramatic presentations of the glory of chemical reactions. Those teachers gave us the gift that keeps on giving—a hunger for truth and understanding—free of fanatical ideology—and sowed in our minds a life-long love of learning. The early drafts of *Common Genius* benefited from the comments and suggestions of a number of those classmates who took a very helpful interest in my project.

My family and friends deserve special mention because they have either supported or tolerated my quasi-intellectual efforts. Their solid confidence and honest comments provided both sufficient encouragement and an accurate compass to see it through to the end. My wife Catherine, along with our nine children and fourteen grandchildren, have been a motivating force—especially when they keep asking, "When will it be done?"

Probably the biggest debt is due to the hundreds of writers who have ploughed this ground before me. Most authors, in their acknowledgments, list all the eminent scholars who they have worked with, but then magnanimously suggest that all errors are theirs alone. I cannot wholly share that sentiment because I have actually relied on the hundreds of authors cited herein. If they are wrong, I may be, but I doubt it. There are just too many writers who have indicated that progress comes strictly from individual human action, and dozens more have lamented the curse that intellectuals place on mature nations. While they all stop short of the obvious conclusions to be drawn, their piecemeal decimation of the great philosophers leaves little room for confusion. All I have done is connect the dots. That is why I owe so much to Julian Simon, Hernando de Soto, Mancur Olson, Thomas Sowell, Paul Johnson, David Landes, Charles Murray, William Mc Neill, E. L. Jones, Adler, Aron, Bailyn, Bloom, Conquest, Dershowitz, Halle, Herman, Horowitz, Kurlansky, McCullough, Muravchik, Podhoretz, Popper, Posner, Stossel, Stein, Tuchman, Voegelin, Von Mises, Wells, and all the other commentators cited in this book. It is their exhaustive, scholarly, and insightful writings that provided the foundation for the new theory of historical progression advanced herein.

Finally, I want to thank a few individuals who provided special assistance: Kathleen Nelson and the people at Laissez Faire Books for the confidence they have shown in *Common Genius*. It is not for the faint of heart to endorse a book that shatters a number of academic icons and challenges traditional orthodoxies. And David M. Brown, whose knowledgeable editing and wise suggestions not only clarified the material but reduced my occasionally erroneous, exaggerated, and outrageous prose to tolerable levels. Chris Burchhardt was very kind to design our website and contribute his teenage genius to guide me through the intricacies of word processing and the magic of transmitting documents over the internet. My thanks to Bruce Greene for the illustrations depicting some of the common people, heroes and other respected characters from the pages of history. His unique renderings emphasize for me the honorable but steely-eyed grit of the uncommon commoners who somehow came forward when needed to advance the well-being of mankind.

Notes

Chapter 1

[1] Niccolo Machiavelli, *The Prince and Other Writings* (New York: Barnes & Noble Classics, 2003), 66.

[2] Marc A. Miles, *Index of Economic Freedom, 2005 Edition* (Washington DC: Heritage Books, 2005).

[3] Richard A. Posner, *Public Intellectuals* (Cambridge MA: Harvard University Press, 2003), 6

[4] Jared Diamond, *Guns, Germs, and Steel: The Fates of Human Societies* (New York: W. W. Norton, 1999), 25.

[5] Ibid.

[6] P.T. Bauer, *Reality and Rhetoric: Studies in the Economics of Development* (Boston: Harvard University Press, 1986).

[7] Julian L. Simon, *The Ultimate Resource* (Princeton: Princeton University Press, 1996), 206. "I do not suggest that nature is limitlessly bountiful. Rather, the possibilities in the world are sufficiently great so that with the present state of knowledge—even without the additional knowledge that human imagination and human enterprise will surely develop in the future—we and our descendents can manipulate the elements in such a fashion that we can have all the raw materials that we desire at prices ever smaller relative to other goods and to our total incomes. In short, our cornucopia is the human mind and heart, not a Santa Claus natural environment."

[8] Ibid, 11.

[9] George F. Will, *With a Happy Eye, But...* (New York: The Free Press, 2002), 20.

[10] Kenneth Pomeranz, *The Great Divergence* (Princeton: Princeton University Press, 2001).

[11] Ricardo Duchesne, "On The Rise of The West: Researching Kenneth Pomerantz's Great Divergence," Review of Radical Political Economics, Winter 2004, 52-81.

[12] Charles Chenevix Trench, *The Road to Khartoum: A Life of General Charles Gordon* (New York: Carroll & Graf Publishers, Inc., 1978), 24.

[13] Arthur Herman, *How The Scots Invented the Modern World* (New York: Three Rivers Press, 2001), 403.

[14] Ibid, 404.

[15] Edward Hallett Carr, *What Is History* (New York: Vintage Books, 1961), 132.

[16] Ibid, 130.

[17] Tim Harford, "Why Poor Countries Are Poor," *Reason*, March 2006, 39.

[18] Thomas B. Carson, *Beyond the American Dream: Work and Wealth in the 21st Century* (Bloomington: First Books Library, 1998), 10.

[19] Thomas Sowell, *Conquests and Cultures* (New York: Basic Books, 1999), 349.

[20] Raymond Aron, *The Opium of the Intellectuals* (New Brunswick: Transaction Publishers, 2002), 227.

Chapter 2

[21] Jared Diamond, *Guns, Germs, and Steel: The Fates of Human Societies* (New York: W.W. Norton, 1999), 24.

[22] Carr, op. cit., 52.

[23] Ibid, 52.

[24] Diamond, op. cit., 24

[25] Jeffrey Sachs, *The End of Poverty* (London and New York: Penguin Books, 2006), 58.

[26] Ibid, 58.

[27] Ibid, 59.

[28] Ibid, 33.

 [29] E.L. Jones, *The European Miracle: Environments, Economies and Geopolitics in the History of Europe and Asia* (Cambridge: Cambridge University Press, 1987).

[30] Ibid, 233.

[31] Henry Grady Weaver, *The Mainspring of Human Progress* (Irvington-On-Hudson, New York: Foundation for Economic Education, 1999), 14

[32] E. L. Jones, op. cit., 225.

[33] Ibid, 234.

[34] Ibid, 236.

[35] Charles Murray, *Human Accomplishment: The Pursuit of Excellence in the Arts and Sciences, 800 B.C. to 1950* (New York: HarperCollins Publishers, 2003), 391-394.

[36] Jones, op. cit., 235.

[37] Murray, op. cit., 361.

[38] James D. Gwartney, *Economic Freedom of the World, 2004: Annual Report* (Washington DC: The Cato Institute, 2004).

[39] Sachs, op. cit., xviii.

Chapter 3

[40] See Gertrude Himmelfarb, *One Nation, Two Cultures* (New York: Alfred A. Knopf, 1999), 9. The author recalls the familiar observation that in the U.S. "there was no aristocratic tradition against which the middle classes had to contend."

[41] *Webster's Encyclopedic Unabridged Dictionary of the English Language* (New York: Gramercy Books, 1994), 738.

[42] Pomeranz, op. cit.

[43] Martin Amis, *Koba the Dread: Laughter and the Twenty Million* (New York: Vintage, 2002).

[44] Jack Cashill, *Hoodwinked: How Intellectual Hucksters Have Hijacked American Culture* (Nashville: Nelson Current, 2005), 13-14.

[45] Ibid, 14.

[46] Martin Amis, op. cit., 273. Quoted in Cashill, op. cit., 14.

[47] *Webster's Encyclopedic Unabridged Dictionary of the English Language*, op. cit., 738.

[48] Ibid, 739

[49] Richard A. Posner, *Public Intellectuals* (Cambridge: Harvard University Press, 2003), 2.

[50] Ibid, 2-3.

[51] Johan Norberg, Entrepreneurs are the Heroes of the World, speech reproduced in Cato's Letter, Winter 2007, Vol. 5, No. 1, 4

[52] Roger Kimball, *Lives of the Mind* (Chicago: Ivan R. Dee, 2002), 5.

[53] Harold Bloom, *Genius: A Mosaic of One Hundred Exemplary Creative Minds* (New York: Warner Books, 2002).

[54] Joseph J. Ellis, *Founding Brothers*, (New York: Alfred A. Knopf, 2004), 234

[55] Russell Jacoby, *The Last Intellectuals: American Culture in the Age of Academe* (New York: Basic Books, 1987), 196.

[56] Ibid, 192.

[57] Ibid, 194-195.

[58] Himmelfarb, op. cit.

[59] Robert Higgs, *Crisis and Leviathan: Critical Episodes in the Growth of American Government* (New York: Oxford University Press, 1987), 53.

[60] Thomas J. DiLorenzo, *How Capitalism Saved America: The Untold History of Our Country, from the Pilgrims to the Present* (New York: Crown Forum, 2004), 33.

[61] Paul Johnson, *Intellectuals* (New York: Harper Perennial, 1990), 306.

[62] Bertrand Russell, *Wisdom of the West: A historical survey of Western philosophy in its social and political setting* (London: Rathbone Books, Ltd., 1959), 5.

[63] Kurt Vonnegut, *Galapagos* (New York: Dell Publishing, 1999), 207.

[64] *Webster's Unabridged*, op. cit., 707.

[65] Joshua Muravchik, *Heaven on Earth* (San Francisco: Encounter Books, 2002), 259.

[66] Tammy Bruce, *The Death of Right and Wrong* (Roseville, CA: Prima Publishing, 2003), 160.

[67] Michael P. Federici, *Eric Voegelin: The Restoration of Order* (City: ISI Books, 2002), xxix.

[68] Ibid, 37.

[69] Mortimer Adler, *Ten Philosophical Mistakes* (New York: Macmillan Publishing Company, 1985), xiv.

[70] Ibid, 200.

[71] Ibid, 197.

Chapter 4

[72] Richard Brookhiser, *Gentleman Revolutionary: Gouverneur Morris, the Rake Who Wrote the Constitution* (New York: Simon and Schuster, 2004), 107.

[73] R. J. Hopper, *The Early Greeks* (New York: Harper & Row), 1976, 107-108.

[74] H. G. Wells, *The Outline of History* (New York: The Macmillan Company, 1921), 293.

 [75] Ken Goffman, *Counterculture Through the Ages: From Abraham to Acid House* (New York: Villard, 2005), 53.

[76] Ibid, 59.

[77] Bryan Magee, *The Story of Philosophy* (New York, DK Publishing, Inc., 1998), 32.

[78] Wells, op. cit., 301.

[79] Adler, op. cit., 174-175.

[80] Herodotus, Aubrey de Selincourt, transl., *Histories* (New York: Penguin Classics, 2003), Book Five, 335.

[81] Ibid, 340.

Chapter 5

[82] Alan Dershowitz, *Rights From Wrongs* (New York: Basic Books, 2004), 21.

[83] Glenn Markoe, *Phoenicians* (Berkley: University of California Press, 2001), p.7.

[84] Ibid. 102.

[85] Ibid. 215

[86] Ibid., xxi

[87] Ibid., xxi

[88] See "Adam Smith for Dummies," a Review of *On the Wealth of Nations* by P. J. O'Rourke, in The American Spectator, May, 2007, p. 67

[89] Ibid., p. 67

[90] Gerhard Herm, *The Phoenicians: The Purple Empire of the ancient world* (New York: William Morrow and Company, 1975), 130-131.

[91] Markoe, op. cit., 101.

[92] Ibid.

[93] Herm, op. cit., 160.

[94] Louis J. Halle, *Out of Chaos* (Boston: Houghton Mifflin, 1977), 407.

[95] Ibid, 413.

[96] Ibid, 415.

[97] Ibid, 415-416.

[98] Bertrand Russell, *Wisdom of the West: A historical survey of Western philosophy in its social and political setting* (London: Rathbone Books, Ltd., 1959), 6.

[99] Ibid, 6.

[100] Halle, op. cit., 417.

[101] Ibid, 434.

[102] Ibid, 433.

[103] Kurt Vonnegut, op. cit., x.

[104] Jesse Byock, *Viking Age Iceland* (New York: Penguin, 2001), 126.

[105] Ibid, 140.

[106] Ibid, 93-94.

[107] Mancur Olson, *Power and Prosperity* (New York: Basic Books, 2000), x.

[108] Mark Kurlansky, *The Basque History of the World* (New York: Penguin Books, 1997), 28.

[109] Ibid, 48.

[110] Ibid, 55.

[111] Ibid, 56.

[112] Ibid, 123.

[113] Ibid, 124.

[114] Ibid, 125.

[115] Vilhelm Moberg, *A History of the Swedish People: From Renaissance to Revolution* (New York: Dorset Press, 1989), 74.

[116] John Julius Norwich, (A History of Venice: London, The Folio Society, 2007), 21

[117] Ibid., 21

[118] Nathan Rosenberg & L. E. Birdzell, *How the West Grew Rich: The Economic Transformation of the Industrial World* (New York: Basic Books, 1986), 55.

[119] Ibid, 55.

[120] Ibid, 59.

[121] Kenneth Clark, *Civilization* (London: The Folio Society, 1999), 68.

[122] Ibid, 71.

[123] Ibid, 96

[124] Paul Johnson, The Renaissance: A Short History (New York: Modern Library Chronicles, ✓ 2000), 5-6.

[125] David S. Landes, *The Wealth and Poverty of Nations: Why Some Are So Rich and Some So Poor* (New York: W.W. Norton and Company, 1997), 37.

[126] Ibid, 37-38.

[127] Mancur Olson, *Power and Prosperity* (New York: Basic Books, 2000), 39-40.   ✓

[128] Bertrand Russell, *Wisdom of the West: A historical survey of Western philosophy in its social and political setting* (London: Rathbone Books, Ltd., 1959), 162.

[129] Ibid.

[130] Jack Weatherford, *Genghis Khan and The Making Of The Modern World* (New York: Three Rivers Press, 2004), 251.

131 F. A. Hayek, Resurrecting The Abandoned Road, from Gregory L. Schneider, *Conservatism in America Since 1930: A Reader* (New York: New York University Press, 2003), 60.

132 Paul Johnson, op. cit., 10.

133 Ibid, 12.

134 Ibid, 15.

135 Ibid, 20.

136 Ibid, 35.

137 Ibid, 53.

138 Ibid, 56.

139 Ibid, 59.

140 Barbara Tuchman, *The First Salute: A View of the American Revolution* (New York: Alfred A. Knopf, 1988), 24.

141 Mancur Olson, op. cit., 185

142 Barbara Tuchman, op. cit., 27-28.

143 Ibid, 30.

144 Ibid, 36.

145 Ibid, 37.

146 Kenneth Clark, op. cit., 146.

147 Barbara Tuchman, op. cit., 5.

148 Arthur Herman, *How the Scots Invented the Modern World: The True Story of How Western Europe's Poorest Nation Created Our World & Everything in It* (New York: Three Rivers Press, 2001), 15.

149 Ibid, 17.

150 Ibid, 16.

151 Ibid, 21-22.

152 Ibid, 22.

153 Ibid, 56.

154 Quoted in Herman, 195.

155 Ibid, 195.

156 Ibid, 240.

157 Ibid, 231.

158 Ibid, 394.

159 Quoted in Herman, 395.

160 David McCullough, 1776 (New York: Simon and Schuster, 2005), 11.

161 Ibid, 19.

162 Herman, op. cit., 231.

163 Ibid, 404.

[164] Rosenberg and Birzell, op. cit., xi.

[165] Ibid, xi.

[166] Hernando de Soto, *The Other Path: The Invisible Revolution in the Third World* (New York: Basic Books, 1989), 222-223.

[167] Landes, op. cit., 44.

[168] De Soto, op. cit., 229.

[169] G. R. Elton, *England Under the Tudors* (London: The Folio Society, 1997), 62.

[170] Ibid, 168.

[171] Ibid, 130-136.

[172] Herman, op. cit., 18-19.

[173] Geoffrey Robertson, *The Tyrannicide Brief* (New York: Pantheon Books 2005), 33

[174] H.G. Wells, op. cit., 776.

[175] Lora S. La Mance, *The Greene Family and Its Branches, from A.D. 861 to A.D. 1904* (Salem, MA: Higginson Book Company, 1989), 40.

[176] H.G. Wells, op. cit., 778.

[177] Ibid, 779.

[178] Robertson, The Tyrannicide Brief, 288 and 327

[179] Bertrand Russell, op. cit., 218.

[180] Quoted in Will Durant, *The Age of Voltaire* (New York: Simon and Schuster, 1965), 96.

[181] Thomas Sowell, *Conquests and Cultures*, op. cit., 58.

[182] Thomas Sowell, *Race and Culture*, (New York: Basic Books, 1994), 212.

[183] Thomas Sowell, *Conquests and Cultures*, op. cit., 91.

[184] Ibid, 87.

[185] Bernard Bailyn, *To Begin the World Anew: The Genius and Ambiguities of the American Founders* (New York: Vintage, 2004), preface.

[186] Richard Brookhiser, op. cit., 99.

[187] Ibid, 100.

[188] Bernard Bailyn, *To Begin the World Anew*, op. cit., 134-35.

[189] Ibid, 135.

[190] Bernard Bailyn, *The Ideological Origins of the American Revolution* (New York: The Belknap Press, 1967), 23.

[191] Ibid, 24.

[192] Herman, op. cit., 263

[193] Bernard Bailyn, *The Ideological Origins of the American Revolution*, op. cit., 33

[194] David McCullough, op. cit., 3.

[195] Ibid, 10.

[196] David McCullough, *John Adams* (New York: Simon and Schuster, 2001), 18.

[197] Ibid, 19.

[198] Ibid, 20.

[199] Ibid, 336.

[200] Jean-Francois Revel, *Anti-Americanism* (San Francisco: Encounter Books, 2000), 169.

[201] Mark Steyn, *America Alone* (Washington DC: Regnery Publishing Co., 2006), 6.

Chapter 6

[202] Carmen Bin Ladin, *Inside the Kingdom: My Life in Saudi Arabia* (New York: Warner Books, 2004), 16.

[203] Jeffrey Hart, *Smiling Through The Cultural Catastrophe* (New Haven: Yale University Press, 2001), 242-243.

[204] Rose Wilder Lane, *The Discovery of Freedom* (San Francisco: Fox & Wilkes, 1993), 4

[205] George F. Thomas, *Christian Ethics and Moral Philosophy* (New York: Charles Scribner's Sons, 1955), 434

[206] Ivan P. Hall, *Cartels of the Mind, Japan's Intellectual Closed Shop* (New York: W. W. Norton & Company, 1998), 101

[207] Ibid., 122

[208] Ibid., 122

[209] Lane, op. cit., p. 15

[210] Lane, op. cit., p. 17

[211] Lane, op. cit., p. 17-18

[212] Johan Norberg speech, printed in quarterly *Cato Institute Letter*, Winter 2007, Vol. 5, No. 1, p. 3

[213] Lane, op cit, p. 5

[214] Mark Elvin, *The Pattern of the Chinese Past* (Stanford: Stanford University Press, 1973), 297-298. Quoted in Landes, op. cit., 55-56.

[215] Ibid, 56.

[216] Ibid, 57.

[217] *The Economist*, July 16-22, 2005, 15.

[218] Ibid.

[219] E. L. Jones, op. cit., xii.

[220] Nathaniel Branden, *Taking Responsibility: Self-Reliance and the Accountable Life* (New York: Fireside, 1996), 16.

[221] Mortimer Adler, op. cit., 118.

[222] Thomas Sowell, *A Conflict of Visions*, op. cit

[223] Bloom, *Giants and Dwarfs*, op. cit., 40

[224] DeSoto, *The Mystery of Capital*, op. cit., 34-35

[225] Thomas Sowell, op. cit., 369-372

[226] E.L. Jones, op. cit., xix.

[227] Michael Paiewonsky, *Conquest of Eden* (Rome: MAPes MONDe, Ltd. 1990), 36

[228] E. L. Jones, op. cit., xxviii.

[229] Jack Weatherford, op. cit., 68.

[230] E.L. Jones, op. cit., 61.

[231] William H. McNeill, *The Rise of the West: A History of the Human Community* (Chicago: University of Chicago Press, 1992), 713

[232] Ibid, 714.

[233] Richard Feynman, *Meaning of It All: Thoughts of a Citizen Scientist* (City: Helix Books, 1998), 115.

[234] E.L. Jones, op. cit., 67.

[235] Ibid, 57-58.

[236] Ibid, 64.

[237] Thomas Sowell, *Race and Culture*, op. cit., 213.

[238] Irshad Manji, *The Trouble With Islam, A Muslim's Call for Reform in Her Faith* (New York: St. Martin's Press, 2003), 3

Chapter 7

[239] Alan Dershowitz, op. cit., 21.

[240] Ibid,

[241] Marvin Olasky, *The Religions Next Door* (Nashville: Broadman and Holman Publishers, 2004), 9-11.

[242] Jean-Francois Revel, op. cit., 13.

[243] Joseph J. Ellis, op. cit., 4.

[244] William McNeill, op. cit., xxix.

[245] Ibid, xxviii.

Chapter 8

[246] George B.N. Ayittey, *Africa Betrayed* (Basingstoke: Palgrave Macmillan, 1993), 283.

[247] Michael Klein and Tim Harford, *The Market for Aid* (Washington DC: International Finance Corporation, 2005), 35.

[248] Ibid, 36.

[249] Ibid, 42.

[250] Ibid, 57.

[251] Ibid, 55.

[252] Edgardo Buscaglia and William Ratliff, *Law and Economics in Developing Countries* (Stanford, CA: Hoover Institution Press, 2000), 2.

253 Klein and Harford, op. cit., 59.

254 Hernando de Soto, *The Mystery of Capital* (New York: Basic Books, 2005), 227.

255 Anne Marie Slaughter, *A New World Order* (Princeton, NJ: Princeton University Press, 2004), 261.

256 Lawrence McQuillan and Peter Montgomery, *The International Monetary Fund: Financial Medic to the World?* (Stanford, CA: Hoover Institution Press, 1999), 126.

257 Nancy Barry, "Tribute to Esther Ocloo," http://womensworldbanking.org/English/3000/tribute_to_esther_ocloo.htm.

258 Muhammad Yunus, Commencement Address at Brigham Young University, August 13, 1998.

259 Ibid.

260 "Breaking the vicious cycle of poverty through microcredit," http://www.grameen-info.org/bank/bcycle.html.

261 James D. Gwartney and Robert A. Lawson, *Economic Freedom of the World, 2004: Annual Report* (Vancouver: Fraser Institute, 2004), 38.

262 Heritage Foundation, 2005 Index of Economic Freedom, Washington, DC, 2005, 57

263 Hernando de Soto, *The Other Path*, op. cit., 239.

264 Hernando de Soto, *The Mystery of Capital*, op. cit., 69.

265 Ibid, 5-7.

266 Ibid, 228.

267 Ibid, 226.

268 Byron R. Wien, Start Packing for Dubai, Investment Perspectives, Morgan Stanley, May 9, 2007, 17

269 Ibid., 17

270 Ibid., 17

271 Ibid., 18

272 Samuel Z. Stone, *Telltale Stories From Central America* (Albuquerque: University of New Mexico Press, 2001), 9

273 Merrie Cave, Letter from Tanzania, *The Salisbury Review*, Spring 2007, p. 26

274 Anne Marie Slaughter, *A New World Order*, op. cit., p. 263

275 Ibid, 263

276 Hernando de Soto, *The Mystery of Capital*, op. cit., 4.

Chapter 9

277 Hernando de Soto, *The Other Path*, op. cit., 202.

278 Hernando de Soto, *The Mystery of Capital*, op. cit., 67.

279 Mark Kurlansky, *Cod: A Biography of the Fish that Changed the World*, (New York: Penguin Books, 1997), 75.

[280] Niccolo Machiavelli, op. cit., 202.

[281] Pomerantz, *The Great Divergence*, op. cit.

[282] Nathan Rosenberg & L. E. Birdzell, op. cit., 92-93.

[283] Joseph F. Johnston, *The Limits of Government* (Chicago: Regnery Gateway, 1987), 323-324.

Chapter 10

[284] Dinesh D'Souza, *What's So Great About America* (Washington, DC: Regnery Publishing Company, 2002), 64.

[285] George Walsh, *The Role of Religion in History* (New Brunswick, NJ: Transaction Publishers,1999), 89-90.

[286] Wells, op. cit., 728-729.

[287] Bertrand Russell, op. cit., 160.

[288] Wells, op. cit., 728.

[289] William McNeill, op. cit., 589.

[290] Kenneth Clark, op. cit., 120.

[291] Niccolo Machiavelli, *Discourses on Livy* (Oxford: Oxford University Press, 2003), book one, chapter 12.

[292] Ibid, 173.

[293] Ludwig von Mises, *Human Action, Fourth Edition* (Irvington-on-Hudson, NY: Foundation for Economic Education, 1996), 29.

[294] Richard J. Ward, *Grampas Are For All Seasons* (Bloomington, Indiana: 1st Books, 2006), 121

[295] Mathew 24:24

[296] George Weigel, *The Cube and The Cathedral* (New York: Basic Books, 2005), 46.

[297] Ibid, 47.

[298] Thomas Cahill, *How The Irish Saved Civilization* (New York: Anchor Books, 1995), 126.

[298] Ibid, 132.

[300] George F. Thomas, *Christian Ethics and Moral Philosophy* (New York: Charles Scribner's Sons, 1955), 52

[301] Cahill, op. cit., 140-142.

[302] Olasky, op. cit., 58.

[303] Dinesh D'Souza, *What's So Great About America* (Regnery Publishing, Inc., Washington DC, 2002), 59

[304] Robert Spencer, *Islam Unveiled* (San Francisco: Encounter Books, 2002), 91

[305] James Bradley, *Flyboys* (Boston: Back Bay Books, Little, Brown and Company, 2003), 56-58 and 190

[306] Philip Short, *Pol Pot: Anatomy of a Nightmare* (New York, Henry Holt and Company, 2004), 10

[307] Ibid, 11

[308] Ibid, 13

[309] Ibid, 12

[310] Ibid, 20-21

[311] Ibid, 19-20

[312] Ibid, 17

[313] Ibid, 73

[314] Arthur Koestler, *Darkness at Noon* (New York: Bantam Books, 1968), 209-211

[315] Ibid, 124

[316] Irshad Manji, op. cit., 2-3

[317] Norma Khouri, *Honor Lost* (New York: Atria Books, 2003), 24.

Chapter 11

[318] Shirer, op. cit., 111.

[319] Maurice Baumont, John H. E. Fried, Edmond Vermeil, *The Third Reich* (New York: Frederick A. Praeger, 1955) 204-205; quoting Nietzsche's Zur Genealogie der Moral and Der Wille zur Macht.

[320] Allan Bullock, *Hitler: A Study in Tyranny* (Old Saybrook, CT: William S. Konecky Associates, 1999). Leonard Peikoff, *The Ominous Parallels* (New York: Signet, 1983).

[321] Daniel Jonah Goldhagen, *Hitler's Willing Executioners* (New York: Vintage Books, 1997), 419.

[322] Ibid, 603.

[323] Walter Phelps Hall, *World Wars and Revolutions* (New York: D. Appleton-Century Company, 1947), 11-12.

[324] Tony Blankley, *The West's Last Chance* (Washington DC: Regnery Publishing, Inc., 2005), 189.

[325] Hall, op. cit., 482-486.

[326] Robert Conquest, *Reflections on a Ravaged Century* (New York: W. W. Norton & Company, 2000) 4

[327] Peter Emberley and Barry Cooper, translators and editors, *Faith and Political Philosophy: The Correspondence Between Leo Strauss and Eric Voegelin, 1934-1964* (Philadelphia: Pennsylvania State University Press, 2004), xvii.

[328] Robert Conquest, *Reflections On a Ravaged Century*, op. cit., 4.

[329] Shirer, op. cit., 98.

[330] Quoted in Shirer, ibid, 99.

[331] Ibid, 101.

[332] Conquest, op. cit., 232-233.

[333] Weigel, op. cit., 105.

[334] Ibid, 104.

[335] Ibid, 33.

[336] Revel, op. cit., 4.

[337] Gerard Alexander, "The Other American Exceptionalism," (Claremont Review of Books, Fall 2005), 53-56.

[338] Robert Kagan, *Of Paradise and Power* (New York: Vintage Books, 2004), 91.

[339] Ibid, 89. Quoting "Half a Billion Americans?" (The Economist, August 22, 2006).

[340] Ibid, 87-88.

Chapter 12

[341] Heather Mac Donald, *The Burden of Bad Ideas* (Chicago: Ivan R. Dee, 2000)

[342] Sowell, *Conquests and Cultures*, op. cit., 352-54

[343] *The World Book Dictionary*, Doubleday & Company, Inc. Chicago, 1976 Ed

[344] *The Canon*, op. cit., 11

[345] Ibid, 11

[346] Barry Goldwater, *The Conscience of a Conservative* (Washington, D.C.: Regnery Gateway, 1990), 31

[347] Ibid, xxv

[348] Hollister, op. cit., 91-92

[349] *The Federalist* (Norwalk CT: The Easton Press, 1979) 308

[350] Ibid, 112

[351] Ibid, 426

[352] Ibid, 333

[353] Ibid, 53

[354] Ibid, 125

[355] Ibid, 127

[356] Alpheus Thomas Mason & Gordon E. Baker, *Free Government in the Making, Fourth Edition* (New York: Oxford Univeristy Press, 1985) 8

[357] Ibid, 9

[358] Ibid, 322

[359] Bicentennial Edition, *Notes of Debates in the Federal Convention of 1787*, Reported by James Madison (New York: W. W. Norton & Company, 1987) 224

[360] Ibid, 209

[361] Geoffrey Robertson, *The Tyrannicide Brief* (New York: Pantheon Books, 2005) 194

[362] Ibid, 21

[363] *American Constitutional History*, Ed by Alpheus T. Mason and Gerald Garvey (new York: Harper Torchbooks, The Academy Library, Harper & Row, NY, 1964) ix

364 Edward S. Corwin, *Liberty Against Government* (Baton Rouge: Louisiana State University Press, 1948) 13-14)

365 Ibid, 25

366 John W. Danford, *Roots of Freedom*, op. cit., 73

367 Bruce S. Thornton, *Plagues Of The Mind*, op. cit., xvii

368 Conquest, *Reflections*, op. cit., 8

369 Ibid, 3

370 Ibid, 4

371 Richard P. Feynman, *The Pleasure of Finding Things Out* (New York: Basic Books, 1999, 23

Chapter 13

372 *The Animal World of Albert Schweitzer*, Transl. and Ed. By Charles R. Joy (Hopewell NJ: The Ecco Press, 1950) 168

373 Ibid., 198

374 Eric Hobsdawn, *The Age of Revolution*, 1789-1848 (London: The Folio Society, 2005), 21-22.

375 Goldhagen, op. cit., 438.

376 Ibid, 398.

377 Shirer, op. cit., 109.

378 Goldhagen, op. cit., 454.

379 James Bradley, *Flyboys: A True Story of Courage* (Boston: Back Bay Books/Little, Brown & Company, 2003), 59.

380 Mark Kurkansky, *The Basque History of the World* (New York: Penguin Books, 2001), 195.

381 Ibid, 200.

382 Bradley, op. cit., 65.

383 Interview with Leonard Peikoff, www.peikoff.com/op/interview.htm.

384 Ibid.

385 Eric Blair, *The Age of Unenlightenment* (Unauthorized Books, 2004) p. 11.

386 Age of the Enlightenment, Professor Gerhard Rempel, mars.wnec.edu/~grempel/courses/we2/lectures/enlightenment.html, p.5.

387 Kenneth L. Grasso, "Christianity, Enlightenment liberalism, and the Quest for freedom," (Modern Age, Fall 2006), 305.

388 Christopher Dawson, *Dynamics of World History*, edited by John J. Mulloy (Wilmington: ISI Books, 2002), p. 88.

389 Grasso, op. cit., 304.

390 Ibid, 306.

391 Ibid, 309.

[392] Dawson, op. cit., 36-37.

[393] Grasso, op. cit., 310.

[394] David L. Jacobson, editor, *The English Libertarian Heritage, Cato's Letters*, April 8, 1721 (San Francisco: Fox & Wilkes, 1994) 61.

[395] Ibid, 62.

Chapter 14

[396] Blankley, op. cit., 137.

[397] Johnston, op. cit., 317.

[398] Charles E. Tomlinson, *A View From My Stump* (Cherokee AL: D. R. Virtue Press, 1992), 45

[399] Thomas Sowell, *Knowledge and Decisions* (New York: Basic Books, 1996), 374

[400] Ibid, 367.

[401] Ibid, 377.

[402] Fareed Zakaria, *The Future of Freedom* (New York: W. W. Norton & Company, 2003), 19.

[403] Ibid, 26.

[404] Joe Scarborough, *Rome Wasn't Burnt In A Day* (New York: Harper Collins Publishers, 2004) 137

[405] Ibid, 151

[406] Dershowitz, *Rights From Wrongs*, op. cit., 6-8.

[407] Sowell, *Knowledge and Decisions*, op. cit., 379-380.

[408] David K. Shipler, *The Working Poor* (New York: Alfred A, Knopf, 2004), 6-7.

[409] Larry Elder, *The Ten Things You Can't Say In America* (New York: St. Martin's Press, 2000), 156.

[410] Barry Goldwater, *The Conscience of a Conservative*, op. cit., 48

[411] Ibid., p. 51

[412] Ibid., p. 48

[413] Joseph F. Johnston, op. cit., 317.

[414] Alan Dershowitz, *The Abuse Excuse* (Boston: Little, Brown and Company, 1994), 318.

[415] Charles E. Tomlinson, *The View From My Stump* (Cherokee AL: DR Virtue Press, 1992, 25

[416] Ibid, 24

[417] Ibid, 28

[418] Ibid, 28

[419] James Pierson, "Investing In Conservative Ideas" (Commentary: May 2005), 49.

[420] Ibid, 49, 52.

[421] Elder, op. cit., 103.

[422] Cashill, op. cit., 9.

[423] George Will, *With a Happy Eye But....* (New York: Free Press, 2003), 26.

[424] David Horowitz, Unholy Alliance, op. cit., 69.

[425] Ibid, 64.

[426] Quoted in Horowitz, ibid, 67.

Chapter 15

[427] Thomas Sowell, *Is Reality Optional?* (Stamford, CA: Hoover Institution Press, 1993), 75.

[428] Ibid.

[429] Ibid, 76.

[430] Jack Cashill, *Hoodwinked* (Nashville: Nelson Current, 2005), 79-80

[431] Thomas Sowell, *A Conflict of Visions: Ideological Origins of Political Struggles* (New York: Basic Books, 2002).

[432] Ibid, 16.

[433] Allan Bloom, *Giants and Dwarfs*, op. cit., 54

[434] Michael Barone, *Hard America, Soft America* (New York: Crown Forum, 2004).

[435] Ibid, 24.

[436] Ibid, 55, 57.

[437] Milton Friedman, *Capitalism and Freedom, 40th Anniversary Edition* (Chicago: University of Chicago Press, 2002), 7-8.

[438] Michael Barone, op. cit., 10.

[439] Michael Savage, *Liberalism is a Mental Disorder* (Nashville: Nelson Current, 2005), 14

[440] Robert M. Persig, *Lila: An Inquiry into Morals* (New York: Bantam Books, 1991), 304.

[441] Ibid, 306.

[442] Larry Elder, *The Ten Things You Can't Say in America* (New York: St. Martin's Press, 2000) 156.

[443] Transcript of Bill Cosby's remarks on May 17, 2004, at NAACP event to commemorate 50th anniversary of Brown v. Board of Education.

[444] Daniel Johnson, "Britain's Neoconservative Moment" (Commentary, March 2006), 53.

[445] Julian Simon, *Hoodwinking the Nation* (New Brunswick: Transaction Publishers, 2000), 1

[446] Ibid, 3.

[447] Ibid, 87-89.

[448] Ibid, 1

[449] Ibid, 93.

[450] Ibid, 95.

[451] James Burnham, *Suicide of the West* (New Rochelle, NY: Arlington House, 1964), 288.

[452] Maurice McTigue, Making Government Accountable: Reform Lessons From New Zealand, speech recorded by Mercatus Center, George Mason University

[453] Eric Blair, *The Age of Unenlightenment* (Unauthorized Books, 2004), 158.

[454] Irshad Manji, op. cit., 18

[455] Tofler, Alvin and Heidi, *Creating a New Civilization* (Turner Publishing, Inc., Atlanta, 1995), 19-20

[456] Daniel J. Flynn, *Intellectual Morons, How Ideology Makes Smart People Fall for Stupid Ideas* (New York: Prima Publishing, 2002)

[457] *The Weekly Standard*, September 27, 2004, 28

[458] James Dale Davidson & Lord William Rees-Mogg, *The Sovereign Individual* (New York: Simon & Schuster, 1997), 82-3

[459] Ibid., 84

[460] Ibid., 87

[461] Tofler, op. cit., 63

[462] Ibid, 64

[463] Davidson, op. cit., 103

[464] Ibid, 86

[465] Spencer Heath MacCallum, *The Art of Community* (Menlo Park CA, Institute for Humane Studies, Inc., 1970), vii

[466] Ibid., 105

[467] Tofler, op. cit., 104-5

[468] Ibid, 99

[469] James Ronald Kennedy, *Reclaiming Liberty* (Gretna LA: Pelican Publishing Company, 2007)

[470] Barry Goldwater, op. cit., xxv

[471] Kennedy, op. cit., 76

[472] Tofler, op. cit., 11

Chapter 16

[473] Karl R. Popper, *The Open Society and Its Enemies,* V2 (Princeton NJ: Princeton University Press, 1971), 270-272.

[474] Milton Friedman, *Capitalism and Freedom* (Chicago: Chicago, The University of Chicago Press, 2002), 3-4.

[475] Sidney Hook, *The Paradoxes of Freedom* (Berkeley: University of California Press, 1962), 138.

[476] Bill O'Reilly, Culture Warrior (New York: Broadway Books, 2006) 193

[477] Ibid., 194

[478] Sheldon Richman, "The Good and Bad News about the Bush Wars," *Freedom Daily*, The Future of Freedom Foundation, Vol. 18, July, 2007, Number 7, page 11

[479] Samuel Huntington, *Who Are We? The Challenges to America's National Identity* (New York: Simon and Schuster, 2004).

[480] Newt Gingrich, *Winning the Future* (Washington DC: Regnery, 2005), xiv-xxiv.

[481] Alexander Deane, *The Great Abdication* (Exeter, UK: Imprint-Academic, 2005)

[482] Maurice McTeague, *Making Government Accountable*, op. cit.

Index